World Agricultural Trade: Building a Consensus

World Agricultural Trade: Building a Consensus

edited by
William M. Miner
and
Dale E. Hathaway

q2·21·05

The Institute for Research on Public Policy/
L'Institut de recherches politiques

and

Institute for International Economics

Printed in Canada

Legal Deposit Second Quarter
Bibliothèque nationale du Québec

Canadian Cataloguing in Publication Data

Main entry under title:
World agricultural trade

Co-published by: Institute for International Economics

ISBN 0-88645-071-3

1. Produce trade. I. Miner, William M. (William Manning), 1928-
II. Hathaway, Dale E. III. Institute for Research on Public
Policy. IV. Institute for International Economics (U.S.)

HD9000.5.W58 1988   382'.41   C88-090263-9

The camera-ready copy for this publication was created
on a Xerox 6085 Desktop Publishing System.

The Institute for Research on Public Policy/
L'Institut de recherches politiques
P.O. Box 3670 South
Halifax, Nova Scotia B3J 3K6

Contents

Foreword   vii

Acknowledgements   xi

Policy Statement   1
    Reforming World Agricultural Trade   3
    List of Signatories   28

Background Studies   33

I. World Agriculture in Crisis: Reforming
   Government Policies   35
   William M. Miner and Dale E. Hathaway

II. Perspectives on Decoupling   111

   A North American Perspective on Decoupling   113
   Barry Carr, Klaus Frohberg, Hartley Furtan,
   S.R. Johnson, William H. Meyers, Tim Phipps,
   and G.E. Rossmiller

An EC Approach to Decoupling   141
John S. Marsh

A Commentary   159
Wilhelm Henrichsmeyer

III. Developing Country Perspectives   167

Agriculture in GATT Negotiations and
Developing Countries   169
Nurul Islam

IV. Exchange Rate Issues   191

Exchange Rates and Their Role in Agricultural
Trade Issues   193
G. Edward Schuh

A Commentary   211
Murray G. Smith

Institute for International Economics   215

Institute for Research on Public Policy   217

Foreword

The international trading system has come under growing tensions in recent years, in the wake of new protectionist actions by numerous countries and increasing disillusion in many quarters over the effectiveness of the GATT in maintaining an open and equitable regime. These pressures have come together more forcefully with respect to agriculture than in any other sector. A major breakthrough in international co-operation on agriculture may in fact be necessary to preserve a liberal trading system in general, and to achieve a successful outcome of the current Uruguay Round of multilateral negotiations in particular.

At the same time, farmers are suffering from agricultural policies that for almost a decade have artificially generated unduly low prices and excess capacity that cannot be sustained in the long run. Reforming agricultural trade would thus help not only the world trading system; it would also promote healthier and more self-reliant agriculture in developed and developing countries alike. In the longer term these reforms would also advance the fundamental goal of achieving more effective utilization of agricultural land and resources, sustainable growth of world food supplies, and improved distribution to meet the basic needs of a growing world population.

In recognition of the critical importance of these problems, leaders of the industrial countries have committed themselves — at the summit meetings of the seven industrial democracies in 1986 (Tokyo) and 1987 (Venice), and at the OECD Ministerial meetings in 1986 and

1987 — to adopt major reforms of national agricultural policies and the rules for farm trade. In launching the Uruguay Round at Punta del Este in 1986, the full membership of the GATT agreed to pursue such reforms. To date, however, there has been little concrete action to implement these pledges. Indeed, some backsliding may be occurring with a failure to coalesce around means for moving the process forward — let alone resolving the issues definitively.

In such an environment, private groups can sometimes help develop the needed consensus on how to proceed. They can do so both by making specific proposals to governments, and by informing public opinion of techniques by which the problems can be addressed. In 1987 the Institute for Research on Public Policy, Canada, and the Institute for International Economics, Washington, D.C., decided to make an effort to develop such a consensus.

The two Institutes therefore brought together a number of persons with considerable experience in agricultural policy from twenty countries representing both importers and exporters. They participated in a series of four meetings: in Washington in November 1987, in Bangkok and Cologne in March 1988, and in Ottawa on April 21 and 22. The group sought to develop a joint view on how governments could best resolve the farm trade problem. At the session in Ottawa they approved the consensus Policy Statement included at the beginning of this book. This statement was released publicly on May 4, 1988 in Ottawa and Washington and disseminated by all signatories in each of their countries to the media and to policy makers and political leaders. Its recommendations set out a framework for action in 1988 — at the upcoming OECD Ministerial meeting, the seven-nation Toronto Economic Summit and the GATT mid-term review meeting in December in Montreal — as well as proposals for policy reform over the longer run.

The Ottawa statement speaks for itself. The signatories, twenty-nine in number, decided to issue it because of the pressing urgency of the problems of agriculture, their concern that the current agricultural trade battles weaken support for the entire GATT system, and their desire to assist governments to develop positive and forward-looking policy responses. Every signatory does not necessarily endorse each phrase of the statement, but they unanimously support its analysis and recommendations and agree on the urgent need for governments to adopt its policy proposals. A number of signatories are having the statement translated into the languages of their countries and are arranging either for separate publication or its inclusion in major periodicals.

The development of materials for these meetings was carried out principally by William Miner, Senior Research Associate at the Institute for Research on Public Policy and former Assistant Deputy

Minister of Agriculture Canada and Co-ordinator of the Advisory Group on Grains for the Government of Canada, and Dale Hathaway, a Visiting Fellow at the Institute for International Economics and former Under Secretary of Agriculture in the United States. They also served as editors for this volume of studies.

Background papers were prepared specially for the group, initially to stimulate discussion and subsequently to focus attention on particular problems identified at the Washington meeting. They are brought together in this volume for the first time.

The principal background paper was prepared by Miner and Hathaway for the group's first meeting in Washington and was revised by them for the Ottawa meeting. It is entitled "World Agriculture in Crisis: Reforming Government Policies." Following from the Washington discussions, additional papers were prepared on specific issues for consideration at the Bangkok and Cologne seminars. Although these papers informed the group's discussions and helped it to reach consensus, no attempt was made to revise the papers so as to reflect the views of the group. In each case they represent only the opinions of the authors. They are, however, being issued because they provide the analytical and empirical foundation for the Ottawa statement.

Peter C. Dobell, Vice-President of The Institute for Research on Public Policy, played a catalytic role in initiating the project and acted as overall project manager. Thomas O. Bayard, Deputy Director of the Institute for International Economics, offered continuous support and advice on all aspects of the project. Murray Smith, Director of the IRPP's International Economics Program, helped guide the background research and assisted in the preparation of the Policy Statement. Frank Stone, Senior Research Associate with the IRPP, provided extremely helpful comments and advice throughout the process.

The project was made possible by generous support from The Charles B. Bronfman Foundation, The John M. Olin Foundation, the Rockefeller Brothers Fund and the Alfred P. Sloan Foundation. Their assistance is gratefully acknowledged.

It is the hope of our two Institutes that this volume of studies and the Ottawa consensus statement will contribute to the resolution of differences among nations on agricultural trade problems, thereby promoting a stronger world economy.

C. Fred Bergsten
Director
Institute for International
  Economics

Rod Dobell
President
Institute for Research on
  Public Policy

Acknowledgements

The preparation of the principal background document and the production of this volume would not have been possible without the advice and assistance of many persons in both Institutes and in several countries. In the preparation of the papers and the organization of the volume, three persons deserve special recognition: Murray Smith for his thoughtful contributions to the paper, Tom Bayard for his administrative skills and Frank Stone for helping to clarify and refine the text. The organization of the project and the two conferences benefited greatly from the leadership and vision of Fred Bergsten and Peter Dobell. Our sincere appreciation is extended to Ammar Siamwalla and the Thailand Development Research Institute for co-hosting the Bangkok seminar and to Hans-Jürgen Rohr for helping to organize the Cologne seminar with the assistance of the Federation of German Industries. Grateful recognition is extended to the staff of the two Institutes for their untiring efforts, particularly to Lynda Lennon for her organizational support and to Marina Horrocks, Melanie McDonald, Chrystine Frank and Ruby Day for their skills with word processing and modern communications. We are grateful to Ann Beasley and Kathryn Randle for their assistance in the preparation of the manuscript.

Finally, the thoughtful and professional contributions of the signatories to the Ottawa Statement and to the deliberations leading to it are acknowledged with respect and gratitude. The breadth and complexity of the issues discussed in this manuscript and the high level of consensus that was achieved through the expertise and understanding of all is a tribute to those who participated in this project. The responsibility for any mistakes, misrepresentations or omissions are entirely our own.

William M. Miner
Dale E. Hathaway
Editors,
May, 1988

Reforming World Agricultural Trade

A Policy Statement by Twenty-nine Professionals from Seventeen Countries

Contents

Introduction   3

The Crisis   4

Agricultural Reform and the GATT Negotiations   9

Bridging the Differences   10

Recommendations for Long-Term Reform   12
    Phased Reductions in Trade-Distorting Policies   14
    Agreements on Decoupled Farm Programs   15
    Policies to Encourage Conservation and
        to Improve the Environment   15
    A Parallel Negotiation of GATT Rules   16
    Full Participation by Developing Countries   16
    Domestic Policy Co-ordination   17
    Dispute Settlement   17
    A Multilateral Program of Early Relief   17

Making the Transition   18

Progress to Date   18

A Framework for Progress in 1988   20
    Defining Trade-Distorting Programs   21

Dealing With Trade-Distorting Programs   22
    Developing Country Issues   22
    Establishing A Surveillance Mechanism   23
    Settling Differences over National Policies   24
    Short-Term Measures   26

The Opportunity   27

Signatories   28

1

Reforming World Agricultural Trade

A Policy Statement by Twenty-nine Professionals from Seventeen Countries

Introduction

The 1980s have been a decade of crisis for much of world agriculture. Following a period of unusual growth in world demand and trade, the 1980s have witnessed a decline in exports, plummeting agricultural prices, widespread economic distress in farming and associated industries, and rising trade tensions as nations have sought to protect their farmers.

It is now widely recognized that the programs governments have developed to assist farmers, maintain farm income, and stabilize market prices are a major factor contributing to global problems. These programs have continued to encourage rapid increases in output in many countries at a time when the growth in world demand has slackened. The result, during the first half of the 1980s, was falling world agricultural commodity prices – to the lowest real levels since the 1930s.

The problems of agriculture have engaged the attention of world leaders and have become a major issue in the Uruguay Round of multilateral trade negotiations under the General Agreement on Tariffs and Trade (GATT). Key proposals for negotiating agriculture issues have been tabled in the GATT, and some countries have begun to confront the issues on their own. There is widespread agreement that policies can be changed more easily, and with much lower adjustment costs, if all countries act together. To date, there is no clear consensus on how to proceed, however, and a danger exists that governments' determination to tackle these complex and sensitive

3

issues will weaken as marginal adjustments are made and markets improve.

World commodity prices have strengthened in recent months. This has resulted from a combination of adverse weather in key producing areas in Europe and Asia, large-scale land retirement programs in the United States, and new programs to reduce dairy production in the European Community (EC) and the United States. As a result, there has been a reduction in excess stocks of grains, meats, and dairy products. But this temporary respite in the worldwide market chaos is not a solution to the fundamental problems of global agriculture. There is an urgent need for immediate and decisive action on the part of governments to move toward fundamental reform of their agricultural policies.

The leaders of the economic summit countries will meet in Canada in June 1988, and agriculture is again on the agenda. This will provide a timely opportunity to move the negotiating process forward. Trade Ministers of the GATT countries will also meet in December 1988 in Canada, for a mid-term review of progress in the Uruguay Round. These opportunities to establish a framework for the negotiations and begin a process of agricultural policy reform through trade negotiations must not be lost. The welfare of millions of farmers and consumers around the world, and of the industries based on agriculture, are at stake. The future of the multilateral trading system may well be at risk.

The Crisis

The cry of "crisis in world agriculture" is heard more frequently today than at any time since the 1930s. The parallel is real and disturbing; there are a number of similarities between agricultural market conditions in the 1980s and those of the depression years. Slow growth in the world economy and declines in inflation rates in the major market economies have exerted downward pressure on agricultural commodity prices in the 1980s. This is in sharp contrast to the buoyant market conditions of the previous decade. Agricultural protectionism rose sharply in the early 1980s as countries attempted to isolate their producers from declining world markets. Farm asset values dropped, and rural communities experienced severe economic stress similar to what occurred in the depression era.

The diagnosis of the underlying sources of problems in agriculture today differs markedly from the 1930s, however. Today there is increasing recognition that subsidies to agricultural producers, price support systems, and trade barriers are largely responsible for excess capacity and over-production on a global basis. National policies intended to promote stability and equity in incomes for domestic agriculture are generating increasing instability in world agricultural trade and are creating international conflicts. Many governments are responding to the economic difficulties with additional subsidies and protectionist measures. In many countries the heavy financial burden of farm support programs and their economic effects create serious domestic conflicts. Internationally, protectionist trade policies and export subsidy programs generate recurring confrontations within the trade system – such as the continuing subsidy war between the United States and the European Community. These trade conflicts are, in turn, creating a crisis in the GATT itself as governments are unable to resolve their differences through the application of existing trade rules.

A number of fora – including the GATT Ministerial Meeting at Punta del Este in September 1986 that launched the Uruguay Round, the Organization for Economic Co-operation and Development (OECD) Ministerial Meeting in May 1987, and the Venice Summit of industrial country leaders in June 1987 – have issued declarations supporting liberalization of agricultural trade and reform of domestic farm policies. It remains to be seen, however, whether these calls for international co-operation to reduce barriers and distortions affecting agricultural trade will actually lead to the negotiation and implementation of international agreements that will deal effectively with these issues.

The crucial question is whether the main countries concerned – having long resisted the application of international rules to agricultural trade – will accept multilateral obligations that would constrain their domestic agricultural policies and open their domestic markets to greater international competition. In the industrial countries, the structure of price regulation, subsidies, and protection against international competition has become woven into the pattern of agricultural activity. Substantial investment in production, processing capabilities, the pattern of land use, and the capitalization of land values are predicated on the continuation of domestic agricultural policies and the maintenance of trade barriers. Entrenched interests are likely to resist unilateral policy moves by national governments. However, a number of forces stemming from domestic stresses and international frictions are increasing the pressure for multilateral co-operation to bring agriculture under strengthened international trade rules at the GATT.

At the same time, governments face pressure for even greater support from economically troubled rural communities. This provokes conflict between primary agricultural constituencies, which are declining in number, and larger, more diffuse interest groups, including consumers and taxpayers. Yet the economic distress of farmers in this decade has reached, and in some cases exceeded, the level of hardship experienced in the 1930s. Governments in wealthier countries have responded with higher subsidies, often resulting in sustained farm production and intensified export competition. Consequently, the economic difficulties of producers in non-subsidizing countries, particularly developing countries, have worsened, further weakening their economies. In short, governments are being forced to recognize that their domestic agricultural policies are not working.

Perhaps the clearest measure of the failure of agricultural policy — and an indicator of growing domestic political conflicts — is the expanding fiscal burden of farm subsidies in the developed countries. Although these subsidies do not account for large shares of total government expenditures, they strain the fiscal capacity of governments attempting to reduce persistent budget deficits. In the United States, public expenditures in support of agriculture still are substantial, especially in light of a massive federal budget deficit. Similarly, in the European Community, the Common Agricultural Policy (CAP) accounts for a high proportion of total EC spending and has created recurring crises in EC financing.

World Bank and OECD sources estimate that the total cost to consumers and taxpayers of agricultural support in the OECD countries ranges from $100 billion to $150 billion annually, a large proportion of which is used to offset the effects of surplus production and to counter the actions of other countries. With the fiscal capacity of governments strained, and a recent history of high real interest rates and unstable exchange rates, the pressures on global agricultural markets from mounting stocks of key commodities provoke tensions between agriculture and other constituencies. The build-up of stocks places severe strains on subsidy programs and makes agriculture vulnerable to sudden policy changes, as governments implement austerity measures in response to pressures to reduce their budget deficits.

Other domestic policy conflicts arise from trade barriers. Certain agricultural producers use other agricultural products as inputs. When the domestic price of those commodities rises above their price in global markets, tension is generated within the agricultural sector. For example, feed grains and protein meals are important cost components for livestock producers, and high domestic prices for those inputs drive the price of meat above competitive levels. Similarly, protection of primary agricultural products increases costs for food-processing industries, creating new demands for protection of those downstream industries. In developing countries, agriculture is often taxed to support economic and industrial expansion; this has the effect of depressing farm prices and farm production, which results in the need to import food. Some governments in developed countries provide subsidies to certain sectors of agriculture to offset the higher costs resulting from protection for other farm products and for the manufacturing sector. The increase in agricultural protection — as governments have responded to pressure from their distressed farm communities — combined with recurring problems with existing agricultural trade regimes and the unprecedented use of export subsidies, have been a source of frequent and severe international friction. Agricultural products account for most of the trade disputes among the industrial countries — particularly if fisheries and forest products are included — and these disputes have often grown into broader agricultural trade wars. The conflicts involve a wide range of commodities, including grains, livestock, sugar, dairy products, vegetable oils, and processed foods. Many frictions between the developing countries and industrialized countries occur as well; the agricultural trade policies of industrialized countries have for many years been protested by developing country groups in GATT and in United Nations organizations. The widespread use of subsidies and protection in agriculture has aggravated the economic difficulties of the developing countries and, in turn, has contributed to the overall crisis in world agriculture. Developing countries have a major stake in agricultural trade and can benefit significantly from a successful Uruguay Round.

The large transfers to agriculture also have significant repercussions for the overall macroeconomic performance of industrial and developing countries. Studies undertaken by the OECD show that agricultural support is wasteful of resources, impairs the competitiveness of manufacturing, and may reduce total employment and discourage the development of efficient agriculture. Moreover, several analyses quantifying these effects show the macroeconomic impact of farm support to be extremely significant. For example, an Australian-sponsored program of international studies suggests that agricultural trade liberalization could make a significant contribution to overall economic growth in industrial and developing countries alike, and could make a substantial contribution to solving many contemporary economic problems such as high unemployment in Europe, the U.S. trade deficit, and the Third World debt problem.

Other dimensions of the world crisis in agriculture must also be considered in the reform of government policies. In addition to a trade crisis, there is a continuing failure to meet basic food needs for millions of people. It is a cruel paradox that, in the midst of a surplus of food and excess capacity in agriculture in much of the developed world, there is widespread malnutrition in many countries and serious famine in isolated areas. The inadequate levels of food consumption in developing countries must be addressed, but an enduring solution can be sought only through long-term development to bring millions now mired in poverty into agricultural markets, as participants with adequate purchasing power. The reform of government policies affecting agricultural trade will assist in overcoming these problems, but the long-run solution is to raise the incomes of people in the developing countries.

The reform of domestic agricultural policies in many developing countries would complement the process of world trade liberalization and would contribute to their overall economic growth. More generally, the global economy is experiencing a significant loss in economic growth because of existing barriers to trade. Policies that discriminate against agriculture in the developing countries and subsidize agriculture in the developed countries cause a significant share of global agricultural output to be produced in the wrong place under inefficient conditions. A more efficient use of the world's agricultural resources would lead to a significant increase in global economic growth, which would ultimately benefit all countries.

Reforms to deal with the problems of agricultural trade will not solve all the problems in the world food system, but if complementary policies are pursued, the liberalization of agricultural trade could have widespread benefits for developed and developing countries. Admittedly, higher and more stable world prices for traded agricultural commodities over the long term, which should result from liberalization of agricultural trade, could increase the cost of food in developing countries that are food importers and maintain internal prices at artificially low levels. But farmers in these countries would benefit; and since agriculture is still the dominant industry in most developing countries, a sound and stable international economic environment for the expansion of their agriculture is vital to their development. In addition, the gains to agricultural producers and rural residents will offer opportunities for improving productivity and reducing poverty in rural areas, thus helping to reduce malnutrition. At the same time, exporters in many developing countries should achieve significant gains from higher and more stable world prices. The overall interests of developing and developed countries will be best served by simultaneous liberalization of trade in agricultural and industrial products, which would stimulate world economic growth while minimizing adjustment problems for agricultural producers.

Finally, in moving toward more liberalized trade in agricultural and industrial products, efforts should be made simultaneously to obtain a more stable and less trade-distorting international monetary environment. Global macroeconomic imbalances, such as occurred in the 1980s, lead to misaligned exchange rates that distort trade and give rise to pressures for protectionist measures from those disadvantaged by such misalignments. (See *Resolving the Global Economic Crisis: After Wall Street, 1987.* Washington: Institute for International Economics.)

Negotiations to improve the functioning of the international monetary system and to avoid distortions in exchange rates need to be conducted in tandem with the general negotiations in GATT on trade liberalization. Greater attention must also be given to ensuring that monetary and fiscal policies will not distort international capital movements, the objective being to reduce both misalignments in exchange rates and the protectionist measures they engender. International surveillance and monitoring efforts to this end should be strengthened.

Agricultural Reform and the GATT Negotiations

Agriculture has historically been treated differently under the GATT. The GATT rules for trade in non-agricultural products impose limits on the type of economic policies that can be used to protect domestic industries. Equally important, non-agricultural trade is subject to strict rules regarding border measures that governments can use to assist domestic industries. With certain exceptions, the use of export subsidies and quantitative import restrictions are prohibited in non-agriculture trade.

The present GATT rules for agricultural products allow for both export subsidies and quantitative restrictions on imports. As a result, there has been a steady proliferation of government intervention in agricultural pricing, production, and trade flows. The use of policy instruments outside, or inconsistent with, the GATT rules has become increasingly common. These include variable levies, voluntary restraint agreements, and state trading operations. In both exporting and importing countries, agricultural production, marketing, and trade decisions have been increasingly separated from world supply and demand conditions and, based on domestic political pressures, have become highly dependent upon government intervention. The result is a series of beggar-thy-neighbour policies, which have sharply increased the level of tensions in world agricultural trade.

The restrictions and distortions in world agricultural trade that have long undermined the GATT system have reached a critical point. Existing GATT rules for agriculture have failed to prevent the rising level of trade tensions, primarily because of the unwillingness of governments to accept effective disciplines over domestic agricultural programs. Governments have been unable to resolve some of the most difficult agricultural trade disputes through the GATT settlement process. This has weakened the GATT's authority and credibility.

Key political leaders recognize this dangerous situation. Heads of government of the seven leading industrial nations called for co-ordinated agricultural reform in their summit statements in 1986 and 1987. Ministers of Trade and Finance of OECD countries echoed the call at their 1987 ministerial meeting. Ministers of Trade of the GATT member nations placed agricultural trade problems at the top of their agenda for the Uruguay Round of Trade Negotiations when they met in Punta del Este in September 1986. For the first time they agreed that all agricultural policies that affect trade should be included in the new round of negotiations, with a view to eliminating their trade-distorting impacts.

In 1987, in the early stages of the Uruguay Round, a number of proposals on agricultural trade negotiation were put forward by key countries and groups of countries. With a few notable exceptions, these proposals call for

- a reduction or elimination of trade distorting subsidies and import restrictions over an agreed period of years; and

- immediate measures to freeze and/or roll back subsidies and to stabilize world agricultural markets.

Major differences remain among individual countries and groups of countries about the pace and depth of these reforms, and regarding the desirability of short-term actions to offset some of the worst market effects of the current distorting measures. These differences must be bridged in the negotiations. Of immediate concern, however, is the increasing acceptance of the view that the process can and should be delayed because of national elections, political fatigue, and the general sensitivity of agricultural issues.

Delay would represent a major error. If agricultural markets have reached their low point and are improving, changing policy directions now would make the necessary adjustment easier and quicker. If the current improvement proved only temporary, however, prompt and decisive action at an early stage of the negotiations could prevent further subsidy wars, which could ultimately jeopardize the successful completion of the GATT Round. It is imperative that governments make every effort in the summer and autumn of 1988 to bridge the differences in national approaches and to develop a framework agreement for the agricultural negotiations for ratification at the mid-term review in December by the Ministers of Trade. The heads of government of the major industrial countries at their summit in Canada in June should set the goal of securing such a framework agreement by December 1988.

Bridging the Differences

The negotiations will proceed most expeditiously if the framework agreement encompasses the principal elements of the positions of the major negotiating countries. It should provide clear directions for policy reform and allow for the maximum degree of trade liberalization without prejudging the ultimate outcome. Most of the proposals tabled in Geneva to date for the conduct of agricultural negotiations are predicated on a comprehensive or aggregate approach, designed to deal with all policy instruments that influence trade and with all commodities. Although there is considerable agreement on the general direction of policy change to be pursued, wide differences persist on the degree of trade liberalization that is acceptable, the time frame for change, and the extent of government involvement in agriculture that is consistent with optimum resource allocation.

Many of the country proposals recommend the use of an aggregate measurement of support, based on the Producer Subsidy Equivalent (PSE) concept, to facilitate the negotiations. A number of the country proposals identify some of the policies and programs to be subjected to negotiation and included in any measurement.

All the countries participating in the Uruguay Round advocate strengthened and enforceable GATT rules and disciplines, including effective ways to maintain surveillance and settle disputes. There appears to be broad support for implementing a process of phased reform of policies affecting trade, combined with the renegotiation of GATT rules to discipline agricultural trade both during a period of transition and after the reforms are in place.

The fundamental problem underlying the current agricultural crisis stems from the fact that national governments chose to use policies that support commodity prices as their major income support for farm people. This distorts both the use of national resources and international trade in agricultural products. The goals of the trade negotiations are, primarily, to reduce the international trade-distorting effects of national agricultural policies and, secondly, to encourage countries to improve the efficiency of resource use within their national economies.

But agricultural producers, governments and segments of the agro-food industry are likely to resist domestic farm policy reforms unless acceptable alternative policies are available. Less competitive agricultural sectors will also oppose trade liberalization. However, there is ample empirical evidence to demonstrate that, in most countries, freer trade enhances economic welfare. Prices for key farm commodities entering world trade would rise, and world trade in agricultural products would increase. In most countries, consumers and taxpayers would benefit. However, some commodity sectors in some countries would suffer from a reduction in farm support and protection. If all agricultural subsidies were eliminated, producer incomes in the more highly assisted industrial countries would decline, at least temporarily. Thus policy adjustments are likely to be introduced gradually, and farm support will be continued, possibly on a declining scale, as world markets strengthen.

Consequently, it is important that governments reach agreement on the types of policy instruments that are the least trade-distorting and begin to reshape farm programs accordingly. This calls for a process of decoupling farm policies from production and the marketplace to minimize distortions in resource allocation and trade. This can be complemented by policies designed to encourage resource conservation and environmental improvement.

There is also a need to ensure that developing countries play a greater role in the agricultural negotiations, both to achieve the maximum possible benefit from them and to broaden the results to the advantage of all trading countries. There are opportunities to support agricultural development and to assist policy reform and structural adjustment to strengthen the economies of less developed countries through trade. Given the significant gains that developing countries can achieve through expanded trade, they should offer reciprocity consistent with their level of economic development.

Agricultural policy reform through trade negotiations would be facilitated by international initiatives to promote world economic growth. Greater macroeconomic policy co-ordination, particularly to reduce global trade imbalances and to achieve greater stability in exchange rates, will aid the agricultural policy reform process.

The GATT rules providing for surveillance of policy commitments and dispute settlement must be strengthened to facilitate and secure progress in the reform of domestic agricultural and trade policies and to reduce the incidence of formal disputes. New mechanisms are needed to oversee and enforce undertakings related to internal policies. Governments will wish to retain considerable flexibility to adjust domestic programs in response to unexpected changes, such as unusual market conditions or trade developments and fluctuations in exchange rates. But in addition to improved processes for dispute settlement, new international mechanisms are needed for regular reviews of domestic farm policies, as well as for the co-ordination and adjustment of these policies. Such procedures would complement but not replace the regular GATT provisions for surveillance and dispute settlement which, in turn, should be strengthened and applied more vigorously.

Recommendations for Long-Term Reform

We propose that the governments of all agricultural trading countries pursue genuine reform of agricultural and trade policies in the context of the Uruguay Round. The long-term objective should be the eventual removal of all trade distortions from agricultural programs.

We believe the following guidelines would provide clear direction and impetus to the negotiations.

- All national measures that restrict or distort agricultural trade, stimulate excess production or limit consumption should be on the table.

- There should be no increase in policies that limit trade or distort production or consumption.

- Agreement should be reached on those programs that have a minimal impact on trade and that may therefore be used.

- There should be a major reduction in all measures that affect trade adversely to allow market signals to guide resource allocation and trade.

- All remaining measures that affect trade adversely should be subject to precise and enforceable GATT rules and disciplines.

- Reforms expected of developing countries must take into account the stage of their economic development, the need for suitable transitional arrangements, and specific problems such as widespread malnutrition.

- Countries should be free to choose their agricultural policies provided they do not limit or distort trade.

We recommend that the GATT negotiations proceed on a comprehensive basis to obtain agreement on the following:

- a program of progressively reducing the adverse trade effects of agricultural policies;

- decoupled or trade-neutral farm policies and positive agricultural adjustment programs;

- policies to encourage conservation of land and water resources and to improve environmental systems;

- stronger and more precise GATT rules, which would be negotiated in parallel with the program of phased reductions in trade-distorting policies;

- arrangements to facilitate full participation by developing countries in the negotiations;

- new mechanisms for surveillance, consultation, and domestic policy co-ordination;

- the strengthening of GATT dispute settlement mechanisms; and

- the implementation of a multilateral program of early relief from severe distortions affecting agricultural trade.

Phased Reductions in Trade-Distorting Policies

Governments should agree to a phased reduction of all policy instruments with significant adverse affects on trade in order to allow market signals to progressively guide resource allocation and trade. The adjustments in national policies, if done on a multilateral basis over time, will be less difficult than if undertaken unilaterally.

Negotiations on agriculture in the Uruguay Round should include all instruments and commodities in a comprehensive manner. This approach is consistent with the negotiating objective and plan for agriculture in the GATT to deal with all subsidies and other instruments affecting agricultural trade and to provide for phased reduction. It treats market access issues and subsidy issues together; these are closely linked and difficult to negotiate independently. It provides the maximum scope for involving as many countries as possible in the negotiation, for sharing the burdens of making adjustments to changes in agriculture systems, and for obtaining the greatest benefits at the least cost. Most important, this approach provides a mechanism for bringing the complex range of domestic agricultural policies and programs into the trade negotiations. The process may be facilitated by the use of empirical measurements such as the PSE to establish target levels of reductions and to assess the effects of policy adjustments.

Countries must enter into contractual commitments to remove the most trade-distorting elements of their national agricultural policies and to restructure these policies in ways that limit their effects on resource use. Individual countries would submit their own plans to implement their undertakings to reduce trade distortions and levels of protection; following a process of negotiations, these plans would become contractual commitments under GATT. Such commitments relating to national agricultural policies would be unique in GATT terms, and their integration into the GATT system may form part of the schedules to the agreement and be implemented through a separate code or other suitable arrangements. To encourage co-operative actions during the negotiation, countries should receive credit for unilateral policy actions that reduce trade-distorting measures.

Agreements on Decoupled Farm Programs

The first step in the multilateral trade negotiation entails adherence by national authorities to the principle, agreed in the OECD, that support for farm people should be progressively 'decoupled' or 'delinked' from production, consumption and trade so as to eliminate the distorting impacts of existing policies and ensure that they are trade-neutral.

Secondly, it will be necessary for the member governments to categorize instruments of farm policy according to their trade-distorting effects. There is an urgent need to reach agreement among governments on the types of farm programs that are trade-neutral or decoupled and the programs that are not and that should therefore be removed or adjusted. The process of negotiating the policy coverage of an overall commitment to reduce trade-influencing measures will be easier if negotiations can identify policies that are trade-neutral and agree that they should be excluded from the negotiations.

For example, government services and general infrastructure support may be excluded, particularly in the case of infrastructure support in developing countries, where such investments are essential to develop and modernize their agriculture. Market stabilization programs, stockpiling and buffer schemes, and programs to remove excess resources and facilitate adjustment might be regarded as interim arrangements and retained subject to specific conditions and review procedures. New programs such as income insurance schemes may be required. The resulting agreements on the reform of farm policies and agricultural adjustment might be incorporated into a GATT code that could also govern countries' commitments to progressively reduce support and protection for agriculture.

Policies to Encourage Conservation and to Improve the Environment

Policies to conserve land and water resources and to improve the environment can complement the reform of domestic agricultural programs. Assistance and incentive programs facilitating the removal of fragile resources from agricultural production will assist in bringing supply and demand into better balance. Similarly, a lowering of commodity price supports toward market-clearing levels will reduce incentives for the use of chemicals and some land resources. Other policies designed to deal with external effects, like landscape values, should be goal-specific, designed to have minimal effect on trade and be a subject of negotiation.

A Parallel Negotiation of GATT Rules

The negotiation of more effective rules and disciplines in the GATT should proceed in step with the progressive reduction in aggregate levels of support and protection. The rules should discipline the use of all instruments that affect trade, including all waivers, grandfather clauses, variable levy systems, state trading practices, voluntary export restraints, and all other non-tariff barriers.

GATT rules should be revised to ensure that all measures affecting access to markets are placed under effective disciplines and that all measures that distort trade are reduced and eventually removed. Among other things, the rules could provide for the conversion of all trade-distorting measures remaining after the transitional period to bound tariff-equivalent forms. The nature of the revised rules will depend on the extent of movement toward free trade in agriculture.

Interim rules will be required to discipline the use of policy measures for agricultural products during the period of transition. These interim rules would cover the progressive reduction of import barriers and trade-distorting subsidies. Precise conditions for any exceptions to the general rules should be agreed to. Termination dates should be negotiated for the removal of all waivers and policies inconsistent with the GATT. The rules should require notification of policy changes and should include procedures for regular international surveillance.

Full Participation by Developing Countries

In the GATT, developing countries are subject to fewer disciplines than apply to the developed countries. But they have paid a price for choosing to remain outside the full GATT system; the developed countries are also subject to less discipline in areas of greatest concern to developing countries, notably agriculture and textiles. The Uruguay Round offers the developing countries an opportunity to press the case for subjecting interventions in agriculture to the same discipline of the GATT as is applied to industrial products. Developing countries must subject their own trade interventions to full GATT discipline. Such a 'concession' will be to their own benefit, because many of these interventions are extremely costly.

However, longer transition periods and the continuation of higher levels of protection and infrastructure development should be permitted for developing countries under agreed conditions, in accordance with their development needs. Opportunities to combine trade liberalization and adjustment assistance should be pursued, possibly with the assistance of the World Bank and the International Monetary Fund.

Domestic Policy Co-ordination

The GATT must be strengthened to oversee the implementation of a comprehensive strategy for the progressive adjustment of farm and trade policies. New institutional arrangements within GATT should be considered for agriculture that would provide for surveillance of the fulfilment of commitments to reform policies, review national policies on a regular basis, and which could help resolve policy differences. This activity might be undertaken by creating a standing GATT committee on agricultural policy. These arrangements would complement and not replace the existing dispute settlement procedures of the GATT. They could be developed as part of broader agreements designed to give GATT new authority to review national trade policies and to strengthen the GATT articles and procedures governing the notification of national policies and consultations.

Dispute Settlement

Within an overall policy framework, the rules governing trade in agricultural products should be strictly enforced. But the effective operation of new rules governing trade in agricultural products will require a strengthened dispute settlement process in the GATT. A number of countries have already proposed changes to the overall GATT dispute settlement process, and these changes will form an important part of the Uruguay Round. In view of the particular problems that have been experienced in resolving agricultural trade disputes, it is essential that clear and enforceable rules be negotiated to enable the GATT dispute settlement process to operate effectively.

A Multilateral Program of Early Relief

The achievement of longer-term reform of policies would be facilitated if governments agree to undertake early actions to provide relief from the most severe distortions currently affecting agricultural trade. These short-term actions should include a freeze of all trade-distorting subsidies and import barriers, undertakings not to introduce new measures with adverse trade effects, and a commitment to roll back those that now exist. The agreement could include steps to curb excess production, encourage demand, and dispose of excess stocks in a manner that avoids serious disruptions in trade. It is critical that commitments to begin early relief actions be undertaken as part of the framework agreement to commence negotiations on the basis of the comprehensive approach and the renegotiation of GATT rules, and they should be consistent with the negotiating guidelines.

Making the Transition

Agricultural policy and trade reforms of the type and scope proposed here will require substantial adjustments in worldwide agriculture. The process will require a more market-oriented global agricultural system, greater influence for competitive market forces, a different role for governments in agriculture, and some reduction in the income transfers to farmers that are made under current types of policies.

Farmers are understandably apprehensive about the impact of these changes on their income and the value of their assets. These effects should not be exaggerated, however, for the income losses associated with reducing protection will be significantly offset by the expansion of effective demand that world trade liberalization will produce. In addition, world market prices for some agricultural products will strengthen, the price of some inputs will fall, and some governments will be able to replace income supports now made through commodity-type programs with alternative policy instruments. Indeed, governments will have ample opportunity to provide assistance to agriculture (for whatever reasons they find compelling, and in amounts desired) as long as they avoid harming the legitimate trade interests of other countries.

Once agriculture has adjusted to a more competitive environment, which will include a reduction of cost structures, commercial farmers will be better off and will face a more predictable environment. They will compete with each other in growing markets, instead of competing with the treasuries of other countries. They will no longer be vulnerable to the whims of their own and other governments, as they are now.

Progress to Date

It is important to recognize that progress is under way to reform domestic agricultural programs and adjust production to market conditions. Farmers in a number of countries already are responding to changes in markets or support programs by reducing their output of surplus crops. Japan lowered its rice support price in 1987 for the first time in 32 years and recently reduced its high internal beef and dairy prices. The United States began implementing the target prices and loan rates contained in its 1985 farm legislation, and land retirement programs involving 70 million acres of cropland have reduced U.S.

production of surplus crops. A buy-out program sharply reduced the growth in U.S. dairy output. Budget expenditures on U.S. government agricultural subsidies have been reduced from a high of $26 billion in fiscal year 1985-86 to an estimated $17 billion in fiscal 1987-88.

The European Community (EC) also has made adjustments in the operation of its Common Agricultural Policy (CAP). A production control program for milk was introduced in 1984 and tightened in 1987. A recent decision by the EC heads of government introduced new constraints on the agricultural budget and aims to reduce surplus production by implementing price cuts for cereals, oilseeds, meats, and certain other products. They also approved the first acreage set-aside program in the CAP.

Important changes also have occurred in a number of developing countries, including trade liberalization, significant removals of exchange rate distortions, and reductions in price distortions in agricultural sectors. Although these changes have been made in response to forces outside the multilateral trade negotiations, it should be recognized that they contribute to the long-run objectives of the Uruguay Round and that appropriate credit should therefore be given.

All of these are moves in the right direction. All required political courage and determination at the highest levels. But these changes are not enough. Reform of agricultural programs must be broadened, institutionalized, and put into a multilateral framework. Both common sense and widespread economic analysis demonstrate that multilateral adjustment is politically and economically easier than unilateral adjustment.

A phased multilateral removal of trade-distorting agricultural policies does not mean that nations must abandon either cherished national goals or their agricultural sectors. These goals can be met in a variety of ways beyond the existing production-encouraging, trade-distorting programs. A search for alternative programs is now under way, and further progress in the agricultural negotiations will add urgency to that search.

Reasonable price stability for basic foodstuffs and secure food supplies have long been major goals of most national policies. A removal of trade-distorting subsidies from the operation of international markets would provide a major stabilizing force in world markets, making it easier for national governments to allow their internal markets to become less isolated from world markets.

Farmers' incomes need not be left entirely to market forces. There is a variety of ways to provide income to agricultural producers that have no adverse effect on agricultural adjustment. These include direct government transfer payments unrelated to current production, land-use conversion programs to encourage conservation, recreation and wildlife use, early retirement programs in exchange for rights to future farm program benefits, and individual and community adjustment programs to encourage the development of alternative employment for rural people. There are also many other programs providing services and support to farmers, some of which give income protection without creating distortions in resource use and trade.

A Framework for Progress in 1988

It is unrealistic to expect that the negotiations on agricultural trade in the Uruguay Round can lead to final agreements before the close of 1988. It is important, however, that momentum not be lost and that the situation not be allowed to drift back into a series of unilateral policies that may be both disruptive and self-defeating. Therefore, it is proposed that a major effort be made during the summer and autumn of 1988 to reach agreement on the elements of a framework to provide general direction for continuing national changes in policy and to outline boundaries within which the final multilateral trade agreement on agriculture would be negotiated.

Several crucial elements must be included in a successful framework agreement. They are:

- identification of the programs to be included in negotiations on reducing trade-distorting policies, as well as clarification of a list of programs that clearly would be considered non-distorting and thus could expect relatively few alterations or constraints as a result of future negotiations;

- agreements, as specific as possible, on the direction of changes in policies to guide the negotiations on trade-distorting programs and the strengthening of GATT rules;

- the role of developing countries;

- a surveillance mechanism under GATT to review current policies, monitor changes in policies, and report publicly to member states on the situation;

- a dispute settlement process that allows speedy and non-confrontational settlement of the disputes that are certain to arise during the subsequent negotiation period and beyond; and

- agreement on short-term measures to be put in place during the remainder of the negotiations and, possibly, during a longer transition period, to deal with urgent severe distortions of international trade.

Those knowledgeable about the economic and political complexity of these elements will recognize that to achieve even this simple framework will require major political will and heroic negotiating efforts. However, a framework agreement that fails to address them will almost certainly be inadequate and could create more problems than it solves. Indeed, if a framework agreement were too vague and unstructured, it would eventually contribute to a breakdown of the negotiations at a later stage. Consequently, the immediate objective for GATT countries is to elaborate these crucial elements along the following lines in a framework agreement as the basis for proceeding with negotiations on agriculture in the Uruguay Round.

Defining Trade-Distorting Programs

Reaching some agreement about which policies seriously distort agricultural trade must be a part of the framework agreement. By necessity, it will take a long time to negotiate what, if any, limits are to be placed on trade-distorting programs, and even longer to bring about the agreed changes. But the direction of change will be determined by an agreement on which programs are to be the focus of the continuing negotiation. It is especially crucial that this occur before an attempt is made to strengthen the GATT rules, an important issue to be addressed later.

It also is important that all national policies, including those covered by GATT waivers and grandfather clauses and those not adequately covered by GATT rules (variable levies, state trading, voluntary restraint agreements, etc.), should be included in the negotiations, starting with a decision as to whether they have significant trade-distorting effects.

We believe that early identification of the policies that create the most distortion in production and trade will serve three useful purposes. First, it will reduce the apprehension of some groups that all governmental programs will be phased out regardless of the economic conditions of farmers and of rural areas. Second, it will focus subsequent negotiations on the important issues of what should be done with the programs judged to have adverse effects and how to do it in the least disruptive fashion. Finally, it will help convince many developing countries, which stand to gain much from the proposed changes, that they can participate fully without jeopardizing their future development goals.

Dealing With Trade-Distorting Programs

We believe that there must be, by the end of 1988, a firm commitment on the direction and the nature of change. This is more important than immediate agreement on the magnitude of change and the time period over which these changes should occur, although these will be essential at the next stage. The world's farm producers and associated industries, private investors and the consuming public have a need to know, and the right to know, the policy directions that governments can be expected to pursue. This is doubly important in a sector where government policy in most countries is a dominant influence on private decisions regarding investment and resource use in agriculture.

Ideally, this commitment would consist of an agreement that the final negotiations should aim toward to complete phasing out of all trade-distorting programs, giving highest priority to those policies with the greatest adverse effects. As an initial step, there must be an agreement that definable and enforceable limits on trade-distorting programs should be negotiated, with the objective of removing or offsetting their negative trade effects. In any case, the objective should be to bring agricultural trade fully under strengthened and enforceable GATT rules and disciplines.

Developing Country Issues

Developing countries are rightly concerned that any new rules limiting domestic agricultural policies should not limit their ability to develop their agricultural potential, increase the productivity of their agricultural industry, and ensure food security for the poor. Developing countries that import food have expressed concern that removing output-distorting subsidies in developed countries will result in higher import costs for food. However, several economic analyses show that any rise in world prices of food and feed grains and oilmeals, which are the main products imported by developing countries, would be modest. For the poorest developing countries, their concerns can be dealt with by strengthening the Food Aid Convention.

To the extent that changes in trade and exchange rate policies in the developing countries lead to higher domestic food prices, targeted feeding programs may be needed for the disadvantaged. Those programs can be strengthened with international financial assistance.

One of the greatest fears of developing countries relates to the instability in world market prices for agriculture products and concern that the shortages of the 1970s will recur. Trade liberalization in agriculture will contribute to stabilizing markets for both importers and exporters. Developing countries can also make use of the compensatory financing facility and the cereal financing facility of the International Monetary Fund, both of which may need further improvement.

Early action on liberalization of trade in tropical products should receive high priority.

Establishing A Surveillance Mechanism

Any functional framework agreement reached in the near future must include the establishment of a mechanism for the surveillance of commitments on national agricultural policies undertaken within the GATT framework. Its purpose would be to review developments in national agricultural policies; to keep track of changes in policies; and to provide a basis for negotiations on changes in policies. Moreover, once such a surveillance mechanism is functioning, it can contribute to the achievement of balance in the negotiations and provide an important basis for resolving differences over policy commitments.

In designing a new surveillance mechanism, it is important to recall the final objectives of the negotiations and to bear in mind that their achievement is likely to involve a long transition process.

As discussed above, the main objectives of the Uruguay Round for agriculture are twofold:

- to agree upon phasing out of trading-distorting agricultural policies and replacing them, as necessary, with non-distorting programs; and

- to strengthen GATT rules in agriculture in a fashion consistent with the first objective, so as to make these rules clear, consistent in scope and coverage, and usable to guide governments both in policy changes and dispute settlement.

It is evident, however, that a long period of change is beginning in world agricultural and trade policies. The surveillance process must therefore be designed to function for an extended period of transition, during which the direction agreed will be clear though differences may exist over the status of commitments.

Surveillance may involve the use of empirical measurements. Over the past year there have been numerous discussions within and outside the GATT about PSEs, Trade Distortions Equivalents (TDEs), price gaps, effective protection equivalents, and other aggregate measuring devices. Each has appeal and thus its advocates. None is perfect, and most require immense amounts of data, some of which are difficult and expensive to obtain. There is a danger that negotiations may become diverted to issues better left to meetings of technical specialists.

Therefore, it is recommended that the surveillance mechanism should begin with an inventory of programs in place in each country in a specified base year. That year probably should be 1984 or 1985, just prior to the beginning of the current round of multilateral trade negotiations. At the same time, information should be obtained on the current status of those programs in 1988, with the same information obtained for programs added subsequently.

At a minimum, information should be gathered on the type of program – price support, import quota, levy, etc. – the commodities covered, the quantities of those commodities produced, consumed and traded, and the local price received by producers.

A system whereby this information is submitted regularly to the GATT will need to be established. The surveillance group should have authority to request more information from individual countries if there are questions regarding the nature and operation of specific programs. The information assembled through the surveillance group would provide much greater uniformity in knowledge across member countries about the agricultural policies and programs affecting trade. This feature of surveillance will be particularly important for developing and smaller developed countries that do not have the resources to remain fully informed about policies and programs in other countries. This increased transparency will broaden the operation and strengthen the GATT as an institution.

On this basis the GATT Secretariat could be requested to prepare and publish an annual review of national agricultural policies, just as the IMF and the OECD present annual reviews of changes and developments in trade, finance, and monetary policies. These annual reviews would facilitate periodic in-depth reviews of national policies. The process could be developed in conjunction with the proposed in-depth GATT review of all trade policies, or it could be developed separetely, then used in a broader GATT review.

Accordingly, the framework agreement should authorize the GATT Secretariat to proceed immediately with the development of a surveillance mechanism and provide the funds required to obtain the necessary professional support for it. At this point it is not crucial to decide whether PSEs, TDEs or other measures should be used as targets or negotiating guides. Those decisions can be made as part of a final package, but the creation of a functioning surveillance mechanism cannot wait, and developing it will be a formidable task.

Settling Differences over National Policies

One of the most difficult tasks in reaching an early framework agreement will be the development of an effective dispute settlement process within the GATT for settling differences on national policies during what will be a long period of negotiating commitments on policy changes and new GATT rules for agriculture. An even longer period will then be required for adjusting to the changes and new rules. However, unless member countries put in place an acceptable and workable process that they trust for resolving policy conflicts, the inevitable disagreements are likely to erupt into battles and wars that could destroy the fragile process of adjustment and change.

It is unlikely that the present GATT dispute settlement procedures will be adequate during this interim period. Resolving disputes may prove more difficult under the present GATT procedures, inasmuch as the interim rules for the transition period will be new and probably, unfortunately, imprecise. However, it is important that recourse to the existing dispute settlement provisions of the GATT also be retained to resolve disputes in relation to rights and obligations under the articles of GATT.

The new dispute settlement rules for GATT as a whole remain to be determined. Meanwhile, the issue of settling differences over national agriculture policies must be faced now if there is to be a viable framework for the negotiations. Therefore, we recommend special procedures, to be in effect for an indefinite period, to deal with surveillance and policy differences in relation to commitments on national agricultural policies.

We recommend that a standing policy review committee and independent panel for resolving disputes over agricultural policies be established within the GATT for an indefinite period. Consultations and surveillance with respect to commitments on national policies would be undertaken by the policy review committee, made up of ministers or senior policy representatives. To resolve disputes that cannot be settled in this committee, an independent panel should be established. It should consist of no fewer than five persons nominated by the Director General and approved by the GATT Council. It could comprise representatives of governments or private citizens. Members would have staggered terms of no fewer than two and no more than five years.

The new mechanism would have dual and closely-related functions: to oversee the policy surveillance activity of the GATT Secretariat and to help resolve disputes over national policy actions. The close relationship between these functions is obvious, for the first exists to enable the second function to be performed. Member governments should agree on time limits for the panel to decide disputes and on its authority to recommend actions to deal with disputes. It is important that panel reports be written, published, and made available to all interested member governments. It is these governments that must ultimately make the political decisions on the course of action to be followed in the event that a member state's policies diverge from its commitments. Member countries would have final recourse to the existing dispute settlement procedures of the GATT in the event of unresolved disputes. We believe that a continuing permanent panel can better interpret the policy commitments and judge whether countries are complying with their commitments than can ad hoc, intermittent panels convened under stress to judge a single national policy action. We believe that establishing a fair and open process of informal review and judgement would facilitate resolution of disputes more effectively than relying upon a court of last appeal in a system where rules and commitments are, of necessity, changing over time.

Short-Term Measures

At present, there is a wide divergence of opinion as to whether short-term measures to deal with serious trade distortions are necessary or desirable. We believe they are, but we recognize that their specific nature must be subject to negotiation.

We believe that, at a minimum, there can be a commitment on three important issues. One is that governments should adhere strictly to their earlier commitment not to introduce any new policies that add further distortions to the system. In other words, a freeze on new export subsidy programs and new trade barriers should be agreed to and implemented, along with a freeze on export taxes.

Second, governments can and should fully implement the positive policy changes already under way in several countries, such as those mentioned earlier in Japan, the European Community and the United States. Those countries that have not already agreed to such policy changes should agree to immediate and commensurate actions consistent with the general objectives of the negotiations.

Third, countries should agree to avoid actions that are clearly inconsistent with the direction and intent of the negotiations. This means that countries will not manipulate present policies and instruments in a way that would encourage subsidized output or destabilize markets, nor will they seek to gain negotiating advantage.

Although co-ordinated actions to reduce the impact on trade of various national measures such as export subsidies could contribute to early relief, overt attempts to manipulate international agricultural markets through commodity agreements, market sharing, or price fixing are highly controversial and, we believe, counter-productive. They are counter-productive because they would be so divisive and could redirect the focus of the negotiations away from the basic issues. Furthermore, they probably would not work, and there will be a tendency to blame someone else if they fail. It is important at this early stage of the negotiations to avoid serious political confrontations whenever possible, for there will be more than enough tough political decisions in the later stages. Now that the agricultural situation is improving, the important political decision is to continue to move it in the right direction and to avoid policy actions inconsistent with the desired final outcome.

The Opportunity

The agricultural trading nations, both developed and developing, are presented with a unique opportunity to achieve fundamental reform of food and agricultural programs in the context of a major trade negotiation. There is a broad mandate from the member nations of GATT to deal with all agricultural policies that affect trade and to proceed with negotiations to reduce the trade impact of domestic and border policies. A number of major trading countries have tabled proposals to begin the negotiations. Although there are important differences between the approaches, there is broad support for dealing with policies and commodities in a comprehensive manner and negotiating major reductions in trade-distorting policies, supported by effective and enforceable GATT rules and disciplines.

For the first time, all of the ingredients for a successful negotiation appear to be on the table. It is now up to governments to translate their political declarations into commitments to policy changes.

The differing capacities of national economies to adjust to change smoothly and equitably suggest that changes will be gradual and must emerge from an understanding of the failure of national policies to respond to the underlying trends affecting modern farming communities today. But there is overwhelming evidence that reform is needed and that it will provide long-term benefits to the global economy and place farmers around the world on a firmer economic footing. This unique opportunity for genuine reform must not be missed because of short-term political and economic considerations.

We urge the leaders of the summit countries meeting in Canada in June to commit their ministers to reaching agreement on a negotiating framework for agriculture in 1988. On this basis, the trade ministers of GATT, when they meet in Canada in December, could begin the process of reforming government policies affecting agriculture trade — a process that may well be crucial to the future welfare of the world's food economy and, indeed, to the multilateral system of international economic co-operation. These two meetings provide a unique opportunity to launch serious negotiations without delay, and to achieve genuine policy reform.

Signatories

C. FRED BERGSTEN
Director, Institute for International Economics
Former Assistant Secretary for International Affairs, Treasury Department
United States

SIR RICHARD BUTLER
Farmer
Former President of the National Farmers' Union of England and Wales; and
    President of COPA (the Farmers' Organization of the European Community)
United Kingdom

FABRIZIO DE FILIPPIS
Professor, Faculty of Agriculture, Università Della Tuscia (Viterbo)
Italy

JAN DE VEER
Director, Agricultural Economic Institute
The Netherlands

WILLIAM HAMILTON
Executive Director, Western Grain Research Foundation
Former Executive Secretary, Canadian Federation of Agriculture
Canada

DALE HATHAWAY
Visiting Fellow, Institute for International Economics, and
    Partner, Consultants International Group
Former Under Secretary of Agriculture for International Affairs and Commodity
    Programs; and Director, International Food Policy Research Institute
United States

DOUGLAS D. HEDLEY
Rockefeller Foundation Overseas Visiting Professor and Winrock International,
    Indonesia
Former Director General, Policy and Planning, Agriculture
Canada

KENZO HEMMI
Professor of International Economics, Asia University (Tokyo), and
    Chairman, International Rice Research Institute (Philippines)
Former Dean, College of Agriculture, University of Tokyo
Japan

WILLIAM HENRICHSMEYER
Professor of Agricultural Economics and Director of the Institute for Agricultural
    Policy, Bonn University, and Chairman of the Advisory Board to the Ministry of
    Agriculture
Federal Republic of Germany

PONCIANO INTAL
Professor of Agricultural Economics, University of the Philippines
Philippines

NURUL ISLAM
Senior Research Adviser, International Food Policy Research Institute
Former Assistant Director-General, United Nations Food and Agriculture
    Organization; and Deputy Chairman (Minister) of the Planning Commission,
Bangladesh

SOREN KJELDSEN-KRAGH
Professor of Economics, Economic Institute of the Royal Agricultural University,
    Copenhagen
Denmark

ARNE LARSEN
Director, Institute of Agricultural Economics
Former Chef de Cabinet to the Commissioner of Agriculture, Commission of the
    European Community
Denmark

JOHN S. MARSH
Professor of Economics and Head of Department of Agricultural Economics and
    Management, University of Reading
United Kingdom

WILLIAM H. MEYERS
Professor of Economics, Iowa State University, and Associate Director, Center for
    Agricultural and Rural Development
United States

WILLIAM MINER
Senior Research Associate (Agriculture), Institute for Research on Public Policy
Former Assistant Deputy Minister, Agriculture Canada and Co-ordinator of the Federal
    Advisory Group on Grains
Canada

JANOS NYERGES
Former Special Representative of the Hungarian Government to International
    Organizations; and Lecturer at the University of Economics, Budapest
Hungary

WILLIAM R. PEARCE
Senior Vice President, Cargill
Former Deputy Special Trade Representative, Executive Office of the President
United States

MICHEL PETIT
Professor, Ecole Nationale Supérieures des Sciences Agronomiques Appliquées, Dijon,
    and President, International Association of Agricultural Economists
France

TONY RAYNER
Chairman, Economic Monitoring Group of The Planning Council of New Zealand, and
    Professor of Agricultural Economics, Lincoln College
New Zealand

HANS-JÜRGEN ROHR
President, DG-Agropartners
Former State Secretary, Federal Ministry of Agriculture
Federal Republic of Germany

GEORGE E. ROSSMILLER
Director, National Center for Food and Agricultural Policy, Resources for the Future
Former Assistant Administrator for International Trade Policy, Department of
    Agriculture; and Professor of Agricultural Economics, Michigan State University
United States

G. EDWARD SCHUH
Dean, Hubert H. Humphrey Institute of Public Policy, University of Minnesota
Former Senior Economist, President's Council of Economic Advisers; Deputy Under
    Secretary, International Affairs and Commodity Programs, U.S. Department of
    Agriculture; and Director, Agriculture and Rural Development, The World Bank
United States

AMMAR SIAMWALLA
Program Director, Thailand Development Research Institute
Former Research Fellow, International Food Policy Research Institute; and Lecturer,
    Faculty of Economics, Thammasat University
Thailand

MURRAY G. SMITH
Director, International Economics Program, Institute for Research on Public Policy
Canada

ANDREW B. STOECKEL
Director, Centre for International Economics
Former Director, Bureau of Agricultural Economics; and President, Economic Society of
    Australia
Australia

ALBERTO VALDÉZ
Program Director, International Food Policy Research Institute
Chile

T.K. WARLEY
Professor of Agricultural Economics, University of Guelph
Canada

JORGE H. ZORREGUIETA
President, Centro Azucarero Argentino
Former Secretary of Agriculture
Argentina

Background Studies

I. World Agriculture in Crisis: Reforming Government Policies

William M. Miner and Dale E. Hathaway

Contents

Introduction   **37**

Imbalances in World Agriculture   **39**

Expanding Supplies   **40**
Demand Weakness   **42**
Agricultural Exports were Hard-hit   **43**
World Food Security   **44**
Government Policies – Why They Are Not Working   **46**
Protection Levels and Impacts   **48**
Production and Trade Distortion   **50**
The Case for Reform   **55**

The Agricultural Crisis and GATT   **57**
Where Have the Difficulties Been?   **57**
Political Commitments for Reform   **59**
A Framework for Negotiations – An Aggregate Approach   **64**
Country Proposals for Strong Rules   **67**
Permanent GATT Rules for Agriculture Trade   **70**
Developing Interim Rules   **72**
Surveillance and Domestic Policy Co-ordination   **74**
Stronger Dispute Settlement Rules   **75**
Agricultural Negotiations and Developing Countries   **76**
The Need For Early Action   **78**

Adjusting Agriculture in a Global Context   **79**
The Decoupling of Farm Programs   **79**
Agricultural Adjustment Programs   **81**
Resource Conservation Programs   **82**
Encouraging Economic Growth   **83**
The Role of Development Assistance   **83**
Early Progress   **84**

35

A Blueprint for Reform   **86**
   Guidelines for the Negotiations   **86**
   Applying the Aggregate Approach   **87**
   Negotiating Stronger Rules   **89**
   Surveillance and Domestic Policy Co-ordination   **90**
   Procedures for Dispute Settlement   **90**
   A Multilateral Program of Early Relief   **91**
   Elements of a Framework for 1988   **94**
   Moving Ahead with Agricultural Reform   **100**

Notes   **101**

Annex I   **104**

Annex II   **107**

Annex III   **110**

World Agriculture in Crisis: Reforming Government Policies

William M. Miner
Dale E. Hathaway

Introduction

A crisis in much of world agriculture has emerged in the 1980s following a decade of unusual growth in international demand and trade. The difficulties are readily apparent from the serious imbalances between supplies and commercial requirements for agricultural products, the rising level of government intervention in international markets, and the economic stress in agricultural industries in all parts of the world. The agricultural problems have arisen from a combination of developments:

- the distortion of production signals to farmers caused by government subsidies;

- steady advances in technology, which have stymied attempts to regulate production;

- reduced demand, resulting from slower world economic growth and high consumer prices in importing countries linked to barriers to trade;

- exchange rate policies and taxes that penalize agricultural exports in developing countries; and

- export subsidy wars among the industrial countries.

Widespread malnutrition and even starvation persist in isolated areas despite the existence of excess capacity and surplus food in much of the developed world. Macroeconomic developments also have given false signals to farmers. The economic boom of the 1970s led to the inflationary expansion of agricultural capacity. This was followed by the global economic recession in the early 1980s and the subsequent unbalanced economic recovery, characterized by misalignment in exchange rates and burdened by the international debt crisis. At the root of many of these problems lie the national policies of governments and, in particular, their reluctance to accept international trade rules that would discipline these agricultural policies.

The difficulty of dealing with these problems within the GATT is well documented. There have been declarations of political will to address the crisis directly and with determination. There is a widespread agreement on the need for major changes in agricultural policies by the developed countries, but consensus is lacking on how international trade measures and domestic policies affecting agriculture should be changed as part of a concerted policy response. This report examines some of the underlying causes of current agricultural problems and proposes a policy approach that could provide a basis for resolving many of the domestic and international conflicts arising out of the policies of both developed and developing countries.

Part two highlights the growing frictions in world markets and international negotiations caused by increasingly extreme government actions to promote agricultural exports, dispose of surplus stocks, and deflect imports of agricultural products. These government actions in turn are accompanied by growing fiscal burdens and escalating domestic controversies over government policies. The symptoms of policy failure are linked to misdirected efforts to support farm incomes in industrial countries through policies based on commodities in the face of expanding supplies and weakened demand. In developing countries, general economic policies often discriminate against agricultural production and trade. The resulting distortions and the misallocation of agricultural resources arising from these failures of government policy are well demonstrated, as are their negative effects on overall economic growth and on agriculture in industrial and developing countries alike. The need for reform is clear.

Part three examines the approaches taken within GATT to deal with subsidies, quantitative restrictions, state trading and other import controls. It reviews the reasons why it has not proved possible to resolve these difficulties in GATT and the risks for the entire trading system if solutions are not found. It sets out a number of proposals for policy reform and for revising the rules governing agricultural trade. The reasons for adopting a comprehensive approach to the negotiations is discussed, an approach that is to be combined with the negotiation of interim rules and a long-term framework of rules in GATT. Great emphasis is placed on the importance of establishing new and strengthened mechanisms of surveillance of national policy commitments, improved policy co-ordination and strengthened dispute settlement procedures. The approach to negotiations must facilitate full participation by developing countries and enable them to reach their agricultural potential and ensure food security for the poor. Early actions are advocated to ease the current difficulties and to demonstrate the necessary political will to deal seriously and in a fundamental way with the current crisis.

Part four sets these proposals in a global context of agricultural adjustment, including the decoupling, of domestic programs and broader policies to encourage economic growth and development. It outlines the contributions that complementary policy actions can make to the achievement of a stronger agriculture, including protection of the environment, stimulating economic growth, and the advancement of the developing countries. The need to begin the process of reform of agricultural policies in a multilateral context is stressed.

Finally, part five sets out guidelines for the GATT negotiations that would substantially remove the distorting effects of farm policies and bring agriculture within an effective set of international trade rules. A comprehensive approach to the reform of farm and trade policies is proposed, together with a renegotiation of GATT rules to deal with all instruments and commodities in an aggregate manner. New proposals are advanced for monitoring commitments and improving domestic policy co-ordination among GATT countries. Strong emphasis is placed on strict enforcement of the rules to govern trade in agricultural products and to settle disputes so as to prevent the recurrence of the current problems. The report proposes the elements of a framework agreement to be reached in 1988 to enable these crucial negotiations to proceed quickly. Governments are urged to translate their political declarations into commitments to policy changes, so that a more open and predictable trading framework and genuine reform of policies affecting agricultural trade can be achieved.

Imbalances in World Agriculture

The heavy build-up of stocks of key commodities, deteriorating prices in world markets, and aggressive export competition despite continuing hunger and malnutrition are the most obvious symptoms of imbalances in world agriculture. Severe economic stress at the farm level and serious international trade conflicts further demonstrate the crisis. These issues have received unprecedented attention at the highest levels of government. Declining farm incomes in many countries, increasing intervention by governments, and growing burdens on taxpayers indicate that world agriculture is experiencing its worst crisis since the 1930s.

Underlying these symptoms are a number of fundamental changes in the structure of supply and demand for farm products, caused in large measure by the growing impact on production and trade of the vast array of instruments deployed by governments that affect agriculture. Most agricultural markets are cyclical, and governments have intervened in agriculture for decades. Indeed in 1988 there is evidence of some recovery in commodity prices. However, the extreme disarray that is apparent in the current situation, affecting most farm commodities and most countries, indicates that the problems are deep-seated and structural.

On the supply side, policies in industrial countries lead to persistent over-capacity and the inevitable fall-out of declining real prices and incomes. In developing countries, agriculture is penalized by policies of controlled prices and taxes. Consequently, at the heart of the crisis lie domestic farm, trade and general economic policies that insulate producers from world prices and lead to increased production of commodities already in excess supply, lower export earnings and, in developing countries, to inadequate food supplies. The resolution of the crisis will require basic shifts in the policies affecting agriculture, particularly in the countries that trade in farm commodities. It will also require stronger rules to govern agricultural trade and to settle disputes in an orderly and efficient manner.

Expanding Supplies[1]

The emphasis placed on increasing food production in the 1970s in many countries, stimulated by a commodity boom and worldwide inflation, set the stage for the over-expansion in farm production that occured in most industrial countries. The increases in agricultural production also reflected persistent advances in technology. The application of modern farming methods aided by scientific improvements, when combined with price support programs and other government subsidies, resulted in a phenomenal increase in productivity and fostered intensive utilization of the agricultural land base.

The long-term trends in world grain production, consumption and trade show that output has increased in recent decades at rates slightly in excess of consumption, despite the variability that has been experienced. Increasing yields are responsible for much of the increase, while weather conditions accounted for most of the variability in production. Projections indicate that these long-term trends will continue, at least into the 1990s, based on existing policies. Periods of relative shortage may occur, but heavy over-supplies can be expected to re-emerge.

As demonstrated by the long-term decline in real prices of most agricultural commodities, the process of achieving greater efficiency in farming and lowering production costs has been under way for decades. Productivity increases, which have exceeded demand growth, have caused this long-term downward trend in real prices. As a result resources in agriculture have gradually moved to other uses or have been redeployed in the sector. The process of productivity improvement, usually requiring more intensive use of farm inputs, may in the short run contribute to economic growth and employment in related industries. But the overall result has been a massive exodus from farming in most industrialized countries and strong resistance to policy change on the part of the producers who remain.

Although surplus production in agriculture is generally not a major issue in developing countries, there is nonetheless evidence that the same trends are emerging. There has been a tendency for production to outstrip demand for a number of export commodities of great importance to the economies of developing countries. In most cases, their domestic farm policies are not important factors; indeed most developing countries discriminate against agriculture. However, some newly industrialized countries appear to be following agriculture policies similar to those that have helped create the problems elsewhere by maintaining high internal prices and restricting low-cost imports. In countries such as Saudi Arabia, the provision of extremely high producer support prices, irrigation and technical inputs stimulated remarkable production responses in agriculture, albeit at prices several times the level of world markets.

Many other developing countries inhibit farm production direct through taxes or price controls imposed on agriculture or indirectly through policies that favour the manufacturing sector. Hence there is also a need for policy reform in many developing countries to encourage more balanced and efficient agricultural production and economic growth.

Malnutrition remains widespread in the developing world as a result of low income levels and the lack of adequate marketing and distribution infrastructure. Increased food aid from abroad may alleviate starvation but may also disrupt indigenous agricultural production. Adjustments in general economic, trade and agricultural policies must be suited to the needs of countries in various stages of development, but reform of domestic farm and trade policies by many developing countries could make a major contribution to alleviating malnutrition and hunger in these countries.

The rapid expansion in productivity and output of crops, encouraged by commodity policies that stimulate greater production, is resulting in the degradation of the resource base in many areas of the world. Loss of the soil resource through erosion, excess salinity, acidity and reduced organic matter is causing widespread concern. Much higher use of chemicals and their impact on the environment is a related problem. Many associate the loss of forests and advancing deserts with agricultural expansion and place much of the blame on government policies. Conserving the agricultural resource base and sound agricultural policies can go hand in hand. The decision of the U.S. government to include a soil conservation program in the 1985 Food Security Act to assist in reducing surpluses is an example of linking two objectives. Similarly, safeguarding the land resources and overcoming poverty in developing countries can be assisted by policy adjustments and the adoption of good farming practices.

There are also examples of policies designed to improve the environment and to develop rural economies that complement the reform of farm programs. In the European Community, assistance is provided to farmers through development programs to adopt approved farming practices in areas with fragile resources. Programs to encourage reforestation are in place in many countries and can be used to help reduce the imbalances between supply and demand.

Expanding supplies have resulted in a long-term downward trend in real prices for most agricultural commodities. The outlook for markets, and the pace of technological improvements in agriculture indicate that these trends will persist. The situation is critical, as structural imbalances now exist for the main agricultural commodities entering world trade.

There is an opportunity for governments to implement programs to remove fragile resources from agriculture, improve conservation and environmental practices and promote good cultural practices while assisting in bringing agricultural supply into better balance with market demand.

Demand Weakness

During the 1970s an expansion in world agricultural trade was especially influenced by rapid growth in middle- and upper-income developing countries where the population was using its rising income to improve its diet. At the same time, the Soviet Union and other Eastern European countries turned to imports to expand domestic consumption.

A combination of high economic growth rates and expanded foreign borrowing by many countries brought increases in world agricultural trade year after year in the 1970s. During much of the period there were rising nominal prices of agricultural products and recurring fears of world food shortage. A review of developments in world agricultural trade demonstrates that the markets expanded rapidly during the last decade. From 1972 to 1980 agricultural imports by developing countries more than doubled and increased by two thirds in the centrally planned economies.

This combination of events came to an end early in the 1980s. A sharp rise in real interest rates and a worldwide recession brought economic growth in many developing countries to a halt. There was increased instability in monetary conditions and in exchange rates, contributing to distortions in trade. The huge external debts that many countries had accumulated could not be serviced, and net capital transfers were reduced or ended. A number of developing countries as well as some centrally planned economies encountered debt servicing problems as their export earnings were depressed. Governments were forced to implement austerity programs, and most of these actions adversely affected real income, employment and imports in the countries concerned. The expansion in world agricultural trade slowed, particularly in developing countries. The previously strong economic growth in these countries, based on investment financed from oil revenues and large flows of foreign capital, dropped to low levels, or their economies contracted.

Macroeconomic policies greatly aggravated the imbalances in world agriculture and have created an uncertain environment for domestic and trade policy reform. The economies of developing countries were particularly affected and this, in turn, contributed to the crisis in world agriculture.

Agricultural Exports were Hard-hit

Many developing countries were forced to reduce their imports of agricultural commodities in the 1980s. Along with lower agricultural imports, self-sufficiency programs were pursued. The success of some developing countries in dramatically improving their domestic farm production, and even exporting, was a factor in the slow-down in trade.

In industrial countries, farmers in protected markets such as Japan and Western Europe did not adjust to the changed market situation. Producers in the United States and other more open economies had invested heavily in farming in the boom years, and some were partially protected by government programs and adjusted slowly to declining demand. Production exceeded requirements on a world basis, stocks accumulated to unprecedented levels, and international prices declined. Policy responses such as higher EC export subsidies and the U.S. Food Security Act of 1985 seriously aggravated the economic difficulties of exporting countries and were particularly harmful to developing exporter nations.

For some commodities the growth in world trade slowed; for others growth stopped or there were declines. For instance, world wheat trade in 1986-87 was only 90.1 million tons, down from a peak of 107 million. World coarse grain trade in 1985-86 was only 83.4 million tons, well below the record of 107.8 million tons. In addition, trade in rice, oil seeds, butter, non-fat dry milk, poultry, and sugar fell below the peak levels reached in the late 1970s or early 1980s.

These developments resulted in a virtual trade war among agricultural exporters, triggered by the United States and the European Community. Government subsidies were used increasingly by these two powerful trading entities to counter the problems in agricultural trade that had been largely created by their own government support programs and the trade protection practised around the world. Those exporters that could not afford subsidies reduced prices and generally maintained production to minimize trade losses. Nonetheless, severe economic stress was experienced, especially in the developing exporting countries.

Faulty farm and trade policies have resulted in offsetting subsidy programs, which are increasingly wasteful and counter-productive. This has placed serious economic strains on many economies, particularly in the developing world.

World Food Security

Against the background of global food supplies growing more rapidly than effective demand — indeed faster than population — concerns about world food security would be expected to diminish. It is a paradox that in the midst of a surplus of food and excess capacity in agriculture in much of the developed world, there continues to be widespread malnutrition in many countries and serious famine in some areas. The causes underlying these problems must be considered in any broad reform of agricultural and trade policies. It cannot be assumed that simply because supplies of food are more than adequate to satisfy market demand, all of the world's people can obtain sufficient nourishment to lead an active and healthy life.

A recent study by the World Bank examined the issues and options for food security in developing countries.[2] The study estimated that in 1980, depending upon the definitions applied, a minimum of 340 million people and up to 730 million had insufficient food. About two-thirds live in South Asia and 20 per cent in sub-Saharan Africa. Almost all live in countries with very low average incomes. According to the World Food Council, the problem of malnutrition has increased in the 1980s. Malnutrition is usually caused by poverty, and its existence represents a heavy cost to many countries through lost productivity and additional health and social expenditures. As populations have expanded, the number of people with inadequate diets appears to have increased. The relatively slow growth of economies and incomes in developing countries predicted for the remainder of the 1980s compared to the last decade suggests that malnutrition and famine may in fact continue to worsen.

The best solution for food insecurity is to raise people's incomes. Thus the solution depends upon overall economic development, including the expansion of exports of both industrial and agricultural products. In countries where agriculture represents a major part of the economy, this can be assisted by stimulating growth in that sector. Farm prices should be market-oriented and provide an incentive to encourage economic production. The improvement of basic infrastructure such as communications, irrigation works and flood control systems may be required. However, policies that lower prices to farmers generally and tax exports have the effect of constraining agricultural production in developing countries. General subsidies to hold down food prices are often expensive and wasteful, although there are circumstances where consumption subsidies directed to certain groups are appropriate.

The goals of improving world food security and overcoming malnutrition and famine are related to general economic and political developments. However, the reform of domestic farm policies and trade liberalization can help alleviate these problems.

Government Policies — Why They Are Not Working

Government intervention in agriculture is widespread and long-standing. Most farm policies were implemented in response to public pressures related to obtaining an adequate supply of food at stable prices and maintaining a prosperous rural society. The pursuit of these widely supported objectives was often in response to problems created by the vagaries of nature, rising productivity in agriculture, and a perception of insecurity in importing food supplies. As a result, governments have created a myriad of well-intentioned policies to assist farmers, achieve rural objectives and improve food security.

Many of the key farm programs in place in industrial countries today were actually developed to counter the price instability, structural problems and rural poverty prevalent during the 1930s. The policies affecting agriculture in developing countries have been designed to respond to general economic and social objectives rather than the needs of agriculture itself. Several of the economic characteristics unique to agriculture remain largely unchanged — the influence of nature on production, the cyclical patterns of output, the fixed form of capital inputs, and the low supply and demand elasticity for basic foods, at least in the short term.

However, farming and the conditions of agricultural production and trade have altered markedly over this period, particularly in the newly industrialized and more advanced economies. The level of education, management skills, information availability and technical knowledge has improved dramatically. Labour has been replaced by machines and other inputs that allow more rapid response to changing conditions. Technological improvements are escalating, as is productivity. In the more advanced economies, farmers represent an increasingly small proportion of the labour force, and their incomes approach or in some countries equal the incomes in urban areas. Increasingly farm output is produced by large, efficient operations that are managed as businesses. A growing proportion of producers supplement their returns with off-farm income. Agriculture is becoming more integrated into the economy.

Yet, the agricultural policy objectives of most countries today are similar to those developed a half century ago — increasing farm incomes, stabilizing agricultural markets, providing an adequate supply of food, improving agricultural productivity and, in the case of developing countries, providing cheap food and fiscal revenues for general economic development. These goals of farm policy have widespread public appeal and have formed the basis for a maze of legislation and policy instruments in all market economy countries, developed and developing and, of course, in the centrally planned economies. The involvement by governments in agriculture appears to be increasing, as evidenced by the experiences of the 1970s and 1980s.

It also appears that the richer the country, the deeper its involvement. Certainly, the costs of government farm programs in industrial countries have risen dramatically in the 1980s.

Governments in all countries provide a wide range of general agricultural services such as research, health inspection, grading and national crop insurance programs. Many countries provide public funding for agricultural infrastructure development, including electricity, education, transportation, irrigation, conservation, environmental programs and, in some cases, general farm credit. Programs are provided in some countries to encourage structural change in agriculture and economic diversification. These programs have limited effects on resource use. In the case of developing countries, they may be essential to attaining optimum development of their agricultural sectors.

Many countries provide market and income stabilizing programs to buffer their farmers against the instability of world markets and natural occurrences. In some cases these programs are insurance-oriented and market-related, but some may provide continuous income support. Such policies may affect production and trade depending on the nature of the instruments, the level of funding and the conditions in each country and in the world market. Programs may be implemented temporarily to remove excess supplies or resources from agriculture, such as set-asides or market quotas, which also reduce trade distortions.

Policies to supplement farm incomes indirectly through commodity price supports, administered pricing and various forms of production and input subsidies are commonly found in industrial countries as well as in some of the emerging developing countries. These subsidies often have significant effects on production and hence on trade. In addition, direct trade measures such as variable levies, quotas, tariffs and voluntary export restraint agreements are applied by many governments to implement their domestic programs. These, in addition to export subsidies and other forms of export assistance, have the greatest direct impact on trade. An illustrative list of agriculture policy instruments, arranged according to their purposes and trade implications, is contained in Annex I to this report.

An examination of the farm programs of the major industrial trading countries demonstrates that all operate some programs that generally raise product prices above world levels, either by direct intervention or through border measures and other indirect means. Many create undesirable cross-commodity effects and frequently lead to offsetting subsidies to compensate for distortions in resource use or higher internal production costs. The benefits become rapidly capitalized into land values. Often they result in over-capacity and surplus production. These policies are at the centre of serious confrontations between the major trading countries in recent years, and the emerging consensus is that agricultural policies are not working and must be reformed.

A wide range of specific and general policies affect agriculture in developing countries. The more advanced nations protect their agriculture with programs that affect trade adversely. Many apply export or other taxes to agriculture or maintain low internal prices, thus limiting the growth of the sector and reducing self-sufficiency and exports. In many developing countries, monetary, fiscal and industrial policies discriminate against agriculture. It is difficult to generalize about the effects of these policies on trade, but obviously there is scope for policy reform to benefit agriculture and the economies of these countries.

Government policies are generally not working effectively and are often counter-productive in relation to the well-being of the farm community. They are becoming increasingly expensive and costly in terms of efficient use of resources and overall economic growth. All industrial nations and some developing countries maintain policies that contribute to the difficulties for trade. There is scope for policy reform to benefit agriculture and the economies of both industrial and developing countries.

Protection Levels and Impacts

An OECD study entitled *National Policies and Agricultural Trade*, presented to a Ministerial Council meeting in May 1987, provided the most comprehensive examination of policies affecting agricultural trade and their effects.[3] This report demonstrates convincingly that there are serious weaknesses in domestic farm policies today and that major reforms are necessary. A number of recent publications have reached similiar conclusions.[4] These studies show that government expenditures to implement agricultural policies in the 1980s are massive. These outlays have escalated in recent years as governments have attempted to offset the effects of excess production, the loss of market share and extreme competition. Obviously expenditures of this magnitude add to government deficits, which in turn are contributing to the large imbalances in trading accounts between countries and to the difficulties in fostering strong economic growth.

There are substantial transfers to agriculture from consumers, which represent important economic losses to industrial countries in the form of higher consumer food prices. The 1987 OECD study made some estimates of the relative magnitude of financial contributions from taxpayers and consumers, although it cautions that these must be interpreted with care. For example, it is estimated that transfers from consumers are more substantial than budget expenditures in Japan and the EC by more than 50 per cent. World Bank and OECD sources estimate that total costs to consumers and taxpayers of agricultural support in OECD countries range from $100 billion to $150 billion annually.

Such large transfers to agriculture have a significant impact on the general economies of both industrial and developing countries. The net losses to industrial countries from agricultural protection have been estimated by several studies and summarized in the *World Bank Development Report, 1986*.[5] These estimates indicate that current programs are an inefficient way of transferring income to the farm sector, as the costs to consumers and taxpayers often exceed the value of the transfer. Expenditures on subsidies to compete in export markets are outstanding examples of wasted resources. A recent analysis by the United States Department of Agriculture estimates that for every dollar producers may lose through trade liberalization, consumers and taxpayers gain more than a dollar ($1.40 in the United States). In addition, the benefits of protection and subsidies in agriculture accrue disproportionately to the wealthier operators rather than reaching those in greatest need. The benefits are generally capitalized into assets, particularly land, and contribute to higher costs of production.[6] The rise in land prices is evidence of this situation.

The OECD report on agricultural trade and the World Bank report present a strong case for reform of agricultural policies in all countries, particularly the industrial nations. These studies demonstrate that agricultural support is not only wasteful of resources but also discourages the development of efficient agriculture and impedes the competitiveness of other economic sectors. Although general economic policies have a relatively greater impact on agriculture in the developing world, agricultural subsidies and other farm policies often distort resource use, production patterns and trade, to the detriment of these countries as well. It appears that developing countries have the most to gain from agricultural reforms and trade liberalization on a multilateral basis, but the economies of all countries will benefit, and efficient agricultural exporters will experience the greatest gains.

To understand the impact of government programs on agriculture and to begin to address reform of this complex set of policies, a number of attempts have been made to measure the relative levels of support or protection in the main trading countries for the principal commodities entering world trade. The most widely used indicator is the producer subsidy equivalent (PSE), which represents the level of income assistance to producers provided by the programs. The OECD regarded this measure as the most appropriate indication of the magnitude of income transfer, although it does not incorporate the effects of all policy instruments and does not relate directly to their production or trade effects. The OECD calculations for 1979 to 1981 have been updated by the USDA to cover the 1982 to 1984 period, and further updates are forthcoming.[7]

Table 1, taken from the USDA report, provides a ranking of PSEs by commodity and country. As expected, the table shows that the farm programs of Japan, the Nordic countries and the European Community provide the highest levels of income support. Canada and the United States have similar levels of support, followed by New Zealand and Australia. With respect to commodities, the greatest amount of assistance is provided for dairy and rice among OECD countries, followed by beef and veal, pork, poultry, sugar, cereals and oil seeds. There are significant substitution effects between commodities, depending on the relative levels of price support and the nature of the products.

Empirical studies demonstrate the costs of supporting and protecting agriculture and indicate the relative levels of protection by country and by commodity. There are serious weaknesses in these policies, which are expensive and wasteful. Fundamental reforms are needed.

Production and Trade Distortion

In terms of influencing production and trade, the OECD analysis as well as other similar work indicates that income support provided through measures that support commodity prices, related border measures and direct export subsidies have the most serious production and trade-distorting effects. Programs designed to stabilize production, marketing and incomes in line with longer-term world market clearing levels are less distorting but may have significant effects on trade depending upon the magnitude of payments and conditions in commodity markets. The effects of this group of instruments are difficult to analyze because the programs are variable and complex and often incorporate offsetting provisions. For example, instruments designed to manage supplies or withdraw acreage impose a 'cost' on producers and a 'benefit' through higher prices. If surpluses do not develop or are kept off world markets, the production and trade

Table 1
Ranking of Producer Subsidy Equivalents by Commodity and Country
1982 - 1984a

Producer Subsidy Equivalent[b]	United States	Australia	Canada	European Community	Japan	Taiwan[c]	South Korea[c]	Mexico	Brazil
0 to 9	Beef Pork Poultry Soybeans	Beef Cotton Pork Poultry Sheep Wheat Wool	Beef Corn Pork Soybeans	Corn		Pork			Poultry
10 to 24		Cane sugar Rice	Poultry Rapeseed Wheat	Common wheat Pork		Corn Soybans Sugar	Poultry	Cotton	
25 to 49	Corn Cotton Dairy Rice Wheat	Milk	Sugar	Dairy Wheat Poultry Rapeseed Rice Sheep Soybeans Sugar	Poultry	Beef Dairy Poultry Rice Tobacco	Pork	Soybeans Wheat	Cotton Rice

Table 1 (cont'd)

Producer Subsidy Equivalent[b]	United States	Australia	Canada	European Community	Japan	Taiwan[c]	South Korea[c]	Mexico	Brazil
50 to 74	Sugar		Dairy	Beef	Beef Pork Soybeans Sugar	Wheat	Beef Corn Milk Rice Soybeans Wheat	Corn	Wheat
75 to 99					Milk Rice Wheat				

Source: U.S. Department of Agriculture, *Government Intervention in Agriculture: Measurement, Evaluation and Implications for Trade Negotiations*, FAER-29 (April 1987).

Notes: a. Some products lack data for some years. References to poultry and sheep are to meat, not live animals.
b. Ratio of value of policy transfers to gross domestic value of production including direct payments, in per cent, based on data for 1982 through 1984.
c. Impacts of input subsidies not included.

distortions would be less than implied by the price differentials between the domestic and world markets.

Similarly, subsidies to develop agricultural infrastructure and provide services have limited impacts on production and trade in the shorter term but may over time be reflected in land values and higher rents. Most government services, if generally available, such as grading, health regulations and crop insurance, are unlikely to distort production or trade, even though examples can be found that do so.

Attempts to measure the trade distortions resulting from agricultural programs indicate that there would be some increase in world prices, particularly for sugar, dairy products and meats, if trade were liberalized in all market economies. The volume of most commodities entering world trade would rise moderately, with significant changes in beef, rice and sugar.[8] Policy changes in the EC and Japan would have the most significant effects on world markets. An estimate (Tyers and Anderson) of the price and trade effects of total liberalization in major commodities is shown in Table 2.[9] Further estimates by the same authors and the USDA of aggregate changes in the welfare of various groups from liberalization show that producers in the EC, Japan and the United States would tend to lose if supports for agriculture were totally removed, whereas their counterparts in other agricultural exporting countries, particularly in the developing world, would gain. Consumers in advanced countries would benefit from lower internal prices, whereas the food importing countries would experience higher costs for some of their purchases. The results of a number of empirical analyses (OECD, USDA, IIASA and the World Bank) give generally consistent results, although the magnitude of the effects varies considerably depending upon the assumptions and data used.

Government programs or trade barriers designed to assist or adjust production of one group of commodities can have undesired cross-commodity impacts. Most governments intervene in the grain and dairy sectors, and these activities have significant side-effects on beef. Substitutes for most commodities exist or can be developed. In the case of sugar, the development in the United States of the high-fructose sweetener industry was stimulated by the high internal price regime for sugar. The expansion in imports of feed grain substitutes by the EC was a direct result of high internal feed grain prices and tariff bindings on protein meals and grain substitutes. Subsidized transport rates in Canada for the main grains have discouraged the production of other crops as well as the feeding of livestock in interior locations. Thus policy adjustments must also take into account the different characteristics of commodities and the ways they are interrelated.

Table 2
International Price and Trade Effects of Liberalization of Selected Commodity Markets
1985

Country or country group in which liberalization takes place	Wheat	Coarse grains	Rice	Beef and lamb	Pork and poultry	Dairy products	Sugar
	Percentage change in international price level following liberalization						
EC	1	3	1	10	2	12	3
Japan	0	0	4	4	1	3	1
United States	1	-3	0	0	-1	5	1
OECD	2	1	5	16	2	27	5
Developing countries	7	3	-12	0	-4	36	3
All market economies	9	4	-8	16	-2	67	8
	Percentage change in world trade volume following liberalization						
EC	0	4	0	107	3	34	-5
Japan	0	3	30	57	-8	28	1
United States	0	14	-2	14	7	50	3
OECD	-1	19	32	195	18	95	2
Developing countries	7	12	75	68	260	330	60
All market economies	6	30	97	235	295	190	60

Source: Tyers and Anderson (background paper).

Note: Data are based on the removal of the rates of protection in effect in 1980-82. Data for the EC exclude Greece, Portugal, and Spain.

The instability of world agricultural commodity prices would be reduced by liberalization. Government actions to buffer domestic markets from variations in international supply and demand destabilize world markets and force all adjustments upon producers and consumers in open economies. Thus adjustments in production, consumption and trade are limited, and some actions such as supply embargoes and import constraints can be quite disruptive to international trade. Studies by the OECD and others indicate that the removal of trade-distorting measures by industrial and by developing countries would significantly reduce price variability in world markets for agricultural commodities.

There is growing recognition that these policies of support and protection to agriculture are responsible for excess production and are adding to the market and income instability that farm policies are designed to overcome. These policies create conflicts among producers who use the higher-priced farm inputs in their own production. The policies also increase the costs to the food processing industries and to the consuming public, thus adding to overall cost structures. The opposite effects are experienced from the policies in many developing countries. Substantial public expenditures on agriculture add to the fiscal burdens and to budget deficits in some industrial countries, giving rise to further domestic policy conflicts.

Ample evidence exists to demonstrate that the policies of agricultural support and protection and resulting trade distortions are causing serious and growing international trade confrontations. These frictions between industrial countries and the policy responses they have triggered are creating severe economic stress in less wealthy countries and a dangerous international trade situation. The policies are responsible for the many trade disputes among industrial countries and between developed and developing countries.

Policies to support prices and farm incomes, related border measures and export subsidies cause severe distortions in production and trade. They give rise to serious domestic and international policy conflicts. There will be gains and losses from trade liberalization, but some increases in world trade and prices and greater stability in international prices are anticipated.

The Case for Reform

It is widely agreed that many farm programs and related border measures are in urgent need of reform. It is clear that most agricultural policies lack flexibility and are not responsive to changes in consumer demand, growth in productivity, or market developments. They contribute to excessive production, lower and unstable prices and reduced economic activity. Larger commercial producers receive a high proportion of the subsidy benefits and continue to expand production at the margin, even though the 'average' producer may be experiencing a loss. The additional benefits encourage more intensive production.

Average farm incomes are often not maintained as real prices decline. The benefits of government programs are capitalized into equity, principally land, and are reflected back to producers in the form of higher cost structures. Consumer costs are greater, government expenditures are rising and public welfare is reduced significantly. Farmers and agricultural support industries are experiencing economic stress in many countries as incomes and asset values fall. These economic pressures, combined with more intensive and larger-scale farming, are placing greater stress on soil and water resources and the rural environment.

There is growing interdependence between farming and other sectors of the economy, and among countries. Farming is becoming more integrated into the economy and national farm policies affect many industries and other countries. These farm and trade problems are causing domestic and international policy conflicts. The distortions and inefficiencies that arise and the costs to taxpayers and to economies provide convincing evidence of the need for reform.

Reform will require adjustments, but the costs of adjustment can be reduced if all key trading countries act in concert. The OECD report demonstrates that a reduction in farm subsidies for all commodities and in all countries would ease the impact on individual farmers of reduced assistance as compared with unilateral or commodity-specific reductions in subsidies. The adjustments required by each country and for each commodity group are less with a multi-commodity and multi-country approach. As production begins to fall overall, world prices should strengthen and become less variable. Commodity earnings of some exporting countries would rise, particularly in a number of developing countries. There would be a decline in government expenditures. Some of the savings would be required for adjustment assistance programs for farmers whose incomes are reduced. A more stable international environment should facilitate the necessary transition in agriculture. The Uruguay Round of GATT trade negotiations provides a unique opportunity for governments to undertake the reform of agricultural policies through trade negotiations.

The case for reforming government farm policies is clear and compelling. Political and social realities indicate that changes must be gradual and emerge from an understanding of the failure of existing farm policies to respond to the current environment, to market realities and to the needs of modern farming communities. But there is overwhelming evidence that reform is needed and will provide long-term benefits to world agriculture after a period of adjustment. Furthermore, the costs of adjustment are reduced if reforms are undertaken on a multilateral basis through agricultural trade negotiations in GATT.

The Agricultural Crisis and GATT

The crisis in world agriculture during the 1980s has further weakened the credibility and authority of GATT, which has again proved unable to resolve an increasing number of trade difficulties and disputes in agriculture. There is a growing belief that GATT as an institution has become irrelevant to deal with the problems of agricultural trade. Similarly, many years of experience with international commodity agreements have proved that these schemes are incapable of coping with the instability of markets for farm products. This loss of faith in multilateral solutions to agricultural trade problems is spreading and could undermine the entire trading system, which has served the world well for nearly forty years. Thus, it is crucial that methods be found to strengthen the GATT rules for agriculture and the processes for resolving disputes over agricultural trade issues in a way that restores health and vigour to the international trading system.

Much of the early discussion in the current Uruguay Round of trade negotiations has focused upon either long-term changes in domestic farm programs or the need for short-term measures to stabilize world agricultural markets. These issues are important, but unless they are accompanied by major changes in the GATT rules regarding agricultural trade and improvements in the GATT dispute settlement process, a lasting solution to agricultural trade problems will not be achieved.

Where Have the Difficulties Been?

From the beginning, the GATT had special, weaker rules for agricultural trade, and even these limited disciplines were often stretched or ignored. In the mid-1950s the United States obtained a waiver from its GATT obligations (over the protests of a number of agricultural exporters, including Canada) to allow it to restrict imports of a range of competing farm products.   The European Economic Community in the early 1960s implemented its notorious Common Agricultural Policy, which included a variety of border measures and subsidies designed to protect its farmers from international competition.   And Japan refused to give up its long-standing restrictions on imports of rice, meat and other homegrown farm products.   Other GATT members, including Canada, have maintained or increased restrictions on imports of various agricultural products by measures that are more or less consistent with the letter, if not the spirit, of the GATT rules.   The developing countries have accepted even fewer of the GATT disciplines that apply to the industrial trading countries.

The major differences in the GATT rules for agricultural products are in the treatment of quantitative import restrictions and domestic and export subsidies.   Quantitative restrictions are generally prohibited under GATT for non-agricultural products, with some exceptions for balance of payments difficulties and other unusual circumstances. However, a number of domestic farm support programs involve restrictions on imports to keep them in place. Consequently for agricultural products, quantitative restrictions are allowed under conditions that significantly limit trade.   In addition, protective devices such as state trading and voluntary restraint agreements (VRAs) are common in agriculture, and their use has increased substantially.   These measures have the effect of quantitative import restrictions in terms of trade flows. State trading is widespread in agricultural trade and many also restrict imports.

The GATT rules that govern the use of subsidies in agriculture create even greater difficulties.   Whereas export subsidies are banned for non-agricultural products, for exports of farm commodities they are allowed as long as they do not result in a more than equitable share of world trade.   Export subsidies for agricultural products have been a major source of disputes in GATT and have created unfair competition in third-country markets for exporting countries. Domestic subsidies that operate to increase exports or reduce imports are frowned on under GATT, but such subsidies are commonly practised for agriculture.   Member countries can request consultations with a view to limiting such subsidies, but in practice this has not been effective in reducing trade-distorting subsidies.

In addition to the special treatment of agriculture, the GATT dispute settlement process has functioned much less effectively for disputes in agricultural trade than in other areas of world trade. GATT panel reports relating to agricultural disputes often have not been definitive, generally because of differing interpretations and the vagueness of the rules. Often the time required to achieve dispute settlement is too long. Moreover, the present consensus rules governing dispute settlements allow countries to block the adoption of a panel report that they do not wish to accept. In some cases, panel recommendations regarding trade practices that violate GATT rules have simply been ignored.

In summary, the present GATT rules for agriculture and the dispute settlement system designed to make them work have proven incapable of dealing with the endless proliferation of trade-distorting agricultural policies that has occurred around the world. Correcting these problems will require substantial revisions of both GATT rules and the dispute settlement mechanisms; and these changes will require parallel reforms of domestic support policies and practices. Unless both are accomplished in the Uruguay Round, there is a real possibility that international conflicts over agricultural trade will destroy the entire multilateral trading system.

Political Commitments for Reform

As noted above, comprehensive reform of the GATT rules for agriculture in the Uruguay Round has been pursued in other international organizations, including the OECD and annual summits of the group of seven. At the Tokyo Summit of May 1986, the leaders of the major industrial nations, for the first time, held a serious discussion of agricultural issues. The resulting declaration expressed concern about global structural surpluses for some agricultural products, arising partly from "long-standing policies of domestic subsidy and protection in all our countries." It recognized that "action was needed to redirect policies and adjust the structure of agricultural production in the light of world demand."

The Ministerial Declaration agreed to in Punta del Este on September 25, 1986 launched member countries of the GATT on the most comprehensive negotiation of agricultural policies ever attempted in the history of the organization. It commits governments to negotiate on all measures affecting import access and export competition, including both domestic and border policies. With respect to agriculture, the Punta del Este Declaration states:

Contracting parties agree that there is an urgent need to bring more discipline and predictability to world agricultural trade by correcting and preventing restrictions and distortions including those related to structural surpluses so as to reduce the uncertainty, imbalances and instability in world agricultural markets.

Negotiations shall aim to achieve greater liberalization of trade in agriculture and bring all measures affecting import access and export competition under strengthened and more operationally effective GATT rules and disciplines, taking into account the general principles governing the negotiations, by:

(i) improving market access through, *inter alia*, the reduction of import barriers;

(ii) improving the competitive environment by increasing discipline on the use of all direct and indirect subsidies and other measures affecting directly or indirectly agricultural trade, including the phased reduction of their negative effects and dealing with their causes;

(iii) minimizing the adverse effects that sanitary and phytosanitary regulations and barriers can have on trade in agriculture, taking into account the relevant international agreements.

Regarding the GATT rules, the Declaration states that:

Participants shall review existing GATT articles, provisions and disciplines as requested by interested contracting parties, and as appropriate, undertake negotiations.[10]

Starting in 1980, the Agricultural Committee of the OECD launched a series of research studies to identify the various kinds of agricultural subsidies that existed in member countries and to measure the level of those subsidies. These studies were completed in late 1985, and a report was presented to the OECD Ministerial Meeting in May 1987.[3] The OECD Ministers agreed on an important statement that is likely to influence the future reform of farm policies.

The full text of the OECD Ministerial Declaration relating to agriculture is reproduced in Annex II. The Ministers stated that "all countries have some responsibilities in the present situation [and that] the situation must be halted and reversed." They called for "a concerted reform of agricultural policies" and set out a number of key principles on which to base the reform.

A further important recognition of the seriousness of the problems in world agriculture was contained in the Declaration that emerged from the Venice Economic Summit in June 1987. With respect to agriculture, the Declaration reaffirmed a commitment by the participants "to work in concert to achieve the necessary adjustments of agricultural policies, both at home and through comprehensive negotiations in the Uruguay Round." The Declaration called upon all countries "to agree to refrain from actions which, by further stimulating production of agricultural commodities in surplus, increasing protection or destabilizing world markets, would worsen the negotiating climate and, more generally, damage trade relations." The full text of the Summit Declaration on agriculture is contained in Annex III.

At the same time as these activities were under way among the major industrial nations and in the OECD, another group was formed with the express purpose of influencing the GATT negotiations in agriculture. Originally called "Fair Traders in Agriculture", it was renamed "The Cairns Group" after the city in Australia where the first Ministerial meeting was held in August 1986. A Declaration issued after that meeting stressed the urgent need to reform and liberalize agricultural trade in order to improve the economic prospects of all participating countries. The Cairns Group Ministers pressed for a marked reduction in the use of agricultural subsidies and a new round of trade negotiations. In subsequent meetings, the Cairns Group has provided specific guidance regarding both the timing and direction of the multilateral trade negotiations. They have urged that negotiations should move forward quickly to reach agreement on a framework to reform and liberalize agricultural trade by the end of 1988.

All the key trading countries have tabled their own proposals for agricultural negotiations in GATT. The United States made its official proposal to the GATT Committee on Trade in Agriculture (CTA) on July 6, 1987.[11] It was comprehensive and sweeping in its scope and approach. The United States proposed that:

- all agricultural subsidies and import barriers be phased out over a 10-year period;

- a two-step process be used to achieve the phase-out of all trade-distorting subsidies:

    a measuring device and overall schedule of reductions should be agreed to for taking aggregate levels of support to zero over a 10 year period;

specific policy changes should be identified by each country to meet its scheduled reductions in subsidies and trade barriers, and these changes should be agreed in the negotiations.

The U.S. proposal is concerned only marginally with the revision of the GATT rules. It merely says that the GATT rules should be revised in negotiations to reflect the trading environment that would exist at the end of the transition period. Should the sweeping U.S. proposals be agreed to, the GATT rules would presumably need to be rewritten to prohibit the use of any forms of assistance to agriculture that distort production, consumption and prices, or that obstruct international trade.

On October 21, 1987 Canada tabled its proposals for negotiating agriculture in Geneva.[12] It proposed a comprehensive approach to eliminate or reduce all trade-distorting measures and called for:

- the elimination of all access barriers over a period to be negotiated, with a major reduction over five years;

- the negotiation of bound access under each tariff line and effective and enforceable rules for all measures affecting access to markets;

- the use of a single measure to convert all access barriers and subsidies affecting trade into a trade distortion equivalent (TDE) for use as a negotiating technique by omitting those policies that have a neutral impact on trade;

- a prohibition on new trade restrictions or trade-distorting subsidies; and

- rules to clarify what practices are permissible in GATT, including practices that would be allowed to offset the non-acceptable policies.

The Cairns Group of agricultural exporting countries presented a joint proposal on October 26, 1987.[13] Its aim is to provide for fully liberalized trade in agriculture, the elimination of subsidies that distort trade, and stronger GATT rules and disciplines. This proposal involves three phases:

- implementing a long-term framework of revised and strengthened rules and disciplines;

- the phase-down of aggregate support using a PSE or equivalent measure to facilitate the reform program; and

- immediate steps for early relief involving a freeze on obstacles to access, to subsidies and to trade barriers, undertakings on stock disposals and an across-the-board reduction of all export and production subsidies. (It would include a commitment to increase access opportunities, effective the end of 1988.)

The European Community also tabled its position in Geneva on October 26, 1987.[14] The approach is comprehensive; it seeks to establish a better balance between supply and demand and a harmonizing of levels of domestic support and protection as preconditions for liberalizing trade. The EC proposal suggests two stages of negotiation:

- in the first stage, parallel short-term actions to restrict support to products in surplus and to harmonize support measures; and

- in the second stage, reductions in support combined with a readjustment of external protection.

These actions would be followed by the negotiation of improved GATT rules and disciplines dealing with obstacles to access and with export competition.

A proposal from the Nordic countries (Finland, Iceland, Norway and Sweden) advocates:

- immediate and long-term measures to reduce those forms of agricultural support that distort agricultural trade most seriously;

- increased market access through reduced import protection and strengthened GATT rules and disciplines; and

- minimizing adverse trade effects of sanitary and phytosanitary regulations.[15]

The Nordic countries envisage a minimum target for the negotiation of reductions in agricultural support and protection and the development of a quantitative measuring device covering policies that have a significant effect on trade.

Switzerland advocates emergency actions relating to subsidized exports, reducing output of products in surplus supply, and maintaining access. In a subsequent stage, the negotiations would focus on improved rules.

The Japanese proposal follows the more traditional approaches to GATT negotiations. It recommends a reduction of import barriers while ensuring stability in trade and sound development of the agricultural sector. Food security continues to be emphasized by Japan. Disciplines are advocated with respect to export restrictions and export subsidies. The Japanese do not envisage a need for a comprehensive aggregate measurement of protection and support, and their position thus could raise difficulties in relation to the use of PSEs in the negotiation.[16]

There is a broad political commitment among member nations of GATT to tackle the tough basic issues that must be addressed in the agricultural negotiations. A number of key trading countries have tabled proposals to begin negotiations. There are important differences in approach between the various proposals, but most support comprehensive negotiations and a revision of the GATT rules. The proposals must now be translated into a framework that will determine the direction and pace of the negotiations.

A Framework for Negotiations — An Aggregate Approach

If agreement is reached that all programs that affect production and trade in agricultural products should be covered by the negotiations, the next logical step is to decide how to frame the negotiations. As noted above, the United States has proposed that all subsidy programs and trade restrictions be negotiated together, using an aggregate measure of their trade-distorting effects. A similar approach is proposed by Canada and the other Cairns Group countries. A complementary, or parallel, approach would be to begin with a negotiation of better rules to apply to the various types of programs. Both approaches would require decisions on:

- the programs to be covered by the commitment and rules;
- the time frame for phasing in the changes;
- the conditions or plans to achieve the changes; and
- surveillance and dispute settlement procedures.

The approach or strategy to follow in framing the negotiations can be crucial to the outcome. A variety of approaches has been used in the past or are now being advocated, as the following summary demonstrates.

The Conventional GATT Approach

Negotiations on GATT rules and disciplines, combined with the traditional 'request and offer' procedure, constitute the conventional means of conducting multilateral trade negotiations. The purpose is to achieve a balanced package of concessions and benefits backed up by strong and enforceable GATT rules. As previously discussed, this process has not been successful in the past for agricultural trade and is not now generally favoured by many countries.

However, the GATT rules have provided some deterrent to protectionist practices and have contributed to the resolution of a number of trade disputes. The improvement of GATT rules is advocated by the key trading countries. It is evident that the reform of the GATT rules will be difficult to achieve unless agreement is reached on parallel reforms of domestic support programs. Clear and enforceable GATT rules will also be essential to ensure that progress in negotiating greater access and in reducing trade-distorting subsidies is made secure.

A Tariff Equivalent Approach
The conversion of existing agricultural trade barriers into customs tariffs, together with the negotiation of bindings and reductions of these tariffs, has been suggested in the past and was discussed in the preparatory work for the Uruguay Round. It should be possible to convert many quantitative restrictions into tariffs where the levels would be reasonable and could be bound in GATT. This approach could also be used to place a cap on variable levies so they would operate within a specific range and make the conditions of trade more predictable. Such conversions can be complex and difficult; they may also be impractical on a broad scale in view of the widely diverse forms of agricultural protection and support now in place. This approach has not been proposed by any of the countries that have tabled negotiating proposals in the CTA to date. However, the concept of establishing a maximum level of protection that is acceptable following the phase-down of trade-distorting policies may be appropriate. It could be developed in terms of a maximum tariff equivalent level, or a maximum fixed import levy, that would be bound in GATT.

The Commodity-Specific Approach
Agreements governing trade in particular commodity sectors have been favoured by a number of countries in the past, particularly by the European Community. It was pursued for dairy, meats and grains in the Tokyo Round but with limited results. The focus on trade in individual commodities detracts from the underlying domestic support policies affecting trade and the need to negotiate disciplines on their use. Attempts to manage international agricultural markets through commodity agreements have largely failed in the past, in part because more fundamental changes in national policies were required. In the current negotiations the commodity-specific approach is likely to be counter-productive. Nevertheless, the negotiation of short-term measures to deal with the problems of surplus production and destabilized markets may be helpful in resolving problems for certain commodities. However, it is important to maintain the focus of the

negotiations on the full range of policies so as to reduce distortions in agricultural production and trade.

The Comprehensive or Aggregate Approach

An approach that would capture all policy instruments for all commodity sectors in a single overall commitment based on an aggregate measure of their trade-distorting effects is clearly now appealing to a number of countries. Proposals tabled to date in the current Round include this concept as a means to facilitate negotiations. It is essential to deal with all farm policies that affect trade and all major commodities entering world markets, in order to address the complexity of the problems for trade arising from domestic farm and trade policies. Since agricultural policies are interrelated and there are significant cross-commodity effects, there are benefits to considering these matters together, at least until a broad and comprehensive negotiation to reform the full range of farm and trade policies is under way.

This comprehensive approach may require agreement on an aggregate measurement device of import restrictions and trade-distorting subsidies (such as the PSE). However, empirical measurement techniques are complex, and ways would have to be found to implement such comprehensive commitments in a contractual manner. Therefore the measurement might be used only to establish negotiating targets and to monitor progress toward that goal. However, the aggregate approach offers a way to structure the negotiations by describing a general commitment to reduce all trade-distorting measures within an agreed time frame and a means of keeping track of that broad commitment for each country.

It is suggested here that a comprehensive or aggregate approach should be adopted as a means to frame the current negotiations, in order to deal with all instruments and commodities in the negotiations. Ideally, a summary measure of the trade-distorting effects of various policies could be developed and used both to measure the trade-distorting effects of current policies and to monitor progress in shifting to a new regime. The United States has proposed that PSEs used in the OECD studies be adopted as such a measure, with the deletion of certain decoupled programs from the calculation. However, the PSE provides an indication of relative income transfers to farmers through government interventions rather than a measure of trade distortion. A modified version of the PSE or trade distortion equivalent (TDE), as suggested by Canada, could be calculated by including only those instruments that usually distort international trade. The approach appears to be supported by the Nordic countries, the European Community and the Cairns Group.

For the conduct of the agricultural negotiations most of the proposals tabled in Geneva during the initial stages of the Uruguay Round have advocated a comprehensive or aggregate approach to dealing with domestic farm programs and border measures together. This has the obvious advantage of avoiding the request and offer procedures of previous negotiations or the commodity-by-commodity approaches, which have not been successful in the past.

> *The comprehensive or aggregate approach appears to offer the most promising means of framing the agricultural negotiations. However, it should be combined with the negotiation of strong, operationally effective GATT rules.*

Country Proposals for Strong Rules

The Punta del Este Declaration represents a commitment by governments to a comprehensive negotiation dealing with both domestic and border measures that affect agricultural trade adversely. Although it remains to be seen whether this Declaration, which launched the Uruguay Round, will be translated into stronger rules and disciplines governing agricultural trade, the opportunity to make progress in that direction certainly exists. The crisis in world agricultural trade has weakened the credibility and authority of GATT, and it is crucial that the GATT rules be strengthened if confidence in the international trading system is to be restored.

The Punta del Este Declaration refers to the need to "bring all measures affecting import access and export competition under strengthened and more operationally effective GATT rules and disciplines ... ". In addition to proposing a comprehensive approach to the negotiations, most proposals tabled in Geneva call for strong and enforceable international rules to govern agricultural trade. The United States proposes that negotiations begin on "the changes necessary to GATT rules to reflect the trading environment that will exist at the end of the transition period" following the phasing out of all agricultural subsidies and all import barriers.[11] Under the U.S. approach, governments would not be allowed to use any domestic or border instruments that distort trade, and this would be specified in the rules.

The European Community proposal is less ambitious; it calls for improved and more detailed rules to apply to:

- conditions for the application of subsidies, including those for agricultural products which are incorporated in processed products;

- treatment of measures to increase demand for agricultural products;

- conditions of access and competition resulting from the existence of state agencies and marketing boards; and

- tighter surveillance of measures taken by the various parties pursuant to their undertakings.[14]

The proposals of the Cairns Group and Canada emphasize the need to secure agricultural policy reforms in a "new framework of strengthened and operationally effective GATT rules and disciplines".[13] The framework is designed to "both underpin and drive the adjustment process during the reform phase" and to take full effect at its conclusion. With respect to market access, in the view of these countries, the permanent rules should remove all restrictions and would include:

- a prohibition on the introduction or continued use of all measures not explicitly provided for in the GATT, including non-tariff barriers and other measures such as variable levies and minimum import prices;

- the elimination when the long-term framework comes into force of all provisions for exceptional treatment whether maintained under waivers, protocols of accession, or other derogations and exceptions; and

- a binding of all tariffs on agricultural products at low levels or zero.

The Cairns Group also proposes a prohibition on the use of all subsidies and other support measures having an effect on agricultural trade; any exceptions would be strictly defined in the rules. They advocate a systematic reduction in overall aggregate support by removing distorting policy instruments, backed up by interim rules to apply during the reform period. These transitional rules would set out the terms and conditions for the phase-down, including:

- targets of reduced support;

- priority in reductions for the most trade-distorting instruments;

- phase-out of direct export subsidies and other trade-distorting subsidies; and

- systematic enlargement of import access.

The Japanese proposal for negotiations on agriculture also supports a degree of strengthening of GATT rules but emphasizes the need for exceptions and flexibility to take into account the specific characteristics of agriculture. Nonetheless, Japan advocates more precision and operational effectiveness in the rules. The Japanese support the prohibition of export subsidies for agricultural and processed agricultural products and the progressive reduction of other trade-distorting subsidies. They call for new GATT rules covering the elimination of quantitative restrictions while maintaining exceptions to stabilize domestic production and to achieve assurances of supply. Rules should also deal with variable levies and export restrictions.[16]

The Nordic countries also call for the negotiation of stronger GATT rules and disciplines. For example, with respect to subsidies they envisage improved rules to encompass undertakings such as:

- bindings of the trade effects of supply management programs in the form of reduced volumes of subsidized exports, including the possibility of eliminating such exports in agreed individual products;

- bindings of reduced levels of direct or indirect subsidies affecting trade in individual products, including the possibility of their complete removal on agreed products; and

- bindings of aggregate ceilings of direct or indirect subsidies either for the totality of a country's agricultural exports or for agreed sectors thereof.[15]

The Nordic countries propose various negotiating techniques to improve market access, including the elaboration of stronger and more effective rules to cover, among other things:

- reductions and bindings of tariffs and import levies;

- agreed criteria regarding variable levies to provide transparency and non-discriminatory applications; and

- clearer provisions with respect to quantitative import restrictions relating to aspects such as production restraints and market access obligations.

In summary, on the basis of the agreed objectives for the Uruguay Round and the proposals tabled to date in GATT, it is likely that the negotiations will begin by efforts to reach agreement on a commitment to a phased reduction in the aggregate support and protection provided by both domestic and border instruments that distort trade. This is likely to be combined with the renegotiation of

GATT rules to discipline agricultural trade, both during the transitional period and to provide a permanent legal framework for trade, including surveillance and dispute settlement procedures.

The present GATT rules for agriculture are not containing the rising level of trade protection and tensions in this area. The failure arises from the lack of effective GATT disciplines over domestic agricultural programs. The main trading countries support the negotiation of much stronger GATT rules to govern agricultural trade, but this will require new disciplines over domestic support programs.

Permanent GATT Rules for Agriculture Trade

If an ambitious proposal along the lines advanced by the United States were to be adopted, it would not be difficult to revise the GATT rules permanently to fit such a regime. The new rules would simply prohibit governments from using any subsidy programs or border restrictions that distort trade. This, of course, would rule out most of the existing programs and restrictions used by governments to transfer income to farm producers. Such an approach would presumably require international agreement on programs that do not distort trade, and which would have to be specified in the GATT rules.

Should the U.S. proposal to phase out all subsidies and border restrictions not be fully accepted, rewriting the rules becomes substantially more complicated. In such circumstances, the revised GATT rules would presumably involve:

- agreement on which farm support programs are not trade-distorting and thus could be used legitimately;

- agreement on what qualifications and/or limitations must be applied if programs and measures are employed that are potentially trade-distorting; these rules must be more precise than the present subsidy rules, where the vague language regarding equitable market share clearly has proven unworkable;

- agreement on those programs and measures that would be prohibited and phased out or brought into conformity with the new rules;

* agreement to bring, within a specified time period, all measures currently outside GATT rules, including derogations, waivers, and grandfather clauses into line with the revised rules; and

* an effective surveillance and dispute settlement process that operates quickly and in a predictable manner.

At this point it is neither possible nor desirable to specify precisely the nature of the new framework of GATT rules, although a number of suggestions have been put forward in preparatory work. Various countries have different views on these issues, and the final GATT rules will be arrived at by the process of negotiation. In drawing up the new rules, however, there are some basic principles that should be observed. For example, the revised rules:

* must be specific enough to provide a definitive guide to governments regarding the agricultural policies they should follow in both domestic programs and border measures;

* must be capable of being internationally monitored; and

* must be written in terms that would allow the effective functioning of the GATT dispute settlement process.

The objective of revising the rules is eventually to bring agricultural trade fully under the disciplines of the GATT. An extended transition period and interim rules are likely to be required to adjust current policy regimes to new permanent rules. Longer adjustment periods for developing countries are likely to be required. Indeed, some governments may be unwilling to accept a prohibition of import restrictions and export subsidies and may insist on continuing exceptions. Thus the interim rules may become part of a permanent framework. It is therefore most important that exceptions should be treated as temporary, so as to ensure that the objective is achieved – that is, the eventual removal of all measures that restrict or distort trade, stimulate excess production or limit consumption – and that all such measures become subject to precise and enforceable GATT rules and disciplines.

The nature of the framework of rules for the 1990s and beyond will depend on the extent to which governments are prepared to move toward free trade in agriculture. But it seems clear that there is a better opportunity now, during the Uruguay Round, to reform the GATT rules for agricultural trade than at any time in the recent past or than is likely to exist following the Uruguay Round.

A rewriting of the GATT rules, based upon commitments to scale back or eliminate trade-distorting programs combined with the opening of domestic markets, is essential to provide a lasting solution to the problem. These changes must be reinforced by a strengthening of GATT dispute settlement procedures so as to provide faster, more effective and predictable settlements of trade grievances.

Developing Interim Rules

Regardless of the outcome of negotiations to revise GATT rules on agricultural trade, it is clear that an extended transition period will be involved in shifting from the present regime to future arrangements. If this process is to proceed smoothly, it will require that specific rules be embodied in GATT to govern the duration of the transition period, the pace at which changes will occur, and how the transition will be measured and monitored.

Some have argued that the transition could best be achieved and monitored by the use of some aggregate measure of trade-distorting policies, such as an adjusted producer subsidy equivalent or trade distortion equivalent. In addition, it has been proposed that countries should be asked to file a schedule of specific policy changes for each of the major policies being altered.

Although the new regime must be determined by a process of negotiations, the report on the preparatory work of the GATT Committee on Trade in Agriculture contained many suggestions that may be considered in the development of interim rules.[17] For example, the GATT prohibition on the use of quantitative restrictions (QRs) might be revised progressively to cover all QRs that currently escape its disciplines, such as waivers, grandfather clauses, protocols of accession and residual QRs. In addition, all similar border restrictions, such as variable levies, minimum import price regimes and voluntary restraint agreements, should also be brought under the disciplines of Article XI of GATT. As this range of QRs and similar instruments are phased out, bound minimum access commitments could be negotiated, possibly including a concept of a minimum share of domestic requirements for imports. If internal prices exceed world levels there should be a net minimum import commitment. Where quantitative restrictions remain, there should be a minimum level of guaranteed access, linked to effective production controls and accompanied by commitments to narrow the gap progressively between domestic and world prices with a view to allowing market signals to guide resource allocation and trade. Where countries are unwilling to accept the free flow of agricultural imports, there should be an agreed maximum level of tariff equivalent protection that is bound against increases and might be reduced progressively. The transitional rules should require notification of all restrictions and of changes in them. New structures and procedures will need to be established for their regular surveillance by a GATT body equipped to carry out this function.

The GATT rules relating to subsidies affecting trade in Article XVI should be revised to apply over an agreed time frame to agricultural products. There should be a standstill commitment on the introduction of new trade-distorting subsidies. The interim rules should achieve a gradual phasing out and a prohibition of any subsidies and other measures having equivalent effects that operate to increase exports. There should be an unconditional prohibition of the use of export subsidies on processed food products. Consideration should be given to the prohibition of direct export subsidies by an early deadline and the gradual phasing out of indirect subsidies. Exceptions might be agreed for producer-financed export subsidies. Any other exceptions would require precise conditions, a fixed period and phase-out schedule, and regular review.

The existing rules relating to state trading enterprises are not adequate, as the agencies can maintain two-price systems and provide export subsidies without adhering to the disciplines of Articles XI and XVI. The rules for state trading should involve similar obligations to those applying to quantitative restrictions and export subsidies, in addition to operating on a non-discriminatory and commercial basis. The requirements with respect to transparency of state trading operations need to be strengthened and implemented. Again, a phase-in of these disciplines would be pursued, consistent with the other transitional rules.

These interim rules are crucial to the future of trade policy in agriculture. Since the transition is likely to go on for a significant period of time, these interim rules could become as important as the final rules for agricultural trade toward which they are aimed. Further, because trade disputes will inevitably arise during this period, the interim rules must be such that they will allow the effective functioning of a process of surveillance and dispute settlement.

Clear and enforceable interim rules will be required to discipline agricultural trade through an extended period of policy reforms.

Surveillance and Domestic Policy Co-ordination

In addition to writing new GATT rules for agriculture and interim rules to use during the transition period, it is important that GATT be organized to exercise surveillance of agricultural policies and commitments to change them. It is equally important that the rules establish far greater transparency in trade-distorting policies than currently exists. At present there is no international catalogue of agricultural programs and trade restrictions even for the major countries, and knowledge about smaller countries' policies is even more sparse. To make the collection and maintenance of such information efficient and available to all countries, this function can best be assigned to the GATT Secretariat.

Monitoring and supervising agricultural policies and changes in them for the 94 member countries of GATT is a formidable task. It will require a nomenclature and classification system that is understood and agreed upon by the member states. Information on these policies must be gathered from member states, and such data will be difficult for some countries to obtain. When the information is gathered and assembled, it should be made available to interested parties on a regular basis. Surveillance may involve the use of empirical measurements such as the PSE or TDE.

It will be necessary to strengthen the institutions of GATT to oversee the implementation of a comprehensive approach to introducing progressive adjustments of farm and trade policies. An effective surveillance and supervisory system will also require the creation of new structures within the GATT, including:

- the establishment of a special unit in the GATT Secretariat for the collection and analysis of the agricultural policies and practices of member countries in the light of their strengthened GATT commitments; expertise on the calculation of PSEs and TDEs may be required; an annual review of national agricultural policies could be published;

- the creation of a standing policy committee of the member countries to scrutinize each other's agricultural policies and practices and to confront member countries that fail to observe their commitments; the committee could undertake a regular agricultural policy review, possibly in conjunction with the proposed in-depth GATT review of all trade policies; and

- precise commitments by member countries to notify GATT, and to provide full details, of their agricultural policies and practices on a regular basis in the light of the new, stronger GATT rules.

An effective system of surveillance and a senior policy review committee is needed in GATT to ensure that commitments are met, to provide for regular policy reviews and greater co-ordination of national agricultural policies, and to resolve policy differences. A catalogue of national programs is needed for the negotiations and the surveillance of commitments.

Stronger Dispute Settlement Rules

The effective operation of new rules governing trade in agricultural products will require a strengthened dispute settlement process in the GATT. A number of changes have been proposed to the overall GATT dispute settlement process, which must be made to function for agricultural trade disputes if the system is to survive. Against the background of extreme difficulties in settling agricultural trade disputes, it is essential that clear and enforceable rules be negotiated to enable the GATT dispute settlement process to operate effectively. A gentleman's agreement will not suffice in a world as complex and competitive as agricultural trade. The system must:

- provide reasonable speed in reaching decisions;

- operate in ways that member states view as 'fair';

- not be subject to manipulation and blocking by individual member states; and

- be transparent and its results made public to all members of GATT.

Moreover, because of the unusual and complex nature of agricultural policies, the dispute settlement process in agriculture should be designed to draw upon qualified non-government agricultural policy experts on a continuing basis.

It is essential to develop a strong and operationally effective dispute settlement process that will provide a basis for confidence in the system of GATT rules.

Agricultural Negotiations and Developing Countries

Developing countries have a significant interest in the GATT negotiations in agriculture and can be expected to play a greater role in these discussions in the Uruguay Round. But the policy problems facing developing countries differ in many ways from those associated with agriculture in the industrial world.

Although some of the newly industrialized countries protect their farm sectors and are beginning to experience problems similar to those already discussed, most developing countries discriminate against their agriculture. Therefore, policy reform in these countries also relates to general economic policies such as over-valued exchange rates, industrial protectionism and other general economic policies. In addition, the economies of most developing countries were severely affected by the economic downturn and by the continuing debt crisis, thus contributing to the overall problems of agricultural trade.

The liberalization of world trade in agricultural products, and especially in manufactured and industrial products, will help developing countries to achieve faster economic growth, which in turn will benefit the economies of both industrial and developing countries, including their farm sectors. This will involve not only the opening of markets in industrial countries but also among developing countries. Exports from developing countries continue to be obstructed by a wide variety of tariff and non-tariff barriers and the reduction or removal of these barriers is a major objective of the Uruguay Round. Lower trade barriers, combined with the reform of domestic agricultural policies, would enlarge world trade in sugar, tropical products, vegetable oils, beef, rice, and other cereals, strengthen and stabilize international prices, and increase exports from a great number of developing countries. Steps to reduce domestic and export subsidies for grains, rice, sugar and a number of other commodities would allow world prices to move toward long-term market clearing levels and be of immediate assistance to many developing country exporters.

The benefits to some developing countries may be offset by higher import prices, although their domestic agricultural industries should be placed on a sounder economic footing by trade liberalization. Several economic analyses show that any rise in world prices of food and feed grains and oil seeds, which are the main products imported by developing countries, would be modest. The overall gains to most developing countries from improved trade in farm products should more than compensate for stronger world prices.

An agreement that places limits on or phases out government subsidies and protection for agriculture needs to consider special provisions for developing countries. Developing countries are rightfully concerned that any new rules limiting domestic agricultural subsidies do not limit their ability to use policies that will enable them to develop their agricultural potential and increase the productivity of their agricultural industry.

Trade liberalizaton provides an opportunity to encourage policy reforms and structural adjustment in developing countries. There are opportunities for these countries to participate fully in the negotiations by pursuing concessions for commodities and processed products of interest to them. By offering to provide reciprocity in accordance with their stage of economic development, these countries would increase their leverage to obtain key concessions and, if appropriate, an extended period for policy adjustment.

During the agricultural negotiations in the Uruguay Round, participating countries might be expected to present national plans to reduce trade-distorting measures and reform their agricultural policies. Developing countries could participate fully in these negotiations by tabling their own plans for reforming their agricultural and trade policies. These could be developed with the assistance of the IMF and World Bank and could include new programs of development aid. For the less developed food deficit countries, consideration should be given to expanding the Food Aid Convention and providing economic assistance in other forms to help offset higher import costs for food and to encourage domestic agriculture.

Among the greatest concerns of developing countries are the instability in world market prices for agricultural products and a possible recurrence of the shortages of the 1970s. There is little doubt that trade liberalization in agriculture will do more to stabilize markets for both importers and exporters than will the various attempts at stabilization through commodity agreements.

Developing countries can obtain significant benefits from trade negotiations, and the negotiating framework should enable them to participate fully. Gains should include improved access to world markets, reduced distortions in the markets, higher and more stable international prices, greater investment flows and expanded trade. In addition, an improved environment to develop efficient farm production should result from successful negotiations in the new GATT Round and be of particular benefit to developing countries.

The Need For Early Action

The present agricultural trade situation is dangerous because it may erupt into a general trade war, which could destroy the Uruguay Round and with it the credibility of GATT. Some nations wanted a 'fast track' for the agricultural negotiations, but consensus was not reached on this approach. However, the Punta Declaration included undertakings to implement a standstill agreement and a rollback of trade-restricting and trade-distorting measures. The OECD Ministerial statement and the Venice Summit Declaration contain commitments by governments to refrain from initiating actions that would stimulate production of commodities in surplus or isolate domestic markets further from international markets.

There continues to be a need for early action to develop a negotiating framework to proceed with the Uruguay Round quickly and to undertake early relief measures to demonstrate the political will of the contracting parties to resolve the tough agricultural issues before them. The first step should be to implement the undertakings of a standstill and rollback for agriculture. There should be a freeze of all trade-distorting subsidies and import barriers, combined with undertakings not to introduce new measures causing adverse trade effects. Short-term measures could include steps to curb excess production, encourage demand and dispose of surplus stocks in a manner that avoids serious disruptions in trade. Moreover, because it is generally agreed that any changes in programs will require a period of adjustment, it would be helpful if governments could take steps to reduce the level of policy confrontation arising from current programs. This could also involve reaching early agreement on the programs regarded as the least trade-distorting. Consideration should also be given to the early establishment of a surveillance and policy review system to reduce trade confrontations and overcome policy differences on an ongoing basis. A speedy and predictable process for settling disputes is also required.

These early actions should be of the type and in the direction that will make completion of the negotiation easier. It is essential that commitments to begin early relief be undertaken as part of a framework agreement to commence negotiations.

It is essential to engage in broad negotiations to deal with all trade-distorting measures through agreeing to a process of reductions and rewriting the rules of GATT to limit or prohibit policy interventions that affect trade. In addition, because the process of negotiation is lengthy and current

*trade problems are severely harming a number of countries,
there are compelling reasons to take early and concrete
actions to ease the frictions and avoid further distortions in
world markets while the process proceeds.*

Adjusting Agriculture in a Global Context

Resolving problems in international trade in agricultural products
raises issues of policy reform and adjustment in the domestic farm
sectors, including the desirability of decoupling farm income support
from production and the market. The transition process will not be
without cost, but once the adjustments have occurred, commercial
farmers will operate in a much more certain environment. Adjusting
agriculture in a global context is inextricably linked to the broader
issues of protecting the rural environment and achieving economic
growth in the world economy. Complementary policies in this larger
context will contribute to the resolution of problems in agriculture.
The process of adjusting agriculture in a global context will continue
over an extended period, and it can be achieved only if nations can
reach agreement on the direction and the framework for change.

The Decoupling of Farm Programs[18]

It has been demonstrated that price and income support policies in
agriculture are responsible for a significant share of the trade
difficulties in this sector. Thus the concept of 'decoupling' or
'delinking' farm programs from production, consumption and trade
has gained support in current circumstances. The purpose is to ensure
that policies are relatively neutral in relation to resource allocation
and trade. If governments are to reform their farm policies in a
negotiation to reduce or remove their trade-distorting effects, it will
be necessary to reach agreement on the types of policies that have
little or no impact on production and markets.

Among the principles adopted by OECD Ministers to guide the
reform process (see Annex II), several are related to the decoupling of
farm programs, such as:

- market signals should be allowed to influence through progressive and concerted reductions of agricultural support and by
  other means, the orientation of agricultural production;

- rather than being provided through price guarantees or other
  measures linked to production, farm income support should be
  pursued through direct income support; and

- adjustment of the agricultural sector should be supported by comprehensive policies for the development of various activities in rural areas.

Some of the country proposals tabled in GATT identify the policies that should be negotiated and those that might be regarded as acceptable and excluded from the negotiations. For example, the United States would allow:

- direct income or other payments decoupled from production and marketing, including those that provide a safety net against natural disaster or other extraordinary circumstances; and

- bona fide foreign and domestic aid programs.[11]

The EC would limit the negotiations only to programs with a significant incidence on trade. The Cairns Group of countries advocates the prohibition of all subsidies and other government support measures, including consumer support programs and consumer transfers having an effect on agricultural trade. However, the following exceptions to the program of reductions would be allowed, subject to prescribed conditions:

- general assistance for structural adjustment that has no negative effects on production and trade;

- aids to domestic consumption of food that do not impede trade or discriminate against imports;

- non-commodity-specific aid for infrastructure development, such as research, extension, education, market information, inspection, grading, pest and disease control;

- measures for specific disaster relief and measures for human-itarian purposes; and

- direct income support that is decoupled from production and marketing.[13]

The Nordic countries recommend actions to reduce the most serious trade-distorting effects of farm policies. Support systems that are production-neutral would be allowed, with special consideration and adjustments for policies of production restraint.

There is a strong economic case for decoupling, but political support for such changes is less forthcoming. However, a number of countries, including the United States, Canada and the European Community, have implemented farm programs that are partially decoupled in order to reduce distortions in production and surplus output. The negotiations would be facilitated by the development of an inventory of national programs and a classification procedure to use as a guide to the trade effects of various types of agricultural programs. A general classification of agricultural policy instruments would serve as a means of engaging in negotiations on types of programs in a broad, comprehensive manner, rather than in a specific commodity and instrument context. This procedure would be based on the purpose of the instruments and their trade-distorting effects. Criteria for developing the categories could include whether the subsidy or program is generally available or targeted to specific commodities or industry sectors. Measures affecting the production, consumption and trade of agricultural commodities might be classified as follows, based largely on the OECD overview of agricultural policy instruments:

- national agricultural services (mainly decoupled) – generally not trade-distorting;

- framework measures (mainly decoupled) – generally not trade-distorting;

- stabilization programs (partially decoupled) – may be trade-distorting;

- indirect income support (not decoupled) – usually trade-distorting; and

- direct trade measures (not decoupled) – trade-distorting.

An illustrative list of agriculture policy instruments arranged according to these categories is contained in Annex I. Agreements by governments on the types of farm programs that are regarded as decoupled and trade-neutral would greatly facilitate policy reform in the context of the Uruguay Round.

Agricultural Adjustment Programs

The reform of government policies affecting agricultural trade can be assisted by domestic policies to encourage the restructuring of agriculture and the development of rural economies. The liberalization of trade and the modification of domestic agricultural policies should provide the basis for overcoming structural imbalances in agricultural markets and establishing a solid foundation for balanced and durable agricultural development in industrial and developing countries. However, political and social realities indicate that the changes must be gradual, and there is a need to develop adjustment policies to facilitate the transition.

A number of industrial countries have implemented programs to ease and encourage change in agriculture. The adjustment process involves the movement of resources within the sector as well as into and out of the agricultural economy. Although the general thrust of these programs is to improve farm structure and increase productivity and viability, rural adjustment programs can be used to minimize the adverse consequences of overall reform of farm policies.

Programs to facilitate adjustment in agriculture may include assistance to withdraw resources from agriculture or to switch from one form of production to another. For example, land diversion schemes, acreage reduction programs and marketing quotas may reduce excess output. Programs to buy out dairy herds or grants to encourage the cessation of farming may also reduce production. The provision of retraining and relocation grants can assist resource removal from the sector. In addition, assistance for early retirement from farming and arrangements to permit inactive farmers to remain on their holdings, as well as incentives for consolidation of agricultural units, can facilitate the adjustment process.

To achieve broad policy reform, such rural adjustment schemes may need to be combined with programs of income support unrelated to production or linked directly with output reduction. In addition, assistance to socially disadvantaged groups should complement programs of adjustment.

Resource Conservation Programs[19]

Widespread concern exists over the deterioration of the land base and the environment in many countries as a result of intensive, modern farming techniques. In the United States, the 1985 farm legislation linked efforts to conserve the land base with steps to remove excess resources from agriculture, by implementing a soil conservation program. Grants for approved farming practices and forestry programs in the European Community aid in resource conservation and in diversifying production. Programs with similar objectives exist in a number of other countries. Such policies should be designed to ensure that the more fragile and sensitive lands are removed from inappropriate agricultural uses. At the same time, it is important to moderate government incentives for intensive utilization of the remaining agricultural land base, including the heavy use of fertilizers and other chemicals.

In most countries there is an opportunity to introduce programs to remove fragile resources from agriculture, improve conservation and environmental practices, and thereby assist in bringing supply and demand into better balance. The World Bank is involved in organizing and supporting agricultural programs in many developing countries, including efforts to conserve and protect the land base. These programs provide useful instruments for supporting agricultural reform and can complement broader efforts to deal with global agricultural trade issues. In many countries there is a need to encourage the non-agricultural use of land resources for rural recreation, forestry and other purposes. The OECD Ministers endorsed the principle of encouraging the adjustment of the agricultural sector through comprehensive policies to develop a range of activities in rural areas. Initiatives relating to resource conservation and improving the environment can make an important contribution to an improved system of world agricultural trade.

Encouraging Economic Growth

The preceding discussion has demonstrated that broad economic developments, particularly as they affect the economies of developing countries, have also contributed significantly to the crisis in world agriculture. For example, there is concern over instability and misalignments in exchange rates and their role in agricultural trade issues. It is not the purpose of this paper to make recommendations concerning general economic policies, but it is evident that the agricultural sectors in all countries are increasingly affected by macroeconomic developments, and that changes in these policies can have a major influence on efforts to reform trade and domestic farm programs.

Clearly, initiatives that stimulate economic growth in all countries, especially in the indebted developing countries, would make a major contribution to correcting the imbalances in world agriculture. Trade negotiations can, of course, aid this process by providing more open access to world markets. But the reform of agricultural and related policies in the industrialized countries, as well as in developing countries, remains at the heart of the world agricultural crisis and cannot be delayed if a deepening of the crisis is to be avoided.

The Role of Development Assistance

Development assistance can also facilitate economic growth in most third world countries. Actions by industrial countries to overcome slow growth and imbalances in international payments, combined with a more liberal world trading environment, are necessary to stimulate economic expansion in the developing world, but higher levels of development assistance on a global scale are also required. Steps by developing countries to reduce export taxes, to limit government expenditures, to promote structural adjustment, and to adjust over-valued exchange rates can be facilitated by external financial support, at least in the short term.

In this respect, there is scope for targeting higher levels of aid in many developing countries to the improvement of rural infrastructure and of domestic markets for food. In some cases, food aid can be used as a development tool – as well as serving to improve nutrition – to provide essential support systems such as transport and storage and to expand demand. The sale of food for national currency, in a manner that protects domestic markets and commercial trade, can provide funds for farm credit schemes, irrigation systems, agricultural research and education.

Food aid will continue to provide a major transfer of resources to the Third World. When it is used well, it can make a major contribution to overcoming hunger and malnutrition and can help ease debt burdens and foreign exchange constraints. Much care needs to be taken to ensure that food aid contributes to, or does not inhibit, policy reform and structural adjustment in agriculture in developing countries.

Early Progress

Agricultural policy and trade reforms of the type proposed by a number of countries will require substantial adjustments in agriculture. However, reform is under way to modify the effects of some government programs on production. Farmers in a number of countries already are responding to changes in markets or support programs by reducing output of surplus crops. Japan lowered its rice support price in 1987 for the first time in 32 years and also recently reduced its high internal beef and dairy prices. The United States has begun to implement the cuts in target prices and loan rates contained in its 1985 farm legislation; land retirement programs idling 70 million acres of cropland have reduced U.S. production of surplus crops, and a buy-out program sharply reduced the growth in U.S. dairy output. Budget expenditures on government agricultural subsidies have been reduced from a high of $26 billion in fiscal 1985-86 to an estimated $17 billion in fiscal 1987-88.

The European Economic Community (EC) also has made adjustments in the operation of its Common Agricultural Policy. A production control program for milk was introduced in 1984 and tightened markedly in 1987. A recent decision by the EC Heads of State instituted constraints on the agricultural budget and aims to reduce surplus production by implementing price cuts for cereals, oil seeds, meats and certain other products. They also approved the first acreage set-aside program in the Community policy.

Major changes also have occurred in a number of developing countries. These have included substantial trade liberalization, significant removals of exchange rate distortions, and reductions in price distortions in the agricultural sectors. While these changes have been made in response to forces outside the MTN, it should be recognized that they do contribute to the long-run objectives of the Uruguay Round, and appropriate credits should be given.

Understandably there is concern among some farmers about the impact of these policy changes on their incomes and the value of their assets. However, these effects should not be exaggerated, because the income losses associated with the reduction of protection will be significantly offset by the expansion of effective demand and trade. Prices for some key agricultural products will strengthen, and the costs of some inputs will decline. It is likely that some of the income supports now made through commodity programs will be provided by other policy means.

A phased multilateral removal of trade-distorting agricultural policies does not mean that nations must abandon either cherished national goals or their agricultural sectors. These goals can be met in a variety of ways beyond the existing production-encouraging, trade-distorting programs now in place. A search for alternative programs is now under way, and further movement in the agricultural negotiations will add urgency to that search.

Reasonable price stability for basic foodstuffs and secure food supplies has long been a major goal of most national policies. A removal of trade-distorting subsidies from the operation of international markets would provide a major stabilizing force in world markets, making it easier for national governments to allow their internal markets to become less isolated from world markets.

Farmers' incomes need not be left entirely to market forces. There is a range of ways to provide income security to agricultural producers that do not have an adverse effect on agricultural adjustment. These include direct government transfer payments unrelated to current production, land-use conversion programs to encourage conservation, recreation and wildlife use, early retirement programs in exchange for rights to future farm program benefits, and individual and community adjustment programs to encourage the development of alternative employment for rural people. There are many other programs providing services and support to farmers, some of which give income protection without creating distortions in resource use and trade.

The case for reforming government farm policies is clear and compelling. Political and social realities indicate that changes must be gradual and emerge from an understanding of the failure of existing farm policies to respond to the current environment, to market realities and to the needs of modern farming communities. The decoupling of farm programs from production and the markets as well as complementary policies to encourage aggregate economic growth, rural adjustment, and the improvement of the environment can help ease the transition to a more open trading regime. There is overwhelming evidence that reform is needed and will provide long-term benefits to world agriculture after a period of adjustment. Furthermore, the costs of adjustments are reduced if reforms are undertaken on a multilateral basis through agricultural trade negotiations in GATT.

A Blueprint for Reform

The GATT member nations have agreed to begin agricultural negotiations on a comprehensive basis in order to deal with both domestic and border measures that affect trade adversely. The present negotiations will be more difficult and complex than any attempted in the past. If governments proceed on the basis of their proposals, they will begin a process of policy change that may continue over an extended period. As a starting point it would be useful to agree upon a set of underlying principles or guidelines that should shape the negotiations. Since the OECD countries have already accepted a number of important principles for the reform of agricultural policies, the approach should follow them and be consistent with the Punta del Este Declaration. These principles should apply to all agricultural programs in all countries.

Guidelines for the Negotiations

It is proposed that the negotiations on agriculture be guided by the following principles, which emerge from the preceding discussion:

- all national measures that restrict or distort trade, stimulate excess production or limit consumption should be on the table for negotiation;

- there should be no increase in policies that limit imports, stimulate excess production or reduce consumption;

- governments should agree on those programs that have a minimal impact on trade and may therefore be used;

- there should be a major reduction in all measures that adversely affect trade, with a view to progressively allowing market signals to guide resource allocation and trade;

- all remaining measures that affect trade adversely should be subject to precise and enforceable GATT rules and disciplines;

- programs decoupled from production and the market, government services to agriculture, infrastructure support and interim adjustment programs may be maintained subject to negotiations; the adoption of new technology and better farming methods should not be inhibited;

- the reform of agricultural and trade policies of developing countries must take into account the stage of their economic development and the need for special transitional arrangements; and

- countries should be free to choose their agricultural policies, provided they do not limit or distort trade.

There are a number of ways in which these basic principles can be applied. Their application does not require that all countries adopt the same agricultural system or the same policies to protect their farmers. However, it is essential for all countries to recognize that their domestic agricultural programs can, and often do, seriously distort agricultural production and trade and that steps should be taken to reduce or eliminate such distortions.

Applying the Aggregate Approach

The GATT member nations have agreed to begin agricultural negotiations on a comprehensive basis in order to deal with both domestic and border measures that affect trade adversely. This approach offers a means of addressing the complex problems for trade arising from the myriad of national policy instruments in all countries and for all commodities. It does not imply a common policy system for all countries but rather a global or aggregate approach to getting the negotiations under way. Because of the complexity of such a negotiation and the need to achieve long-term fundamental reform and early results wherever possible, it would be desirable to include the elements for developing stronger trade rules and negotiating guidelines in a framework agreement for agriculture. Strong and enforceable GATT rules will be needed to guide the transition period as governments adjust their policies, to settle disputes and to provide the basis for a permanent rule of international trade law for agriculture.

The negotiations will proceed most expeditiously if the framework agreement encompasses the principal elements of the positions of the major negotiating countries. It should provide clear direction for policy reform and allow for the maximum degree of trade liberalization without prejudging the outcome. As already indicated, most of the proposals tabled in Geneva to date for the conduct of agricultural negotiations are based on a comprehensive or aggregate approach. There is considerable agreement on the general direction of policy change to be pursued, but wide differences persist on the degree of trade liberalization that is acceptable, the time frame for change, and the extent of government involvement in agriculture and trade that is consistent with optimum resource allocation.

Once an aggregate commitment on the depth of a cut in trade-distorting measures has been agreed to, each country would propose the programs to be modified to fulfil their part of the agreement. Individual countries would submit a plan to implement their commitment. There would be a process of negotiation to finalize a balanced and acceptable package. To facilitate the negotiations, it would be useful to develop a general classification of agricultural policy instruments based on their purpose and trade effects. It would be designed as a guide to assist in reaching agreement on which policy instruments to include in the general framework agreement. An independent group, working with the GATT Secretariat and drawing on expertise from the OECD and elsewhere, could develop the measurement techniques and the classification system.

Although such an agreement would form part of the GATT, either by incorporation in the schedules or as a separate understanding or code, it would be difficult to describe the undertakings in clear, unambiguous legal terms that could be subjected to the usual dispute settlement procedures. Consideration will need to be given to the development of unique arrangements to administer such an agreement, including a senior policy committee as mentioned previously. These arrangements should provide for an annual review, and possibly for negotiated adjustments, to take account of changes in conditions such as fluctuations in exchange rates and prices outside the control of the countries concerned.

Combining the aggregate approach with a renegotiation of the GATT rules will ensure that the principal policy instruments responsible for distorting world trade are subjected to specific disciplines that can be included in the articles of the GATT and subjected to dispute settlement procedures.

Negotiating Stronger Rules

The Punta del Este Declaration and the proposals tabled in GATT have indicated the need to negotiate strengthened and operationally effective rules and disciplines. It is proposed that the rules of GATT be rewritten to apply fully to agriculture based on the principles suggested to guide the negotiations. The objective would be to alter or remove over time all programs that seriously distort production, consumption or trade patterns. The rules should be renegotiated to reflect the situation that would prevail on implementation of the aggregate commitments. They would deal with all import barriers, subsidies, state trading, variable levies, voluntary restraints and other measures. Negotiations on the two complementary approaches would be undertaken in parallel.

The rules should be changed to discipline the full range of instruments that affect trade, to limit the types of policy intervention that are allowed, and to establish strict conditions for those remaining instruments that affect trade. For example, the GATT prohibition on the use of quantitative restrictions might be revised explicitly to include agricultural products, and the exceptions permitted for agricultural products could be severely constrained and subject to specific conditions. All waivers and grandfather clauses should have termination dates attached to them or be removed at once. Concurrently, all forms of quantitative import restrictions should be brought under the revised rules. Where quantitative restrictions remain, these should provide for a minimum level of guaranteed access, should be linked with effective controls over domestic production of the products concerned, including close substitutes, and should be administered so as to safeguard traditional import shares. The rules should also require notification of such restrictions and changes in them and provide for new procedures for their regular surveillance by a GATT body equipped to carry out this function.

The GATT rules on subsidies should be redesigned to embody commitments to phase out and terminate those that distort production and trade over an agreed period of time, with standstill commitments on the introduction of new subsidies. They should envisage the conversion of certain subsidies to direct income payments, which might also become a subject of GATT discipline. The GATT prohibition on export subsidies should be extended to cover agricultural products, with provision for their phasing out and termination by some agreed future date. Subsidy programs, and especially export subsidies, should be brought under arrangements for notifications and surveillance.

The GATT rules governing state trading, particularly for agricultural products, should be strengthened and elaborated and should embody new commitments to operate these systems on a non-discriminating and commercial basis as well as commitments relating to price mark-ups. The rules governing quantitative restrictions, production subsidies and export subsidies should be applicable to state trading systems.

Reforming the GATT rules for agricultural trade along these lines would involve, as well, the establishment of new institutional arrangements for notification, consultations, surveillance and dispute resolution.

Surveillance and Domestic Policy Co-ordination

Strengthened consultation and surveillance procedures should be developed to facilitate and secure progress in the reform of domestic agricultural policies and to ensure the implementation of revised GATT rules governing trade in agricultural products. The institutions of GATT must also be strengthened to oversee the implementation of the aggregate approach and the effective application and enforcement of GATT rules. New institutional arrangements within GATT should be considered for agriculture to undertake the surveillance of commitments on policy reform, to review national policies on a regular basis, to negotiate any adjustments and to settle policy differences. The policy co-ordination, adjustment and enforcement activity might form part of a GATT code on agricultural trade. These commitments might be administered by a standing policy committee on agriculture and be developed as part of broader agreements to give GATT new authority to review national trade policies. Only agreement on an overall policy framework, policy surveillance and the strict enforcement of rules governing trade in agricultural products will prevent the recurrence of similar problems in the future.

Procedures for Dispute Settlement

The enforcement of specific commitments under the strengthened GATT rules, whether of an interim or a permanent nature, should be achieved through the regular GATT provisions of Articles XXII and XXIII covering consultation, nullification or impairment. However, stronger surveillance and dispute settlement procedures appear to be necessary for the effective operation of new rules governing trade in agricultural products. A number of countries have already proposed changes to the overall GATT dispute settlement process as part of the Uruguay Round of negotiations. In view of the particular problems that have been experienced in resolving agricultural trade disputes, there may be a need for special dispute settlement procedures during the period of transition. An independent panel of trade specialists could be considered to complement and facilitate the regular dispute settlement mechanisms of the GATT until clearer and stronger rules and procedures have been negotiated. The rules and disciplines must be made effective and operational, and the dispute settlement procedures must operate expeditiously and in a manner that is transparent and fair.

A Multilateral Program of Early Relief

Even the most optimistic observers understand that the agricultural negotiations will last for several years. A transition from the present programs to a new structure will require an even longer period. Therefore, it is in the interests of all nations, and the special responsibility of those with heavy subsidies, to agree to some short-term measures as an adjunct to the trade negotiations. In addition to a framework agreement on how to structure the negotiations, these measures should include a standstill or cease-fire on all agricultural subsidies in all countries and market stabilization measures to offset some of the most damaging trade effects of present subsidy programs.

A Cease-Fire: Freezing the System

Assuming that governments are committed to a comprehensive negotiation aimed at reducing all trade-distorting measures and have reached agreement on a negotiating approach, there is a need for immediate action to set the stage for the negotiations. The first step must be an end to the escalation of subsidies that has been occurring over much of the last decade; a related action would be to freeze import barriers apart from emergency safeguard actions.

The concept of a freeze should have several characteristics: it should be simple and understandable, measurable, and universal, in terms of both countries and products. Freezing market shares, and using government programs to enforce them, will add to levels of protection and subsidies rather than reduce them. Freezing public expenditure is the wrong approach: countries are not certain of their actual expenditures on agricultural programs; it is not possible to monitor expenditures until after the fact; some kinds of protection do not involve public expenditures, nor do the import controls run by most state trading organizations; and freezing expenditures cuts off the possibility of using public funds to achieve other objectives, such as adjusting production and protecting farmers' incomes.

The simplest and most transparent way is to freeze the upper limit of producers' prices in local currencies and the quantity upon which producers receive that price or payment. A freeze should involve internal subsidies, direct export subsidies, and price premiums achieved by the use of state trading.

Applying limits to the benefits resulting from the use of import quotas is more difficult in practice but the goal should be the same: that is, that controls be operated so that the domestic price to producers does not rise and the quantity of domestic output receiving the high guaranteed price does not increase. It is important to understand that a freeze is not intended to limit output, nor is it intended to limit exports; it is intended only to limit output and exports receiving subsidies of any kind. A freeze is not intended to raise commodity prices; it is meant to stop the further depression of world commodity prices by subsidized output.

A freeze should not place a country at a relative disadvantage compared with the base period insofar as subsidies are concerned; its effects will be to end the open-ended entitlement programs. A standstill would require the choice of a base period; it should be a recent base period, even though that period contains the greatest levels of protection and subsidies for producers in most countries.

Curbing Excess Production

As a second step, there is a need for some production restraints for some short period of time to avoid further stock building. Many countries already have such programs under way. The concept is understood and accepted in major trading countries, and most have methods of implementing it. However, stock accumulation has continued because current output exceeds demand even at sharply lower world commodity prices.

More comprehensive action is needed, with wider participation by a larger number of countries. This participation could take several forms, including production controls, land retirement where such programs are feasible, and accepting obligations to carry additional commercial reserves. The object of the agreement would be to bring current production and consumption into better balance without further depressing world commodity prices. Such a market stabilization program should not have a minimum world price or price fixing as its objective. It should not try to cut production to bring about substantially higher commodity prices. Instead it is designed to offset the excessive incentives to increase output embodied in present programs.

Expanding Demand

There are some possibilities to increase demand, even in the short term. In countries where consumer prices are maintained at high levels relative to world prices, reductions in prices could be implemented. Special programs to increase domestic consumption could be considered, such as subsidies to the very poor. Similarly, in the less developed countries, subsidies directed to certain groups may be appropriate. Food aid, if carefully targeted to stimulate economic growth, to increase strategic food reserves, or to assist the poorest groups, can increase demand.

Disposing of Excess Stocks

There also is a need to deal with the problem of managing and disposing of surplus stocks. Countries will not agree to a freeze on subsidies to their producers if there is a possibility that another country will further depress world markets by dumping accumulated stocks into a market. Countries will be equally reluctant to participate in a production restraint program if they believe that supplies from accumulated excess stocks will be put into world markets and offset any reductions in output they make.

A general agreement on guidelines for surplus stock disposal is needed as an integral part of the solution to the present problems; in its absence, a freeze on direct subsidies is likely to be unattainable, and a production restraint agreement would be unworkable. Guidelines should be developed to prevent serious disruptions of trade in the stock disposal process. Among the principles that should be included in guidelines are:

- stock reduction for food aid use, including expanded levels of food aid, are acceptable as long as they meet the long-established guidelines for surplus disposal;

- surplus stocks could be used in lieu of cash for payment to producers to reduce production as long as the reduction in output exceeds the volume of stocks used as payment;

- the sale of surplus stocks into international markets should be offset by an equal reduction in export subsidies or other export aids so that no country should gain market share as the result of stock sales; and

- any reduced-price sale of stocks in the domestic market should be done in a way that increases total consumption and does not displace consumption of imports or other close substitutes.

Excess stocks are the direct result of specific programs of governments designed to aid their producers. It should be the primary responsibility of those same governments either to hold those stocks indefinitely or to dispose of them in ways that do not have an adverse impact on trade.

Elements of a Framework for 1988

It is unrealistic to expect that the negotiations on agricultural trade can lead to final agreements before the end of 1988. It is important, however, that the momentum not be lost and that the situation not be allowed to drift back into a series of unilateral policies, which may be both disruptive and self-defeating. Yet there is a danger that this may occur. In the United States, preparatory work is beginning on a new Farm Bill for 1990, work that will be influenced by experience with the 1985 Act. Already there are forces actively promoting a continuation of similar legislation, perhaps with reduced farm income support but the maintenance of massive export subsidies.

In the European Community, following a protracted debate and deadlock between the heads of state of the member countries, a compromise was reached that at best may hold the problems of their agriculture in check. Some improvements in supply and demand imbalances and reduced government outlays are evident in the United States, assisted by the withdrawal of resources from production, but the underlying policies leading to over-capacity, increasing protection and continuing high levels of government subsidies remain essentially unchanged. Japan, under severe pressure from its trading partners, has liberalized parts of its regime of agricultural trade protection, but there is no evidence of a shift in basic policies. Apart from New Zealand, where agricultural protection and support policies have been largely dismantled, the traditional farm policies of other industrial countries are being maintained and in some cases strengthened. These contradictory farm and trade policies are causing severe economic hardship for many developing countries by eroding their purchasing power, weakening their economies and helping to perpetuate the global crisis in agriculture.

The leaders from the seven economic summit countries meeting in Toronto have an opportunity to commit their Ministers to reaching agreement to a negotiating framework in 1988. On this basis, when GATT Ministers meet later in Montreal they could reach agreement on a negotiating framework setting out the direction and pace of the negotiations in the Uruguay Round. It is to be hoped that they will also agree on the types of farm programs that do not distort trade and that assist rural communities to adjust, an agreement that would make an essential contribution to the negotiating process. The role of developing countries should be clarified and mechanisms put in place for surveillance of commitments and settling of disputes during the transition phase. These two meetings provide the opportunity to launch serious negotiations without delay and to maintain the momentum for reform so carefully nurtured in 1987.

Therefore, it is suggested that a major attempt be made during the summer and autumn of 1988 to reach agreement on the elements of a framework that will provide general direction for continuing changes in national policies and that would outline boundaries within which the final multilateral trade agreement in agriculture would be negotiated.

Several crucial elements must be included in a successful framework agreement. They are:

• agreements, as specific as possible, on the direction of changes in policies to guide the negotiations on trade-distorting programs and the strengthening of GATT rules;

• identification of the programs that are to be included in negotiations on reducing trade-distorting policies, as well as clarification of a list of programs that would be considered clearly non-distorting and thus could expect relatively few alterations or constraints as a result of future negotiations;

• the basis for full participation by developing countries;

• a surveillance mechanism under GATT that would detail current policies, monitor changes in policies, and report publicly to member states on the situation;

• a dispute settlement mechanism to allow a speedy and non-confrontational settlement of the disputes that are certain to arise during the subsequent negotiation period and beyond; and

• an agreement on short-term measures, to be used during the remainder of the negotiations and, possibly, during a longer transition period.

Those knowledgeable about the economic and political complexity of these main points will recognize that to achieve even this simple framework will require major political will and heroic negotiating efforts. However, a framework agreement that fails to address them will almost certainly be inadequate and could create more problems than it solves. Indeed, if a framework agreement is too vague and too unstructured, it would eventually contribute to a breakdown of the negotiations at a later stage. Consequently, the immediate objective for GATT countries is to elaborate these crucial elements along the following lines in a framework agreement as the basis for proceeding with negotiations on agriculture in the Uruguay Round.

Setting Policy Directions

It is imperative that a firm commitment be reached by governments, by the end of 1988, on the direction and the nature of policy change. This is more important than an immediate agreement on the magnitude of change and the period over which changes should occur. The world's farm producers and associated industries, private investors, and the consuming public have a need to know — and the right to know — the policy directions that governments can be expected to pursue.

Ideally, this commitment would consist of an agreement that the final negotiations should aim toward the complete phasing out of all trade-distorting programs, giving highest priority to those policies with the greatest adverse effects. As an initial step, there must be an agreement that definable and enforceable limits on trade-distorting programs should be negotiated, with the objective of removing or offsetting their negative trade effects. In any case, the objective should be to bring agricultural trade fully under strengthened and enforceable GATT rules and disciplines.

Agreeing on the Programs that Distort Trade

As a first step, agreement must be reached on which policies seriously distort agricultural trade and will be subject to negotiations. It will take some time to negotiate what, if any, limits are to be placed on trade-distorting programs and the timing for phasing in the agreed changes. The direction of change will be determined by an agreement on which programs are to be the focus of the continuing negotiation. All national policies that significantly affect trade must be subjected to negotiations, including those covered by GATT waivers, grandfather clauses, and those not adequately covered by GATT rules, particularly variable levies, state trading, and voluntary restraint agreements.

The early identification of policies that create the most distortion in production and trade will reduce the apprehension of some groups that all governmental programs will be phased out, regardless of the economic conditions of farmers and of rural areas. It will also focus subsequent negotiations on the important issues of what should be done with the programs judged to have adverse effects, and how to do it in the least disruptive manner. Finally, it will help convince many developing countries, which stand to gain much from the proposed changes, that they can participate fully without jeopardizing future development goals.

Provisions for Developing Countries

An agreement that places limits on or phases out government subsidies and protection to agriculture needs to consider special provisions for developing countries. However, because agriculture makes up a higher proportion of employment, income, and export earnings in most developing countries, they have much to gain from reducing the distortions in world agricultural markets.

Developing countries are rightfully concerned that any new rules limiting domestic agricultural subsidies should not limit their ability to use policies that will enable them to develop their agricultural potential and increase the productivity of their agricultural industry.

Importing developing countries have expressed concern that removing output-distorting subsidies in developed countries will result in higher import costs for food. However, several economic analyses show that any rise in world prices of food and feed grains and oilmeals, which are the main products imported by developing countries, would be modest. For the poorest developing countries, their concerns can be dealt with by strengthening the Food Aid Convention. For other developing countries the internal price of food will be more dependent upon their own domestic agricultural policies than upon likely changes in world markets.

Among the greatest concerns of developing countries are the instability in world market prices for agricultural products and the possibility that the shortages of the 1970s will recur. There is little doubt that trade liberalization in agriculture will do more to stabilize markets for both importers and exporters than will the various attempts at stabilization through commodity agreements.

Establishing A Surveillance Mechanism

A functional framework agreement reached in the near future must establish without delay a surveillance mechanism for agricultural trade issues within the GATT framework. Its purpose would be to establish where nations are now in their agricultural policies on an easily understood basis; to keep track of changes in policies; and to provide a basis for negotiations about changes in policies. Moreover, once such a surveillance mechanism is functioning, it can contribute to discussions regarding balance in the negotiations and provide an important basis for a dispute settlement mechanism.

Over the past year there have been numerous discussions within the GATT and outside it about producer subsidy equivalents, trade distortion equivalents, price gaps, effective protection equivalents, and other aggregate measuring devices. Each has appeal and thus its advocates. None is perfect, and most require immense amounts of data, some of which are difficult and expensive to obtain. There is thus a danger that negotiations will be diverted to issues better left to meetings of technical specialists.

It is therefore recommended that the surveillance mechanism begin with a simple but complete cataloguing of all programs in place in each country in a specified base year. That year probably should be 1984 or 1985, a period just prior to the beginning of the multilateral trade negotiations. At the same time, information should be obtained on the status of all the base year programs in 1988, with the same information added for programs introduced subsequent to the base year. As a minimum, information should be gathered on the type of program (price support, import quota, levy, etc.) the commodities covered, the quantities of those commodities produced, consumed and traded, and the local price received by producers.

A system whereby these data are submitted regularly to GATT also needs to be established. The surveillance group needs to have the authority to request more information from industrial countries if there are questions regarding the nature and operation of specific programs.

It is recommended that the GATT Secretariat be requested to prepare and publish an annual review of national policies based on this information, just as the IMF and OECD present an annual review of changes and developments in trade, finance, and monetary policies. Eventually, it is desirable to conduct periodic in-depth reviews of national policies. This could be done separately or in conjunction with the proposed in-depth GATT review of all trade policies and then used in a broader review when it occurs.

Member countries should authorize the GATT Secretariat to proceed immediately with the development of a surveillance mechanism and should provide the funds required to obtain the necessary professional support for it. At this point it is not crucial to decide whether PSEs or TDEs or something else are to be used as targets, negotiating guides, or GATT bindings. Those decisions can be made as part of a final package, but for obvious reasons a functioning surveillance mechanism cannot wait, and developing it is a formidable task.

Settling National Policy Differences

Probably the most difficult task in reaching an early framework agreement is the development of a dispute settlement process within the GATT that would operate during what will certainly be a long period of negotiating new GATT rules for agriculture and an even longer period of adjusting to them. However, unless member countries put in place an acceptable and workable dispute settlement process that they trust, the inevitable disagreements are likely to erupt into battles and wars that could destroy the fragile process of adjustment and change.

It is unlikely that the present GATT dispute settlement procedures will be adequate during this interim period. It may prove more difficult under the present GATT rules, inasmuch as the interim rules for the transition period will be new and probably, unfortunately, imprecise. However, it is important that the existing dispute settlement provisions of the GATT be retained to resolve disputes in relation to rights and obligations under the articles of GATT.

The new dispute settlement rules for GATT as a whole remain to be agreed; meanwhile the issue of settling differences over national agricultural policies must be faced now if there is to be a viable framework for the negotiations.

It is recommended that a standing policy review committee and independent panel for agriculture be established within GATT for an indefinite period. Consultations and surveillance with respect to commitments on national policies would be undertaken by a policy review committee made up of ministers or senior policy representatives. To resolve disputes that cannot be settled in the committee, an independent panel should be established. It should comprise no fewer than five persons nominated by the Director General and approved by the GATT Council. It could include representatives of governments or private citizens. Members would have staggered terms of not less than two years and not more than five years.

The new panel would have dual and closely related functions: to oversee the policy surveillance activity of the GATT Secretariat and to hear disputes over national policy actions. The close relationship between these functions is obvious, for the first exists to enable the second function to be performed. Member governments should agree on time limits for the panel to decide disputes and on its authority to recommend actions to deal with disputes. It is important that the panel reports be written, published, and made available to all interested member governments. It is these governments that must ultimately make the political decisions as to the course of action to be followed in the unfortunate event of continued divergence of a member state's policies from the commitments.

Member countries would have final recourse to the existing dispute settlement procedures of the GATT in the event of unresolved differences. However, a continuing panel can better provide and judge these norms than can ad hoc, intermittent panels convened under stress to judge a single national policy action. The establishment of a fair and open process of informal review and judgement is more appropriate than relying upon a court of last appeal in a system where the underlying laws are, of necessity, changing over time. It must be emphasized that these new procedures are designed to assist in settling differences in national policies during the period of transition and would not replace the regular dispute settlement process of GATT.

Measures for the Short Term

At present, there is a wide divergence of opinion as to whether short-term measures are necessary or desirable. It is extremely important to begin the process of reform to ensure that key policy decisions in 1989 and beyond in the United States, the European Community and elsewhere are influenced by the reforms under way in the Uruguay Round. However, the specific nature of short-term measures must be subject to negotiation. As a minimum, there should be a commitment on several important issues. One is that governments should reaffirm their earlier commitment not to introduce any new policies that add further distortions to the system. In other words, a freeze on new subsidy programs and new trade barriers should be agreed to and implemented as well as a freeze on export taxes.

Governments can and should fully implement the positive policy changes already under way in several countries, such as those in the European Community and the United States mentioned earlier. Those countries that have not already agreed to such policy changes should agree to immediate and commensurate actions consistent with the general objectives of the negotiations. Countries should also agree to avoid actions that are clearly inconsistent with the direction and intent of the negotiations. This means that countries would not manipulate present policies and instruments in ways that would encourage subsidized output, destabilize markets, or seek to gain negotiating advantage.

Although co-ordinated actions to reduce the impact on trade of various national measures (such as export subsidies) could contribute to early relief, overt attempts to manipulate international agricultural markets through commodity agreements, market sharing, or price fixing are highly controversial and, we believe, counter-productive. They are counter-productive because they will be so divisive that they could divert the focus of the negotiations away from the basic issues. Besides, they probably will not work, and there will be a tendency to blame someone else if they fail. It is important at this early stage of the negotiations to avoid serious political confrontations whenever possible, for there will be more than enough tough political decisions in the later stages of the negotiations. Now that the agricultural situation is improving, the important political decision is to continue to move it in the right direction and to avoid policy actions inconsistent with the desired final outcome.

Moving Ahead with Agricultural Reform

The political leaders should be commended for squarely facing the fact that a major reform of the GATT rules relating to agriculture is long overdue and that to do so successfully will require a multilateral adjustment of national policies. It is crucial that recent momentum not be lost and that the opportunity be taken to further the process at the Economic Summit in Toronto in June 1988 and the subsequent GATT Meeting of Trade Ministers in Montreal in December.

A successful agreement on a framework for negotiating agriculture reached in 1988 would be a clear signal that the Uruguay Round is moving forward and that there are good prospects for a successful negotiation that will strengthen the world trading system. An agreement of the type outlined would be constructive and is obtainable. It would be a significant step in the process of completing the commitments of the Punta del Este Declaration – a process that may well be crucial to the future welfare of the world's food economy and, indeed, to the multilateral system of international economic co-operation. This unique opportunity to launch serious negotiations without delay must not be missed.

Notes

1. For a fuller discussion of agricultural trade developments with supporting statistical tables, see Dale E. Hathaway, *Agriculture and the GATT: Rewriting the Rules* (Washington, D.C.: Institute for International Economics, September 1987).

2. The World Bank, *Poverty and Hunger, Issues and Options for Food Security in Developing Countries* (Washington, D.C.: February 1986).

3. OECD, *National Policies and Agricultural Trade* (Paris, May 1987).

4. For a more complete discussion of national policies, see D.G. Johnson, Kenzo Hemmi and P. Lardinois, *Agricultural Policy and Trade: Adjusting Domestic Programs in an International Framework* New York: New York University Press for The Trilateral Commission, 1985) and Dale E. Hathaway, *Agriculture and the GATT*.

5. The World Bank, *World Development Report, 1986* (Washington, D.C.).

6. USDA, *Impacts of Removal of Support to Agriculture in Developed Countries*, P. Dixit, V. Roningen, J. Sullivan, and J. Wainio, Paper presented at the International Research Consortium Meetings, Airlie House, Virginia, December 1987 (mimeo).

7. USDA, *Government Intervention in Agriculture*, Economic Research Service, Staff Report No. 229, April 1987.

8. USDA, *Preliminary Estimates of Producer and Consumer Subsidy Equivalents*, 1982-1986 (mimeo).

9. R. Tyers and K. Anderson, *Distortions in World Food Markets: A Quantitative Assessment* (World Bank, 1986).

10. GATT/1396, *Ministerial Declaration on the Uruguay Round* (Punta del Este, September 25, 1986).

11. U.S. Government, *United States Proposal for Negotiations on Agriculture* (The White House, Office of the Press Secretary, July 6, 1987).

12. Government of Canada, *Canadian Views on the Negotiating Approach for Agriculture* (Department of External Affairs, October 20, 1987).

13. GATT, *Cairns Group Proposal to the Uruguay Round: Negotiating Group on Agriculture* (Secretariat, October 26, 1987).

14. GATT, *European Communities Proposal for Multilateral Trade Negotiations on Agriculture* (Secretariat, October 26, 1987).

15. GATT, *Proposal of the Nordic Countries: Negotiating Group on Agriculture* (Secretariat, December 1, 1987).

16. Government of Japan, *Japanese Proposal for Negotiations on Agriculture* (December, 1987).

17. GATT, Committee on Trade in Agriculture, *Recommendation: Draft Elaboration* (Geneva, June 1986).

18. W.M. Miner, *Foreign Aspects of Decoupling: The Use of Measurements in Relation to Decoupling and Trade Negotiations,*

Institute for Research on Public Policy, Ottawa, January 1987 (mimeo).

19. The World Commission on Environment and Development (The Brundtland Commission), *Our Common Future* (Oxford, 1987).

Annex I

Agriculture Policy Instruments
— An Illustrative List —

Policy	Purpose	Example

1. National Agricultural Services – generally not trade-distorting

• research, development and extension	• improve productivity and social welfare	• publicly funded research
• technical and health standards	• protect health and safety	• plant and animal inspection, labelling regulations
• grading and inspection services	• consumer protection and marketing efficiencies	• compulsory grading
• farm tax and financial services	• tax incentives, debt management	• farm tax programs, debt deferral
• emergency/disaster payments	• compensation for unusual losses	• flood damage
• national insurance programs	• reduce risks of natural hazards	• farmer premium crop insurance (actuarially sound)

2. Framework Measures – generally not trade-distorting

• rural development	• economic and social assistance	• education, regional development grants
• infrastructure development	• capital investment	• irrigation, electrification, transportation
• conservation and environmental programs	• conserve the basic resource	• erosion control
• farm loan programs (non-commodity-specific)	• capital purchases, low-cost financing	• farm credit, adjustment assistance

- national direct
  income transfers

- minimum income
  support

- direct income
  supplements
  unrelated to
  production

- international
  development
  assistance

- economic growth,
  humanitarian aid

- grant aid including
  food aid

3. **Stabilization Programs** – may be trading-distorting

- income stabilization

- income averaging

- shared cost
  programs

- stockpiling and
  buffer schemes

- reduce variability,
  provide food security,
  support international
  commodity agreements

- storage payments,
  inventory
  purchases export
  controls

- market flow
  controls

- orderly
  marketing

- delivery quotas,
  farm reserve
  program

- resource inventory

- land idling for
  market purposes

- acreage and output
  reduction
  programs

- marketing
  advances and
  guarantees

- market-related
  financing support
  (low net transfers)

- advance payments,
  loan rates, initial
  payments

- state trading
  (commercial)

- discretionary pricing
  and trading

- national purchase/
  sales agencies

4. **Indirect Income Support Programs** – usually trade distorting

- price/market support,
  deficiency payments

- maintain farm
  income

- target prices and
  deficiency
  payments

- administered
  pricing, state trading
  (non-commercial)

- increase farm
  income from the
  market

- import agencies,
  two-price systems

- production subsidies

- increase farm
  income

- processing
  payments

- input subsidies
  (commodity-specific)

- reduce production
  costs

- irrigation and
  fertilizer subsidies

5. **Direct Trade Measures** – trade distorting

• border measures	• protect internal prices, incomes	• variable levies, quotas, tariffs, VERs, import controls
• export assistance programs (concessional)	• expand exports	• export credits, barter and tied development aid
• export subsidies	• expand exports	• export enhancement programs, export restitutions, commodity-specific transport subsidies on exports

Source: This Table draws on OECD and USDA sources.

Annex II

OECD Communique – Agriculture
Paris, 13th May 1987

The joint report of the Trade and Agriculture Committees* was approved. This important work clearly highlights the serious imbalances that prevail in the markets for the main agricultural products. Boosted by policies which have prevented an adequate transmission of market signals to farmers, supply substantially exceeds effective demand. The cost of agricultural policies is considerable, for government budgets, for consumers and for the economy as a whole. Moreover, excessive support policies entail an increasing distortion of competition on world markets; run counter to the principle of comparative advantage which is at the root of international trade; and severely damage the situation of many developing countries. This steady deterioration, compounded by technological change and other factors such as slow economic growth or wide exchange rate changes, creates serious difficulties in international trade, which risk going beyond the bounds of agricultural trade alone.

All countries bear some responsibilities in the present situation. The deterioration must be halted and reversed. Some countries, or groups of countries, have begun to work in this direction. But, given the scope of the problems and their urgency, a concerted reform of agricultural policies will be implemented in a balanced manner.

Reform will be based on the following principles:

a.   The long-term objective is to allow market signals to influence by way of a progressive and concerted reduction of agricultural support, as well as by all other appropriate means, the orientation of agricultural production; this will bring about a better allocation of resources which will benefit consumers and the economy in general.

b.   In pursuing the long-term objective of agricultural reform, consideration may be given to social and other concerns, such as food security, environment protection or overall employment, which are not purely economic. The progressive correction of policies to achieve the long-term objective will require time; it is

---

*   "National Policies and Agricultural Trade".

all the more necessary that this correction be started without delay.

c. The most pressing need is to avoid further deterioration of present market imbalances. It is necessary:

— on the demand side, to improve prospects as much as possible inside as well as outside the OECD area;

— on the supply side, to implement measures which, by reducing guaranteed prices and other types of production incentives, by imposing quantitative production restrictions, or by other means, will prevent an increase in excess supply.

d. When production restrictions are imposed or productive farming resources withdrawn by administrative decision, these steps should be taken in such a way as to minimise possible economic distortions and should be conceived and implemented in such a way as to permit better functioning of market mechanisms.

e. Rather than being provided through price guarantees or other measures linked to production or to factors of production, farm income support should, as appropriate, be sought through direct income support. This approach would be particularly well suited to meeting the needs of, amongst others, low-income farmers, those in particularly disadvantaged regions, or those affected by structural adjustment in agriculture.

f. The adjustment of the agricultural sector will be facilitated if it is supported by comprehensive policies for the development of various activities in rural areas. Farmers and their families will thus be helped to find supplementary or alternative income.

g. In implementing the above principles Governments retain flexibility in the choice of the means necessary for the fulfilment of their commitments.

The Uruguay Round is of decisive importance. The Ministerial Declaration of Punta del Este and its objectives provide for the improvement of market access and the reduction of trade barriers in agriculture and will furnish a framework for most of the measures necessary to give effect to the principles for agricultural reform agreed upon by OECD Ministers, including a progressive reduction of assistance to and protection of agriculture on a multi-country and multi-commodity basis. As agreed in paragraph 16, the Uruguay Round negotiations will be vigorously pursued and comprehensive negotiating proposals tabled over the coming months, in this as in other fields. In the Uruguay Round appropriate account should be taken of actions made unilaterally.

In order to permit a de-escalation of present tensions and thereby enhance prospects for the earliest possible progress in the Uruguay Round as a whole, OECD governments will carry out expeditiously their standstill and rollback commitments and, more generally, refrain from actions which would worsen the negotiating climate: they will, *inter alia*, avoid initiating actions which would result in stimulating production in surplus agricultural commodities and in isolating the domestic market further from international markets; additionally, they will act responsibly in disposing of surplus stocks and refrain from confrontational and destabilising trade practices.

Agricultural reform is not solely in the interests of Member countries. Developing countries which are agricultural exporters will benefit from a recovery on world markets. Developing countries which are importers of agricultural produce will be encouraged to base their economic development on more solid ground, by strengthening their own farm sector.

Agricultural reform poses vast and difficult problems for Member countries. Strengthened international co-operation is needed to overcome these problems. The OECD will continue to contribute to their solution by deepening further its work; by updating and improving the analytical tools it has begun to develop and which will prove particularly valuable in many respects; by monitoring the implementation of the various actions and principles listed above. The Secretary-General is asked to submit a progress report to the Council at Ministerial level in 1988.

Annex III

The Venice Economic Summit Declaration – Agriculture

At Tokyo, we recognized the serious nature of the agricultural problem. We agreed that the structure of agricultural production needed to be adjusted in the light of world demand, and expressed our determination to give full support to the work of the OECD in this field. In doing so, we all recognized the importance of agriculture to the well-being of our rural communities. In the past year, we have actively pursued the approach outlined at Tokyo, and we take satisfaction from the agreement in the Ministerial Declaration adopted in Punta del Este on the objectives for the negotiations on agriculture in the Uruguay Round.

We reaffirm our commitment to the important agreement on agriculture set out in the OECD Ministerial communique of May 13, 1987; in particular, the statement of the scope and urgency of the problem which require that a concerted reform of agricultural policies be implemented in a balanced and flexible manner; the assessment of the grave implications, for developed and developing countries alike, of the growing imbalances in supply of and demand for the main agricultural products; the acknowledgement of shared responsibility for the problems as well as for their equitable, effective and durable resolution; the principles of reform and the action required. The long-term objective is to allow market signals to influence the orientation of agricultural production, by way of a progressive and concerted reduction of agricultural support, as well as by all other appropriate means, giving consideration to social and other concerns, such as food security, environmental protection and overall employment.

We underscore our commitment to work in concert to achieve the necessary adjustments of agricultural policies, both at home and through comprehensive negotiations in the Uruguay Round. In this as in other fields, we will table comprehensive proposals for negotiations in the coming months to be conducted in accordance with the mandate in the Ministerial Declaration, and we intend to review at our next meeting the progress achieved and the tasks that remain.

In the meantime, in order to create a climate of greater confidence which would enhance the prospect of rapid progress in the Uruguay Round as a whole and as a step towards the long-term result to be expected from those negotiations, we have agreed, and call upon other countries to agree, to refrain from actions which, by further stimulating production of agricultural commodities in surplus, increasing protection or destabilizing world markets, would worsen the negotiating climate and, more generally, damage trade relations.

II. Perspectives on Decoupling

Contents

A North American Perspective on Decoupling 113
Barry Carr, Klaus Frohberg, Hartley Furtan, S.R. Johnson,
William H. Meyers, Tim Phipps, and G.E. Rossmiller

Introduction 113

Achieving Decoupling in North America 116
  Evolution of Decoupling in the United States 116
  Evolution of Decoupling in Canada 119
  Extent of Decoupling in Current Programs 120
  Decoupling Strategies for North America 124

Impacts and Problems with Decoupling 126
  Commodity Markets 126
  Processing and Marketing Industries 128
  Environmental Quality and Asset Values 129
  Input, Labour, and Land Markets 130
  Farm Structure and Rural Communities 131
  Canadian Decoupling 133
  Decoupling vs. Phased Elimination 134
  Partial Decoupling Options 135
  The Role of a Conservation Reserve in a
    Decoupled World 136

Political Problems of Decoupling 137

Summary and Conclusions 138

References 139

An EC Approach to Decoupling 141
John S. Marsh

Prologue 141

Why Decouple?　142
　　The economic argument　142
　　The political argument　144

Mechanisms for Decoupling　146
　　The economic base line　146
　　Justification for direct transfers　148
　　Decoupling and the flow of world trade　149

Some Practical Problems of Decoupling within the EC　150
　　Administration, complexity and cost　151
　　Financial 'borders', who pays?　151
　　Diversity of goals　152
　　Present policies and new opportunities for distortion　153
　　'Compensation' or 'Welfare Payments'　154

Epilogue – Would Decoupling Solve our Problems?　154

Conclusions　156

Notes　157

A European Community Approach to Decoupling:
A Commentary　159
Wilhelm Henrichsmeyer

An EC Approach to Decoupling　159
　　EC Performance on Decoupling　159
　　Prospects for Decoupling in the EC　162

General Considerations on Decoupling　163

A North American Perspective on Decoupling

Barry Carr, Klaus Frohberg, Hartley Furtan,
S.R. Johnson, William H. Meyers,
Tim Phipps, and G.E. Rossmiller*

Introduction

The term 'decoupling' has recently entered the lexicon of agricultural economists and policy makers. In general, the term refers to the concept of providing support to farmers in ways that do not distort production, consumption or trade. The objective is to minimize the effect of domestic agricultural programs on other countries. Because the term has often been used without precise definition, confusion has arisen over the extent of coupling or decoupling implicit in the agricultural programs of different countries. With the emphasis on agricultural trade distortions and the inclusion of domestic agricultural policies in the GATT Round, a more complete understanding of decoupling will be necessary.

This paper reviews current agricultural programs in North America in the context of the decoupled concept, then evaluates the probable impacts of decoupling measures that might be taken. The paper focuses on the relatively short-term economic effects and

---

*   Authors are listed in alphabetical order. Carr, Phipps, and Rossmiller are with the National Center for Food and Agricultural Policy, Resources for the Future (RFF), Washington, D.C., and Frohberg, Johnson, and Meyers are with the Center for Agricultural and Rural Development (CARD), Iowa State University, Ames, Iowa. Furtan is Professor of Agricultural Economics, University of Saskatchewan, Saskatoon, Canada.

adjustments that would likely take place with the removal of programs affecting the prices and production of agricultural commodities. The paper generally describes the economic impacts of phasing out existing government programs without going into detail as to how income support and other transition assistance programs might be constituted or implemented in a form that is consistent with decoupling principles. Other than making the point that global decoupling is better than North American decoupling by itself, which in turn is better than U.S. unilateral decoupling, the paper does not attempt to address the question of longer-term impacts following a period of transitional adjustments. Indeed, some of the short-term negative effects could turn positive in the longer term under any of the scenarios described.

Several agricultural proposals tabled at Geneva involve, to varying degrees, a substantial reduction or elimination of trade distortions caused by domestic agricultural programs that affect producer prices and thus production decisions and trade. The U.S. proposal, the first to be tabled, outlined the most ambitious agenda. It calls for the elimination of all production and trade-distorting subsidies and all barriers to market access over a 10-year period.

The EC proposal takes a much more measured and less extensive approach. It calls for a balanced and significant reduction in levels of agricultural support through policy harmonization, reductions in trade-distorting support on a reciprocal basis, and improved GATT rules and disciplines. This restructuring of agricultural policies is to be accomplished, however, on an unspecified timetable and only after short-term measures are taken to stabilize markets and reduce government budget costs.

The Cairns Group proposal incorporates elements for potential compromise between the U.S. and EC positions. It suggests three phases — early relief measures, an intermediate reform program, and a long-term GATT framework. Upon agreement on the provisions of a long-term GATT framework, or at latest by the end of 1988, the early relief measures would be implemented. They consist, inter alia, of a freeze on access barriers and subsidies affecting trade, nondisrupting stocks management, reduction of trade-distorting subsidies, and increasing trade access by an agreed percentage.

The intermediate reform program of the Cairns proposal would operate over a 10-year transition period in which reduced trade-distorting support measures would evolve into the provisions of the long-term GATT framework agreement. At the end of the transition period, the long-term GATT framework would apply. It would prohibit the use of all measures not explicitly allowed in the GATT, such as non-tariff measures, variable levies and minimum import prices. It would eliminate all special treatment provisions, such as waivers, protocols of accession, and derogation. It would bind all tariffs at low or zero levels and prohibit subsidies and other support measures affecting agricultural trade. Exceptions would apply to various non-commodity-specific agricultural programs and direct income support decoupled from production, marketing, and trade.

All three proposals, while possessing differences in timing, process, and extent, imply significant *decoupling* of government support from domestic producer prices and production decisions and *recoupling* of domestic and international markets on a multilateral basis. However, none explicitly addresses the trade-distorting effects that would result if consumer prices were not decoupled. In the European Community or Japan, and for the North American sugar and dairy industries, consumers pay a major portion of the cost to support producers. Present programs that provide producer price supports also maintain domestic consumer prices consistent with the supported levels.

If consumer prices were decoupled along with producer prices, the income transfers now paid directly by consumers would be shifted to taxpayers. This decoupling would add significantly to the already large budget costs of agricultural programs and, therefore, may become a major point of contention in the GATT negotiations. If the domestic consumer price is not decoupled, the quantity demanded by consumers is constrained, and international trade remains distorted.

Another issue in the definition of decoupling is the treatment of resource allocation distortions. In a partial equilibrium framework, it is theoretically possible to devise a combination of producer price increases and supply controls that leaves world prices and trade undistorted. The feed grains and wheat titles of the U.S. Food Security Act of 1985 may be viewed by some as approaching this concept of partial decoupling. Although some would call this a decoupled program, it still distorts resource allocation among agricultural enterprises or among inputs within an enterprise, indirectly affecting trade and market access.

The motivation for decoupling in North America arises from continuing internal pressures to rationalize agricultural policies and from the anticipated benefits of more open markets in world trade (see trade liberalization studies cited later). The benefits that Warley (1987) has argued for Canada can also be enjoyed by the United States:

> Canada is playing a leading role in this latest and most ambitious attempt to rationalize and discipline world agricultural production and exchange. Success in agricultural policy and trade reform on a multilateral basis would provide larger opportunities for the release of

Canada's comparative advantage and international competitiveness in agriculture, and thereby for increases in national income and the recovery of farmers' incomes and asset values.

Achieving Decoupling in North America

A useful approach to refining decoupling issues is to review the extent to which it exists and is implemented. The evolution of the decoupling concept, the degree to which current programs are decoupled, and selected alternative programs for decoupling North American agriculture are reviewed here.

Evolution of Decoupling in the United States

The modern era of U.S. agricultural policy began with the Agricultural Adjustment Act of 1933, which contained a number of enduring concepts. Major farm legislation has been enacted approximately every four years since 1933. Over time, what evolved as primary program instruments were voluntary programs, price support loans that maintained market prices at predetermined levels with government acquisitions, and crop acreage allotments that attempted to keep production under control.

The first major proposal for decoupling income support from production decisions was in the Brannan Plan proposed in 1949. Direct income payments rather than price supports to increase farm income were proposed. A limit on payments to a level of production determined by farm size was also included. This proposal was defeated in favour of continued price supports, but some of its provisions were later adopted.

By the 1960s, a technological revolution was under way, and farmers were setting production and yield records year after year. Neither lower price supports nor politically acceptable acreage diversions could control mounting agricultural surpluses. After the Kennedy administration made an unsuccessful push for mandatory production and marketing controls, the 1964 legislation set up a marketing certificate for wheat that provided a supplemental producer payment, the value of which depended on whether the wheat was intended for domestic or foreign consumption. (A similar plan had been initiated for feed grains in 1962.)

In effect, this 1964 legislation provided three price levels for wheat: domestic consumption was supported at $2.00 per bushel, the portion of production for export covered by certificates was supported at $1.55, and all other wheat was supported at $1.30. The low support rate for the marginal unit of production was to reduce the supply response of program participants. Producers participating on a volunteer basis were required to reduce planting to qualify for these payments.

In the Agricultural Act of 1970, at the beginning of the Nixon administration, an increased export demand prompted a more flexible approach to supply control. The Act replaced existing crop-specific acreage control programs with a general acreage set-aside program. The set-aside required that, for each acre planted to a particular crop, a portion of an acre had to be idled. This feature reduced overall planted acreage. Although the 1970 Act eliminated rigid acreage allotments, it did not dictate to producers which crop had to be cut back or what could be grown on the remaining acreage. For the first time, a payment limit of $50,000 per producer per crop was imposed. These changes reduced the linkage between support programs and crop production decisions.

In 1973, the Agriculture and Consumer Protection Act introduced a new concept of target prices and deficiency payments. Deficiency payments were tied to the difference between the target price and the higher of either the market price or the loan rate, rather than being fixed in value like earlier certificates. Price support loans were set at levels intended to put greater reliance on market prices. The payment limitation was reduced to $20,000 per producer. This limit was subsequently raised in 1977 to $50,000 per year in combined payments from all crops, where it remains, with some exemptions, today.

Economic conditions in the farm sector were depressed as the 1985 farm bill debate began. Exports had fallen by 23 per cent in the previous three years. Nearly one-third of all farms were under severe financial stress. The index of farm real estate values had fallen by 19 per cent in four years. The government-sponsored, farmer-owned Farm Credit System was experiencing loan losses and payment delinquencies of magnitudes sufficient to threaten its financial viability. And government program costs under the four-year Act of 1981 had risen to over $60 billion, more than double the amount during the previous four years.

The administration proposed the Agricultural Adjustment Act of 1985 in late February of that year (AAA85). Significant changes proposed included allowing loan rates to adjust to a moving average of the market price, phasing down target prices by setting them at a declining percentage of the market price, lowering payment limits, phasing out the dairy program, banning program payments to farmers who convert erodible land to crops, and eliminating supply controls after 1988. The AAA85 would have phased out farm price and income support measures over a five-year period – decoupling by elimination.

Reactions to the proposed program were negative; neither the House nor the Senate agriculture committee gave the bill serious consideration. The concept of complete decoupling first emerged in the farm bill debate when Senators Boschwitz and Boren introduced an Omnibus Bill on May 1, 1985. The bill had three goals: to maintain farm income; to encourage full, market-based production; and to make the United States price-competitive in world agricultural markets. The domestic part of the Boschwitz-Boren bill would have reduced loan rates to market clearing levels and replaced government price and income supports with "transition payments", gradually reduced over a five-year period and skewed to favour smaller farms. The transition payments would have been based on previous levels of production and would have been made regardless of current production decisions. There was no supply control in the proposal. The proposed transition payments were generally feared to be too expensive. This concern, the late introduction date, and the general aversion of Congress to major program changes led to failure of the proposal in the Senate Agriculture Committee.

A second decoupling proposal, from the American Soybean Association, appeared late in the 1985 farm bill deliberations. This proposal combined gradually declining lump sum payments per acre with market-related price supports and no supply controls. The ASA proposal fell under the gathering momentum of the Food Security Act of 1985 (FSA85).

The objectives of the FSA85 have been described as lowering commodity prices to make the United States more competitive, expanding export markets, controlling crop production, maintaining farm income and gradually reducing the role of government in agriculture. The Act made a number of changes in existing programs. Price support loan rates were reduced and tied to a moving average of world market prices. Marketing loans, allowing farmers to escape a loan quickly when the market price is below the loan rate, were implemented for rice and cotton and were made discretionary for other program crops. But to protect farm income, target prices were frozen for two years then allowed to decline slowly – assuring high deficiency payments and high program participation.

To curb the production incentives associated with the high target price, the Act froze the program yield by farm at the average of 1981-85; in addition the opportunity to expand acreage eligibility for program participation was constrained. A long-term conservation reserve was established to remove up to 45 million acres of highly erodible or frail land from crop production for 10 years. The intent of freezing yields and constraining eligible acreage expansion was to "decouple" marginal production decisions from support payments.

But again, government influence was retained over resource allocation decisions through the acreage reduction program. The FSA85 also incorporated the 50/92 provision, which some view as a step toward decoupling. Under this voluntary provision, farmers can plant as little as 50 per cent of eligible acreage and receive 92 per cent of the maximum deficiency payment. Initially, it was proposed that land not planted under the 50/92 provision could be planted to any non-program crop or no crop at all. Strong protests by growers of certain non-program crops and by livestock producers led to a requirement that land not planted under the 50/92 provision be allocated to conserving uses and only grazed or harvested for hay when approved by the state committee that administers farm programs. Farmers did not make extensive use of the 50/92 provision in 1986 and 1987.

Congress expanded the 50/92 provision to 0/92 in the recent Fiscal Year 1988 budget package. This change was stimulated by the need to reduce the budget deficit. The major choices before the Agriculture Committees were to raise loan rates, lower target prices, decrease paid land diversion or adopt 0/92. By adopting 0/92, the Congress lessened necessary adjustments in the other program parameters. This action illustrates a difference between the concept of decoupling in The Boschwitz-Boren proposal and the 50/92 or 0/92 provisions. The current program provisions are for land retirement or supply management and budget savings. Boschwitz and Boren proposed a goal of full, market-based production. The FSA85 remains a policy with strong commodity orientation where benefits accrue to producers in direct proportion to production levels, and the government continues to influence producers' decisions.

Evolution of Decoupling in Canada

The current set of farm programs in Canada has its roots in the desire for farmers to achieve a stabilized price for their products. There are three major periods in Canadian history when the federal government put in place significant farm programs. Before World War II, farm programs were introduced to control railway pricing, development of the western grains sector (i.e., Canadian Wheat Board and Canadian Grain Commission), expansion of agricultural research, and health of animals regulations. Government support to agriculture by provincial governments was directed at infrastructure such as roads, electricity and schools. There was very little, if any, direct subsidization of agriculture.

After the war, government agriculture policy changed significantly. Labour started to leave agriculture in the 1950s and 1960s, especially in the province of Quebec. It was during this time that supply management got started in Canada as a means of supporting farm prices and incomes. The major force for supply management was the Quebec and Ontario dairy sector, which achieved non-tariff barriers and industrial milk subsidies in the mid-1960s. Products such as eggs, turkey and chicken meat followed the supply management path in the mid-1970s.

Stabilization programs for red meats and grains were developed in the 1970s on an ad hoc basis. The grains sector had two programs, one for western Canada (Western Grains Stabilization Act, WGSA) and one for the rest of Canada (Agricultural Stabilization Act, ASA). The WGSA is a partially decoupled program that pays out money to farmers if their current net revenue falls below a five-year moving average. Because a farmer does not know what payment will be made when planting the crop, and because farmers contribute one-third of the cost of the program, the WGSA has a minimum impact on production. The ASA program is a straight deficiency payment to farmers if the net return falls below a moving average return. Farmers cannot be certain of this payment at the time of planting, so it too has a minimal impact on production.

Support to the red meat industry is largely provincial. Individual provinces put stabilization programs in place to encourage the production and feeding of livestock within their boundaries. These programs largely influence where cattle are fed rather than increase overall production. Quarterly deficiency payments are made to red meat producers if the average return falls below the cost of production.

In 1986, the federal government announced a major deficiency payment to grain producers. The Special Canadian Grains Payment program is tied to production, but announced after the crop is harvested. Again, it is difficult for farmers to adjust their production in the short run to maximize the returns from the program; therefore, it is partially decoupled.

The recent interest in further decoupling of agricultural support programs stems from the GATT negotiations. Canada has taken the position that it wishes to have agricultural markets opened up for trade and that one of the means to achieve this objective is to decouple farm programs from production and trade. The extent to which Canadian farm programs will move in this direction will be determined by similar moves in the agricultural and food policies of other GATT countries.

Extent of Decoupling in Current Programs

Clearly, the degree to which current programs affect production, consumption, trade, prices, and resource allocation varies. The major agricultural programs employed in the United States and Canada are listed in Tables 1 and 2, with indications of likely effects on production, consumption, and resource allocation.

United States. There are programs to assist farmers or facilitate marketing that can be considered to be fully or almost fully decoupled. These are programs like the Farm Credit System, the Federal Crop Insurance program, and bilateral trade agreements that do not include subsidized prices. Research, extension, education, and grading and inspection services are generally considered to be in this category as well.

Under the FSA85, some changes in commodity programs were made to reduce the market impacts of the programs. Commodity loan levels for grains and cotton were reduced substantially, which also significantly reduced their influence on commodity markets. In this mode of operation, their major effect is to provide credit at slightly below commercial rates and to reduce the cost of carrying commodities through the low-price months after harvest.

In theory, acreage control and deficiency payment programs can be operated so that the idled acreage exactly offsets the increased stimulus afforded by the payment. The grain programs appear to have operated closer to this 'ideal' during the first two years of the FSA85 than under previous legislation. However, if unbalanced, these programs have the potential to stimulate production and lower market prices. Even in ideal circumstances, resource allocation is affected because producers are required to plant particular crops to reap program benefits.

The conservation reserve is another program with impacts that are not clear-cut. The current program will remove between 40 and 45 million acres from production. By reducing plantings, the program has a net effect of reducing production, consumption, and trade while increasing domestic and world prices. However, production might be even lower if the full costs of off-site externalities were taken into account in production decisions.

Export subsidy programs, including the expert enhancement program, export credit, PL480, and targeted export assistance, all stimulate domestic production and exports and raise domestic prices while depressing world prices. In the context of the FSA85, the domestic effect is to reduce the cost of deficiency payments rather than to stimulate increased production.

The most highly trade-distorting interventions are the sugar loan and import quota and the dairy price support and import quota. High domestic sugar prices have led to increased substitution of other sweeteners and continuing reductions of the import quota. The dairy program responds in some degree to market signals. Dairy price supports are required to drop $0.50 per hundredweight each year that

Table 1
Effects of some current U.S. programs on production, consumption, trade, and prices

Programs	Effect on[1]					
	Production	Consumption	Trade	Domestic Price	World Price	Resource Allocation
Bilateral trade Agreement[2]	no	no	no	no	no	no
Farm credit system	no	no	no	no	no	small
Crop insurance	no	no	no	no	no	small
Low commodity loans[3]	no	no	no	no	no	small
Acreage control and deficiency payment[4]	small(+)	small(+)	small(+)	small(-)	small(-)	yes
Export subsidies	yes(-)	yes(-)	yes(-)	yes(+)	yes(+)	yes
Conservation reserve	yes(-)	yes(-)	yes(-)	yes(+)	yes(+)	yes
Sugar loan and import quota	yes(+)	yes(-)	yes(-)	yes(+)	yes(-)	yes
Dairy support and quotas	yes(+)	yes(-)	yes(-)	yes(+)	yes(-)	yes

1. (+) or (-) indicates the probable direction of influence.
2. Without subsidy.
3. Below market price (wheat, feed grains, soybeans, cotton).
4. Cotton effects depend on size of acreage reduction requirement relative to payment.

government purchases exceed 5 billion pounds milk equivalent. Current indications are that this decrease will occur in 1988 and again in 1989, after which removals will be below the trigger level. Even after these adjustments, domestic prices and production will be higher, and consumption, trade and world prices will be lower as a result of these policies.

This discussion on the policies and programs subsidizing agriculture in the United States, though not exhaustive, covers the major policies and programs of representative design. The intent is to define the extent of decoupling imbedded in existing programs qualitatively and broadly.

Canada. Trade in agricultural commodities is extremely important to Canada. Canadian agricultural and trade policies have evolved in such a way that livestock products are traded in a continental market and grains and oilseeds in an international market, while poultry and dairy production are solely for the domestic market.

Safety net farm programs are different for each type of commodity. There are regional differences in Canadian farm programs because of the institutional arrangements for marketing some commodities, such as the Canadian Wheat Board, and because of the dual authority for agriculture shared between the federal and provincial governments.

The dairy, poultry, egg, and turkey sectors have been protected by import tariffs and domestic production quotas. This has become known as supply management. While farmers who produce supply-managed commodities do not receive a deficiency payment from the government, they do receive prices above border prices. The supply management system is trade-distorting in the sense that imports are not allowed into the domestic market.

The programs that support incomes of grain producers are regional. The Western Grains Stabilization Act and Western Grain Transportation Act affect only the farmers in the Canadian Wheat Board Area. The Agricultural Stabilization Act applies to most commodities in other regions of Canada, excluding livestock and supply-managed commodities. The WGSA and ASA support commodity incomes if net cash receipts fall below some moving average of cash receipts (farmers enrolled in WGSA contribute to the program, which is not the case for the ASA). The WGTA is a payment to the railways by the federal government for the movement of some export grains.

The effects of the WGSA and ASA on production are likely to be quite small. In times of relatively strong markets, the programs do not make payments to farmers. It is in periods of low prices, such as those currently experienced by grains and oilseed producers, that payouts are made. Payout in periods of low prices will keep resources in agriculture and cause some resource inefficiency.

Several ad hoc programs also support grain incomes, including the Special Canadian Grains Program and provincial programs. Most of these government programs are in the form of deficiency payments. The livestock programs are mostly provincial in nature (currently the industry is moving toward a national stabilization plan) and tend to support farmers' net cash flow from production. Each province has had a different program in the past.

Not all the Canadian programs are covered here, but the most important are included. The application of the programs is so diverse that it is not possible to generalize on the overall trade-distorting effect of the programs. However, in Table 2 the individual programs are assessed qualitatively.

Decoupling Strategies for North America

Given the broad and and narrow concepts of decoupling and the nature of current programs in the United States and Canada, there is a fairly wide range of strategies that could be developed for responding to a decoupling mandate. Under the broadest and most inclusive definition of decoupling, all programs that influence production, consumption, trade, domestic and world market prices, and resource allocation would need to be dismantled. All support for farmers would come through direct payment schemes. Payments, though they might be linked to current levels of support and provide similar compensation, would be as much as possible decoupled from production decisions. An alternative payment scheme could be designed around the objective of aiding in sectoral adjustment rather than merely compensating current program recipients. The broad decoupling goal could, of course, be reached by phased elimination of current programs as well.

Under a narrower definition of decoupling, stabilization programs and supply management programs that are demonstrated to offset production incentives might be considered admissible. The criterion would be that there should be no trade effects or world price effects. This narrow definition will be referred to subsequently as 'partial decoupling'. Under this rule, some stabilization and supply management programs in North America may be able to comply after relatively small adjustments in program provisions. The narrow definition would also admit two-price schemes where commodities produced for the external market would have to be based on price inducements that reflect world market conditions. The higher domestic price would need to be for a specified quantity, not a

Table 2
Effects of some current Canadian programs on production, consumption, trade, and prices

Programs	Effect on[1]					
	Production	Consumption	Trade	Domestic Price	World Price	Resource Allocation
Bilateral trade agreement	no	no	no	no	no	no
Farm credit corp.	no	no	no	no	no	small
Crop insurance	no	no	no	no	no	small
ASA*	small(+)	no	small(+)	small(−)	n.s.[2]	small
WGSA*	small(+)	no	small(+)	no	n.s.[2]	small
WGTA*	small(+)	no	yes(+)	no	n.s.[2]	small
Industrial milk subsidy	yes(−)	yes(−)	yes(−)	yes(+)	n.s.[2]	yes
Supply management	yes(−)	yes(−)	yes(−)	yes(+)	n.s.[2]	yes
Livestock stabilization	yes(+)	no	small(+)	yes(+)	n.s.[2]	yes
Two-price wheat	yes(+)	no	small(+)	yes(+)	n.s.[2]	yes
SCGP*	yes(+)	no	yes(+)	no	n.s.[2]	yes

* Agricultural Stabilization Act, Western Grains Stabilization Act, Western Grain Transportation Act, Special Canadian Grains Program.

1. (+) or (−) indicates the probable direction of influence.
2. Trade effects are expected to have no significant world price effect because of the small country assumption.

percentage of production. But in many of these cases government constraints on producer decisions must be retained or increased.

Impacts and Problems with Decoupling

The major economic argument underlying decoupling is that it would bring about an increase in the efficiency of resource use in agriculture in domestic and international markets. Indeed, there is little argument among economists about the preferability of decoupling in relation to current programs. Arguments arise, however, about political feasibility. This section deals with two issues that generally fall outside the economic efficiency criterion but are of relevance in determining political acceptability. The first is equity or incidence of effects, as in who gains and who loses from decoupling. The second is environmental quality, an issue that is sometimes neglected by narrow measures of efficiency.

The impacts and problems associated with decoupling are evaluated for the alternative programs reviewed at the end of the previous section. This qualitative impact assessment is for commodity markets, the processing and marketing industry, environmental quality, asset values, inputs and factor markets, and farm structure and rural communities. Full decoupling is evaluated generically, with current programs replaced by direct income payments that are production-neutral. We leave aside the question of whether a purely neutral income transfer program can be devised. Under full decoupling, we only indicate when impacts are influenced by the type of payments scheme. Since a phase-out of current programs is one decoupling option, we indicate how this approach would alter the impacts. Finally, selected partial decoupling options are assessed.

Commodity Markets

Commodity market impacts of full decoupling can be viewed in two parts: the impacts for current programs in North America, and the offsetting effects of decoupling elsewhere in the world. Recall that the interest in decoupling by North American policy makers is motivated in part by the improved international market conditions anticipated from decoupling programs elsewhere. There have been studies on full decoupling and phased elimination of U.S. programs (FAPRI 1987, NCFAP 1987, and Wharton 1987), but the effects of global decoupling must be imputed from trade liberalization studies (Frohberg 1987, Krissoff and Ballinger 1987, Meyers et al., OECD 1987, Parikh et al. 1988, Ronigen et al. 1987, Tyres and Anderson 1986, Zietz and Valdes 1986).

Unilateral full decoupling of current U.S. grain programs could be accomplished by replacing the current deficiency payments and supply reduction programs by lump sum payments. Thus, the 60 million acres (24 million hectares) currently in the acreage reduction programs would be available for planting. Given the reduced level of profit on an added unit of production, not all of this land would be cropped. If the conservation reserve program were permitted to continue, the increased area available for production would be reduced by the expected enrollment of 40 to 45 million areas (16 to 18 million hectares). If the conservation reserve were not continued, the short-run effect would be increases in U.S. program crop production and general reductions in market prices. In the longer run, prices would increase again, but would probably remain below the price path under the continuation of the current programs.

The release of producers from the requirement to produce program crops for subsidy eligibility would lead to increases in acreages of non-program crops: potatoes, peas, dry beans and sunflowers, as well as hay and pasture. The lower market price for feed and the expansion of hay and pasture land would initially increase profits and stimulate expansion of livestock production. Over time, the short-term livestock profits would be reduced and the ultimate benefits of lower livestock prices passed on in lower meat prices to consumers.

Impacts on net farm income would depend upon the level of decoupled farm income payments, the level of commodity prices and production, and the level of production expenses after decoupling. For payment levels equal to the total current programs, net farm income would decline, as increased volumes of production and sales would reduce commodity prices. It is unlikely that political support could be sustained for increased government payments to fully offset the lower cash receipts.

With multilateral decoupling in the rest of the world, these impacts would be modified. The consensus from available studies is that global trade liberalization would raise world market prices above those expected under the continuation of current programs. This suggests that, with global decoupling, U.S. commodity prices would be likely to rise rather than fall. Increases in prices would not be large enough to eliminate lump sum payments to maintain net farm income. However, the payments for maintaining net farm income could be smaller than those implied by an extension of the FSA85. Thus, for commodity markets and net farm income relative to government cost, the degree to which decoupling is extended to rest of the world is extremely important to North America.

Eliminating the conservation reserve would merely exacerbate the production expansion and downward pressure on commodity market prices. The conservation reserve currently has 22 million acres enrolled (8.9 million hectares) and can increase to 45 million acres (18.2 hectares) by 1990. Since this program is for a 10-year land retirement contract between producers and the government, it probably would not be dismantled even as part of full decoupling. The separate conservation compliance program is designed to internalize external or off-site costs and would have little effect on commodity markets.

According to some analysts, the largest commodity market effects would be for sugar and dairy. It is possible that sugar beet and cane production would not survive in the United States without price supports and import restrictions. Falling U.S. sugar prices would also affect the corn market, because substantial quantities of corn are now used in the sweetener industry. It is doubtful that high-fructose corn syrup would continue to be competitive with sugar as a sweetener if world market prices remained below 10 cents per pound, especially if corn prices were rising. However, some analysts argue that global decoupling would raise sugar prices well above 10 cents per pound. Thus, the effects on the use of corn for high-fructose syrup would be dependent upon the world price impacts of a global decoupling for sugar and grains. Decoupling of income supports for dairy would probably lead to reduced production, increased consumption and increased trade, with significantly lower domestic prices for fluid milk and milk products. Resulting world prices of dairy products would increase, and pasture and labour resources could be released for other uses.

Processing and Marketing Industries

The expected effects on processing and marketing differ by commodity. For feed grains and wheat, decoupling would lead to increased volumes flowing to domestic and export markets. Benefit would accrue to exporters, manufacturers, and soybean and feed processing. The exception among grains would be rice, where the United States could not sustain existing production levels without substantial subsidies. Livestock processing and marketing would benefit from expanded volume and increased consumption levels.

For sugar, coastal refining plants could see an expansion in volume as more of the domestic sweetener market was taken by imported raw sugar. Inland beet processing facilities would be affected adversely as domestic beets were replaced with imported raw cane sugar. The high-fructose sweetener industry that has developed in recent years would suffer substantially. In fact, long-term survival of the industry would depend on the degree to which international sugar and corn prices responded to the global decoupling.

The dairy processing industry could suffer even in a fully decoupled world. Increased imports of dairy products would probably more than offset the increased domestic demand generated by lower market prices.

For other manufacturers using agricultural commodities as primary inputs, the outcomes are less clear. Trade in the products of final demand of these industries could significantly affect their status in a decoupled world. One North American agricultural industry – contingency market – is likely to expand. With less government intervention to stabilize prices, markets for transferring and spreading risk would expand. Also, higher risk premiums would be paid by the more risk-averse participants in the transactions. This would likely imply an improvement in incomes for the industry buying and selling contracts in contingency markets.

Environmental Quality and Asset Values

Full decoupling would be expected to have significant impacts on environmental quality and farmland prices (and hence landowner wealth). It is assumed here that payments made to farmers under decoupling are not tied to a particular use of the land. The split of transition payments between landlords and farm operators would be important to the acceptability of a decoupling program but would not affect the ultimate resource allocation.

The effects of decoupling on resources include an output substitution effect, an output price effect and an input substitution effect. The output substitution effect is a result of a shift in the relative net returns for program and non-program crops. With decoupling, producer returns for program crops are expected to fall relative to non-program crops, leading farmers to shift production toward non-program crops. The output substitution effect would act to improve environmental quality if non-program crops tended to be less erosive than program crops or if the former require less intensive use of the land (less fertilizer and fewer pesticides).

The output price effect results from change in absolute, not relative, levels of producer returns. The logic is that decoupling will ultimately cause producer returns for all crops to fall. First, the returns for program crops will fall. The resulting shift toward production of non-program crops would cause returns in those crops to fall. If all agricultural producer returns fall, land rents will fall, the extensive margin will decline, and the total amount of cropland will be reduced. The environmental effect is generally positive, with marginal crop land dropping out of production or shifting to less intensive agricultural uses. The FSA85 ties payments to land in general, so the combined impact of markets and subsidies is currently to increase land prices over levels that would obtain in a decoupled era.

The input substitution effect results from removing constraints on land use (acreage reduction program) and shifts in the relative input prices. The output price effect will lead to a reduction in land rents, which, *ceteris paribus*, will lead to a substitution of land for inputs that are technical substitutes for land, such as fertilizer. (The price of fertilizer may also fall, but assuming fertilizer supply is more elastic than farmland, land rents will fall relative to fertilizer.) The lifting of constraints on land in program crops will tend to increase the acreage in both program and non-program crops. The net effect for environmental quality is probably positive. The land in production will be farmed less intensively because it has a price no longer tied to government payments. This should result in reduced fertilizer use. However, if the total land in row crops increased as constraints on land use are lifted, soil erosion might increase.

Land rents would fall with decoupling, relative to the FSA85. Land prices, therefore, would also be expected to fall. However, current land prices are based on the present value of expected future land rents. To the extent that landowners have already anticipated a move to decoupling, or at least continued reductions in government involvement in agriculture, current land prices may already reflect reduced future land rents. The point is that anticipation of future policies or uncertainty about current support levels may have already reduced farmland prices to be more consistent with decoupling.

Input, Labour, and Land Markets

The effects of full, unilateral decoupling on input (chemicals and machinery) and labour markets can be analyzed using a logic similar to that for environmental quality. The output substitution effect, shifting production away from program crops, could reduce the demand for fertilizers and pesticides to the extent that non-program crops require less intensive cultivation. Effects on labour and machinery markets are uncertain.

The output price effect, since it involves a reduction in the producer returns for all crops, will lead to a reduction in demand for all normal inputs. This would be expected to reduce the demand for cultivated land, chemicals and machinery, and probably also for labour. The effect on labour demand is less certain, because some enterprises might shift to a more labour intensive form of production compared to that under the FSA85. However, the overall effect of a decline in farm income would put pressure on labour to move out of agriculture to other sectors where earnings are higher. Generally we would expect decoupling to accelerate the exit of labour from agriculture. Many of the current subsidy policies are, in fact, designed to hold labour in agriculture.

The input substitution effect, by reducing the cost of land relative to all other inputs and factors, will tend to reduce the demand for factors that are substitutes for land and raise the demand for factors that are complements to land. Fertilizers are generally viewed as a land substitute, so the input substitution effect would lead to a reduction in fertilizer use. Pesticides are generally viewed as substitutes for labour, management, and mechanical cultivation. Their relationship with land is more difficult to classify. While they may be net substitutes at the margin, they may also be necessary to the cultivation of certain crops in particular regions, such as cotton farming in the southern United States. For this reason, the net effect on pesticide demand is uncertain. The impact of the input substitution effect on labour demand is equally difficult to predict.

Again, the effect of decoupling on input and factor markets will depend on the net result of all three effects. The output substitution effect and the input substitution effect should tend to reduce fertilizer and, to a lesser extent, pesticide use. The effects on labour and machinery use are uncertain. The output price effect should reduce the demand for all inputs and factors. The net result, then, would be that demand for all factors would be less than or equal to demand before decoupling, with fertilizer demand probably experiencing the greatest decline.

Farm Structure and Rural Communities

In the earlier discussion of the impact of decoupling on resource use, three effects were identified. Because of the output substitution effect, we expect that the effective acreage base (planted acreage plus acreage idled under required acreage reduction programs) of program crops would decline as a result of a shift to production of non-program crops. Because of the output price effect, we expect that total agricultural output would be reduced from the full production levels that would occur with the current support levels in the absence of production controls. The result of this effect would be a reduction in total cropland acreage, land rents, and the value of farm real estate. This adjustment process would generally consist of moving some cropland out of agriculture. Because of the input substitution effect, lower land costs would lead to the substitution of land for those inputs that are technical substitutes — for example, fertilizer.

The dislocations caused by the resource adjustments described in the preceding section would be spread throughout the entire agricultural sector with respect to commodities, geographic regions, and classes of farm operators.

With respect to commodities, attention has been focused on the current program commodities where producers of feed grains, wheat, soybeans, and cotton are major beneficiaries. Many producers of these commodities are efficient enough to maintain production at world market prices after decoupling. The discrepancies between current world market prices and current domestic prices for sugar, rice, peanuts, milk, and wool are such that producers of these commodities would be hard pressed to remain competitive with unilateral decoupling. With global decoupling, U.S. producers of certain commodities may gain greater access to world markets and world prices may rise. In some cases, producers of non-program commodities have also enjoyed indirect benefits from the current programs, which would be lost at the same time they come under competition from resources released from the program crops by decoupling.

With respect to geographic regions, the commodity-specific adjustments just mentioned could have significant local effects in rural communities. For example, sugar beet production from a fairly large area may be processed in a single mill. The same is true for milk and, to a lesser degree, for rice and peanuts. If a local community is heavily dependent on the production and processing of one commodity, it will suffer severe economic impacts from the loss of that industry.

When one looks at larger geographic areas, such as states or groups of states, there is generally enough diversification of commodities to minimize the impact of dislocation in a single commodity. However, there are exceptions with respect to some marginal production of crops that currently enjoy income supports. Where low soil fertility, arid conditions, or weather variability cause production costs to be high, complete decoupling could lead to large areas of cropland being converted to less valuable forage production or being abandoned.

The expected decline in farmland values could also affect local governments that depend heavily on *ad valorem* taxes on farm real estate to finance local services such as schools. Unless ways can be devised to reduce the costs of providing these services or to share revenues from other sources, a significant deterioration in the quality of rural life could result at least in some areas.

With respect to the effects on the structure of the farm sector, the commodity price effects of total decoupling will likely accelerate the process of removing the least efficient producers from agriculture. The provision of transition payments or permanent income maintenance not tied to commodity production would be a further incentive for inefficient producers to leave agriculture and would reduce the trauma associated with their relocation. The retention of farm operators could be encouraged by payment schemes that target income assistance to smaller farm operators. It would be desirable to provide local governments in regions where structural impacts are concentrated with assistance in vocational education and rural job creation.

Canadian Decoupling

If Canadian agricultural policy moved toward decoupling price supports and removing of non-tariff barriers, the impact on production and trade would range from minimal to substantial. The difficulty in assessing the outcome of such a policy change arises because the current markets are distorted to the point where there is little empirical evidence about Canada's comparative advantage.

In the supply-managed commodities, the removal of non-tariff barriers would immediately result in a drop in consumer and producer prices. Canadian fluid milk producers would likely maintain their market because of the cost of transport. Whether Canadian producers could export fluid milk to the United States would depend on the cost of production in the two countries. Industrial milk production would most certainly decline in Canada because countries such as New Zealand can produce much cheaper industrial milk products.

Livestock production could increase in Canada in a decoupled world. Compared with grain producers, livestock producers have received a fairly low level of support from governments; as a result, they should be in a favoured position to expand production. Canadian red meat producers currently compete very successfully in the North American market.

The effect of decoupling on grain producers would be substantial. The removal of the freight subsidy, the Special Canadian Grains Program and the Western Grains Stabilization Act would lower the price received by producers. The price increase from free world trade would probably not compensate for this loss in transfer payments.

The immediate effect on the grain producer would be a reduction in land rents. Because the grain land has few alternative uses, especially in western Canada, and if producers could cover variable costs, then in the short run production of wheat and canola would remain at present levels. The depressed feed grains market would likely result in a reduction in feed grain production. Barley production would be only for the domestic market, at least until the world price increased substantially.

The major impact of decoupling would be on the structure of the agriculture sector. The supply-managed sector would see a reduction in numbers of producers. To be competitive on world markets, Canadian producers would have to greatly increase their size.

The structural change in the grains sector would depend on the new equilibrium grain prices and on the income support afforded these producers in the decoupled programs. The pressure to remove farmers from agricultural production in the prairie region would be substantial. If, however, prices rose to the current producer support levels (market price plus subsidy), the impact on structure would be quite small.

The impact of decoupling on smaller farm commodities such as fruits and vegetables would be minimal. These agricultural commodities are largely protected by tariffs that are to be removed under the Canada-U.S. Free Trade Agreement.

The final important consideration for the Canadian case is the regional impact of decoupling. Because the production of commodities tends to be concentrated in specific regions (e.g., wheat in the prairies), the manner of decoupling will be important. If only the grain subsidies are decoupled and not the non-tariff barriers in the supply-managed commodities, the regional effects would be important.

Decoupling vs. Phased Elimination

Removal of distortions could be achieved gradually, through a phase-out of current support programs, or, by full decoupling. The goals of these two approaches are the same: both attempt to achieve an unrestricted market for agriculture. The difference lies with how they achieve that result. Radical decoupling represents an instantaneous jump to a free market with transition payments used to cushion the impact of that jump on farmers and landowners. A gradual decoupling plan provides a cushion by slowly reducing the difference between support prices and world prices over time until support prices are eliminated.

Because their end results are the same, in the long run both can be expected to have the same effect on land prices, environmental quality, factor markets, and farm structure. With gradual decoupling, since it is a phase out of the current system, land prices would be expected to fall to their long-run equilibrium more slowly than with the sudden alternative. Other input and factor markets, such as the fertilizer supply industry, would also have more time to shift their resources to other uses as the demands for their products fall. For this reason, the gradual plan would be expected to be less disruptive of capital, credit, and other input markets than a sudden shift to decoupling.

We do not see a clear-cut distinction between the two alternatives as far as environmental quality is concerned. Sudden decoupling may induce faster adjustment in resource use, thus speeding the improvement in environmental quality. A rapid adjustment may cause problems, however, by making it more difficult to assure that marginal land goes into conserving uses such as grassland and is not just abandoned.

A recent analysis of the Food Security Act of 1985 with assumptions of its continuing for the next decade (FAPRI 1988), indicates that the continuing of gradual reductions in target price support for several commodities would lead to the convergence of target prices with market prices in about ten years. This represents a much more gradual adjustment toward decoupling in the United States than was proposed by the administration in 1985. Whether this result would actually come to pass depends both on the political will to continue the current path of support reductions and on future developments in market conditions. Should market prices rise more rapidly than in this analysis, effective decoupling would occur earlier. On the other hand, if prices do not recover or recover more slowly, the period of adjustment would be longer. This type of uncertainty may not be acceptable in the negotiating process, since decoupling could not be assured within a specific period of time.

Partial Decoupling Options

The previous section discussed full decoupling as well as the gradual phasing out current programs over some period of time. In contrast to these, partial decoupling options involve adjustments that correspond to the narrower definition of decoupling. Examples of partial decoupling would involve current U.S. or Canadian supply management and stabilization programs to ensure that support transferred to producers under these programs did not distort trade or world prices. This limited definition of decoupling focuses on trade distortions rather than on the broader distortions that may occur in domestic resource allocation or domestic production and consumption patterns. Warley has argued, for example, that the programs operated under the Agricultural Stabilization Act, the Agricultural Boards Act and the Lesser Grains Stabilization Act have "so small an effect on production and consumption as to be for all practical purposes trade neutral." Even if that were not strictly true under current provisions, modifications could be made to ensure that such programs were trade-neutral, though there would still be distortions in resource allocation.

Similarly, the former Assistant Secretary for Economics of the U.S. Department of Agriculture, Robert Thompson, has argued that the freezing of the program yield and constraints on program base have the effect of decoupling U.S. crop production from the support payments currently provided. It is not yet clear how successful this attempt at decoupling has been. A more certain way to ensure that U.S. support payments under these programs are trade-neutral would be to make the payments on the basis of a fixed quantity for each producer. This would ensure that any quantities produced over that amount would have to be produced for the market price. A program of this type already exists in the U.S. peanut sector. Under this program the domestic allotment for peanut production is protected at a relatively high price, but producers are free to produce additional quantities, which must be sold on the international market. This provision ensures that marginal production occurs in response to world market price signals. This represents a two-tier price scheme, which may be acceptable under the narrow definition of a trade-neutral program.

The Role of a Conservation Reserve in a Decoupled World

As stated earlier, the major economic argument behind decoupling is improvement in the efficiency of resource use in agriculture. This increased efficiency is achieved by allowing prices to adjust to their market clearing levels. In the absence of externalities and other forms of market imperfection, these market prices will reflect social scarcity values, and resources will flow naturally to their socially best and highest uses. When externalities are present, as they are in agriculture, it may be possible to improve the efficiency of resource allocation with policies that alter the market allocation.

A program such as the conservation reserve could be justified on economic efficiency grounds as an attempt to reduce a negative externality (soil erosion and water pollution) by removing erosive land from production. The socially optimal level of production for the exporting nation would be something less, and world price would be higher than the free market level.

An optimal conservation reserve would be one that would shift the market supply curve to coincide with the socially optimal level. Similar arguments could be made in the case of positive externalities for programs to preserve stone fences and hedgerows in England or subsidies to preserve terraces in Italy. Unfortunately, all these programs also alter production and trade relative to an unregulated market, so there will be great temptation to use environmental and cultural preservation arguments to justify domestic price enhancement policies. There will be a distinct trade-off in the GATT negotiations with regard to giving countries the flexibility to improve their environmental quality or preserve cultural values without allowing the same types of market distorting policies we have now, though with different names.

Political Problems of Decoupling

Hearings held during March 1987 before the Subcommittee on Wheat, Soybeans, and Feed Grains of the U.S. House of Representatives Committee on Agriculture indicated that opposition to decoupling at that time was widespread and formidable. Producers of wheat, feed grains, rice and cotton liked the current programs and seemed unwilling to trade them for decoupled programs. Producers of non-program crops felt that decoupling would doubly penalize them, since they have no present eligibility for transition payments and would face new competition from shifts of decoupled acreage. Input suppliers feared lower farm income and possible reduced input use decoupling might bring. Support for decoupling has come mainly from exporting interests and economists who are philosophically dedicated to the free market.

Dubbed as welfare or paying farmers for nothing by such diverse sources as the *Baltimore Sun* and the distinguished agricultural economist, Harold Breimyer, decoupling may be more susceptible to political criticism than the current programs. Several U.S. farm state legislators have also labelled decoupling as welfare. In the words of one, Terry Bruce of Illinois, "I don't think the American farmer wants something for nothing and I don't think the federal government wants to encourage that sort of mentality." In the eyes of these critics, decoupling drops all efforts to conduct farm programs as economic policy and instead treats them as social policy. The public perception of welfare would become a political problem because, unlike traditional means-tested social programs such as food stamps, the transition payments under current decoupling proposals would not likely be based on need. Rich and poor alike could receive a government check in proportion to their past production history.

History has taught us that new policy initiatives take a long time to become accepted and implemented. The concept of decoupling is a mere babe in the policy arena, although various limited forms of partial decoupling are part of current policy. Vested interest groups are responsible for the creation of policy, and vested interest groups are also responsible for maintaining those policies from which they benefit. The decoupling proposals currently under discussion in the United States and in international forums have been opposed by those who feel they would lose if current programs are abolished. That is not to say, however, that policy makers cannot devise a successful decoupling proposal that fairly compensates the various affected parties. Such a task is worthy of our efforts if it leads to broader global decoupling of agricultural programs.

Summary and Conclusions

There is some question about how farmers would react in a truly decoupled environment. Analysts expect that most of the land currently idled under farm programs would return to production, but not all would end up in the current program crops — wheat, feed grains, soybeans, cotton, and rice. It seems reasonable to expect that some land would shift to crops not currently supported, for example, potatoes, dry beans, and sunflowers, as well as hay and pasture. Thus the process of dislocation and adjustment would be spread throughout the entire agricultural sector.

Significant structural change could occur as less efficient producers leave agriculture and their land and other resources are acquired by the better entrepreneurs. The environmental benefits could be positive, as the shifts in crops and production practices result in less intensive use of fertilizer and pesticides. Part of this benefit would be offset, however, if crop acreage expanded on erodible land (in the absence of the provisions in FSA85 that discourage this) or if support for the conservation reserve was lost.

The effect of decoupling in North America depends greatly upon how broad the definition of decoupling is and on the world market effects of decoupling by other countries. Global decoupling that includes consumption effects would be preferable from a North American perspective, since the market impacts would be more favourable. The impact on the North American agricultural sector would be smaller under the narrow definition of decoupling that focuses only on trade distortions and ignores distortions in resource use. Under this narrow approach, some of the current programs could achieve the decoupling objective with relatively small modifications. This narrow approach obviously would also limit the degree to which North America would benefit from improved domestic resource use and larger program changes in other countries.

This paper should not be viewed as an endorsement or condemnation of the decoupling concept. Nor does this paper put forth specific decoupled programs to take the place of existing market intervention. We have attempted to provide an assessment of the economic and social impacts of reducing or removing direct governmental intervention in agricultural markets. The assessment leads to a recognition of the political forces that would need to be addressed before an effectively decoupled set of agricultural and rural programs could be acceptable to the body politic.

References

Breimyer, H.F. 1988. "Agricultural Policies: The New Reality."
Summary of a seminar held at the University of Missouri-
Columbia, Nov. 12-13, 1987. *Economics and Marketing
Information for Missouri Agriculture* 31(1). Missouri
Cooperative Extension Service, Columbia, MO.

Food and Agricultural Policy Research Institute. 1988. "FAPRI Ten-
Year International Agricultural Outlook." FAPRI Staff Report.
1-88. Iowa State University, Ames, IA and University of
Missouri, Columbia, MO (March).

Food and Agricultural Policy Research Institute. 1987. "Comparative
Analysis of Selected Policy Options for U.S. Agriculture." FAPRI
Staff Report 1-87. Iowa State University, Ames, IA and
University of Missouri, Columbia, MO (February).

Frohberg, Klaus. 1987. "International Institute for Applied Systems
Analyses Basic Linked System World Agricultural Model." in
*The International Agriculture Trade Research Consortium:
Agricultural Trade Modelling, the State of Practice and Research
Issues.* Staff Report No. AGES861215. USDA (June).

Guither, H.D. 1986. "Tough Choices: Writing the Food Security Act
of 1985." AEI Occasional Paper. American Enterprise Institute
for Public Policy Research, Washington, D.C. (December).

House Committee on Agriculture. 1987. "Policy Alternatives to the
Food Security Act of 1985." Hearings held before the
Subcommittee on Wheat, Soybeans, and Feed Grains, March 10,
12, 17, 19, 31. Serial No. 100-31, Washington, D.C.

Krissoff, B. and N. Ballenger. 1987. "Effects of Protection and
Exchange Rate Policies on Agricultural Trade: Implications for
Argentina, Brazil, and Mexico." ERS Staff Report No.
AGES870825. USDA (September).

Meyers, William H., S. Devadoss, and Michael D. Helmar. 1987.
"Analysis of Cross Commodity and Cross Country Linkages with
an Econometric Agricultural Trade Model." *Journal of Policy
Modelling* 9: 455-482.

National Center for Food and Agricultural Policy. 1987. "The 1985 Farm Bill Revisited: Midstream Correction or Stay the Course." Resources for the Future, Washington, D.C. (April).

Organization for Economic Co-operation and Development. 1987. "National Policies and Agricultural Trade." Paris.

Parikh, K.S., G. Fischer, K. Frohberg, and O. Gulbrandsen. 1988. "Toward Free Trade in Agriculture." Amsterdam: Martinns Nijhoff.

Roningen, V., J. Sullivan and J. Wainio. 1987. "The Impact of the Removal of Support to Agriculture in Developed Countries." Paper presented at the 1987 AAEA Meetings. East Lansing, MI (August).

Tyers, R. and K. Anderson. 1986. "Distortions in World Food Markets: A Quantitative Assessment." Background Paper No. 22 for *World Development Report, 1986.* World Bank (January).

Warley, T.K. 1987. "Issues Facing Agriculture in the GATT Negotiations." *Canadian Journal of Agricultural Economics* 35: 515-534.

Wharton Econometric Forecasting Associates. 1987. "An Economic Analysis of Alternative Agricultural Policies." Bala Cynwyd, PA (April).

Zietz, J. and Alberto Valdez. 1986. "The Costs of Protectionism to Developing Countries: An Analysis for Selected Agricultural Products." World Bank Staff Working Paper No. 769.

An EC Approach to Decoupling

John S. Marsh

Prologue

Words that attain the status of negotiating symbols generally embody some comfortable ambiguities. Thus they may be uttered in good faith and with due reverence by each side while leading to actions that participants may find surprising or even shocking. Agricultural trade debates have their own library of such terms: 'food aid', 'reciprocity' and 'voluntary restraint' to name but three.

'Decoupling' may be at the top of today's chart of agricultural policy jargon because it shares something of these characteristics. What is to be decoupled are policy decisions that affect production from those that are pursued on social or environmental grounds. Within the European Community such an approach would mean that price policy could not be justified on the basis of the need to maintain farm incomes or rural populations. Those goals would have to be pursued through separate instruments such as direct income aids or regional policy.

This is an important idea and one that has been much discussed within the Community. Its strongest advocates have been economists; its opponents the the leaders of farm organizations, who rightly fear that explicit payments for such social goals might be more difficult to defend than the implicit benefits of a high price.

This paper argues that the distinctions between production goals and others are often difficult to define, and it may be far from straightforward to determine whether a policy is 'decoupled'. Hence those who seek salvation through this term will need to exercise eternal vigilance if they are not to be disappointed.

Why Decouple?

The economic argument

Orthodox western economic analysis attaches central importance to the working of the price mechanism in a competitive environment. By allowing prices to move, production takes place where costs are lowest; entrepreneurs adopt cost-reducing techniques; the mix of goods produced reflects the priorities of consumers, and the owners of resources (not least those who supply their own labour) receive the highest reward possible. Such a 'Parero efficient' economy is regarded with some enthusiasm, and variations from it are commonly labelled distortions.

The European Community embodies such a perception of the world in much of its constitution, the Rome Treaty. Goods and services are to move freely between member countries. Articles 85 to 102 establish rules of competition. Government actions that distort the conditions of competition conflict with these rules. It is inconsistent with such an approach that the Community should have devised a policy for agriculture that represents a substantial inter-sectoral distortion. It is also inconsistent with the conceptual basis of the Community that this distortion should be imposed on its trade with the rest of the world. Although the existence of a common market implies some element of Community preference, the benefits of such an arrangement depend directly on whether its trade-creating effects exceed its trade-diverting effects. In terms of this analysis the Common Agricultural Policy (CAP) is massively trade-diverting and so makes the Community poorer.

An essential element in understanding this situation is the CAP's dependence on price policy. For most commodities the Council of Ministers fix a level of price. This takes account not so much of what the market will bear, but of what the farmers will receive. The need to do so is built into the expectations embodied in the Treaty (Article 39 (b)), to ensure thereby a fair standard of living for the agricultural population, particularly by the increasing of the individual earnings of persons engaged in agriculture. Still more it is a perceived current political necessity: a sharp contrast to the political weight attached to clause (V) or Article 39, which requires reasonable prices for consumers.

Concentration on the income distribution implications of price determination has meant that production has not been controlled. Given rising productivity, the consequence has been a rate of production growth that substantially exceeds consumption increases. Two immediate results ensue. Community spending on price support has risen, forcing the EC into a budget crisis. The Community has diminished its imports of competitive products and, with the aid of subsidies, increased its exports. In economic terms this trend represents a growing waste of resources within the Community and a rising level of economic loss imposed on the rest of the world.

The economic case for decoupling is that this waste could be avoided. By allowing prices genuinely to represent the value of incremental output to consumers, production would be constrained. The benefits of new technology would materialize as lower prices for food and in the form of the additional non-food goods and services that the resources released from farming would provide. The separation of the production targets of policy from social and regional elements would permit these to be addressed directly. In terms of cost effectiveness this seems likely to lead to a higher return than an exclusively price policy could deliver.

It is logically possible, although practically difficult, to conceive of direct social and regional policies that are even worse than product price manipulation. Prices are however very bad instruments of income policy. In the short run, they benefit most those with most to sell: the rich farmer rather than the needy peasant. In the long run, they are capitalized into higher land prices, benefiting landowners but penalizing new entrants and farmers who seek to expand to exploit economies of scale. The geographical distribution of benefits is most favourable to the richest farming regions; for areas facing depopulation price policy may do little to help.

Most important, price policy traps resources in obsolete uses. Because the farmer gains only as long as he produces, his incentive to move to a more market-determined use of his labour and capital is weakened. However, as the short-run benefits of price increases disappear, his income is likely to come under renewed pressure. In reality a purely price-based policy sustains agricultural poverty rather than enables farmers or farm workers to become rich.[1] Insofar as policies may attract young people to enter the industry and invest on the basis of inappropriate prices, it can even be said to add to the problems.

This economic assessment of the case for decoupling rests heavily upon the assumption of the competitive model central to classical economics. The model is inadequate in several dimensions. It assumes that resources displaced from one use will move into alternative employments. For many unemployed people in Europe that seems simply to be invalid. It assumes that farmers and consumers operate in competitive markets, but in this industry food distribution and manufacture are increasingly concentrated. Thus the assumption of competition provides an unsafe basis for policy. On a global scale the analysis assumes that prices open to the influence of world markets will reflect the underlying comparative advantage of industries in various countries. That has not been the case. Its prescription relies wholly on market signals to guide production, ignoring externalities that represent an authentic part of the benefits and costs resulting from agricultural activity.

The actual impact on employment of a lowered price combined with some form of direct income aid would depend critically upon assumptions made about the working of the rest of the economy. Lower land prices would probably encourage a less capital-intensive agriculture, but the savings in cost would not offset the reduction in revenue, so that unless farmers chose to accept lower incomes their numbers would fail and farm sizes tend to enlarge. The contrast between the structure of UK and German farms is at least in part a result of differences in past policy of this nature. At the same time the reduced burden of farm support on the rest of the economy should strengthen growth.[2] This should tend to encourage an outflow of manpower as real incomes in other sectors rise. Much of this moreover might be associated with an expansion of part-time farming or a decrease in the dependence of existing part-time farms on income from farming.

The implication of these reservations is not that decoupling becomes unattractive but that to attain its economic benefits it has to be applied within a consistent economic system. One important advantage of a decoupled policy may be that it can address some of these imperfections directly, for instance by rewarding people for positive externalities, rather than by price increases.

The political argument

The political merits of decoupling depend on the standpoint from which it is assessed. At one extreme is the concept of the overall welfare of society. Here the virtue of decoupling is that it requires the policy maker to identify, assess and respond to the various elements that constitute societies' goals for agriculture. By separating issues, policies may be designed to meet more precisely the purposes for which they are intended. Typically, for example, a direct income policy for farmers can be directed at specific vulnerable groups, while a policy that tries to raise income exclusively through price manipulation will benefit these groups least.

The reverse situation is that of the farm lobbyist. Here, as it sometimes says at French railway crossings, "one train can conceal another". The opportunities to attain substantial net income transfers to wealthy farmers and landowners while arguing for small farmers, for depressed regions or for food security, are highly prized. The politician stands between these positions. He has multiple goals reflecting a diversity of interest groups. His ability to satisfy one group depends upon actions that avoid arousing too much opposition amongst the generality of his supporters. In principle, he likes the results of his policy, where they meet goals, to be highly visible, whereas he would prefer the costs to be invisible. The CAP provides clear evidence. Economists assess the costs of the policy to consumers in terms of the increased prices it forces them to pay for their food. The total amount involved is vigorously disputed but seems likely to be not less than 40 billion ECU. Total public expenditure costs of farm support include substantial payments made by national governments in aids to their own agriculture. Again, this is hard to measure satisfactorily, but it probably accounts for a further 10 to 12 billion ECU. At a Community level, however, both consumer transfers and national aids are largely invisible; debate focuses instead on the visible charges falling on the common budget, the way these are to be financed, and their division among member countries. It is the growing visibility of the effects of price policy on the EC budget that now makes decoupling practical politics within the Community.

Recent policy developments are indicative of this. The application of integrated development programmes — especially for the Mediterranean region — embodies visible direct support that reduces the pressure for price increases. The agreement to allow countries to provide aids to farmers who pursue approved farming practices in environmentally sensitive areas (ESA), enables visible specific payments to replace indirect inducements via price to maintain farming in such regions. Developments in the EC's Forestry Action Programmes may also help to relieve the pressure to sustain agriculture in order to maintain population in vulnerable areas.

Decoupling has thus become part of the political reality of the Community. In a situation where visibility has become inescapable, policy makers may well find it easier to defend policies that directly address the goals of policy rather than prices, which lead to surplus. At the same time, the decoupled policies are more suited for national financing. Both the goals they pursue and the financial resources available vary greatly among EC member countries. In a single market product prices must be commonly regulated, but such a necessity does not prevail for many of the non-production goals of farm policy. Hence, the concept of a CAP less reliant on price support but acting as the orchestrator of varying national activities may well develop from the Community's current financial problems. For many people, both within and outside the Community, the key issue may well be the authority of the conductor and the score he presents to the players. This theme will be resumed later in this paper.

Mechanisms for Decoupling

The economic base line

Decoupling implies allowing prices to reflect market conditions. The key question is which market prices or, as implied here, what represents an economically rational base line? In current circumstances, where markets are seriously over-supplied, reflecting market conditions means allowing prices to fall. Within Europe at least, a free fall is regarded as politically non-negotiable. Apart from the hardship it would impose on the European farm sector, a price of collapse is also rejected because it is feared, probably erroneously, that it would threaten food security and lead to wasteful price instability. In principle, the EC could decouple to a global economic base line, or to one peculiar to itself, lower than at present but not directly vulnerable to changes in world markets. Memories of war-time and post-war food scarcity are still sufficiently alive to make the idea of dependence upon outside sources for a large proportion of food supplies unattractive to many Europeans. Thus, while European policy makers may accept the concept of decoupling as a useful avenue of escape from the absurdities of the CAP as its stands, it is unlikely that they would be prepared to contemplate an economic base line that amounted to current import prices. Two types of approach might be considered for some more acceptable relationship to world markets.

First, the base line might be related to world markets by a formula that allowed internal prices to rise and fall in sympathy with the world market. In its purest form such a base line based on free trade would not be acceptable, but a possible variant would be a fixed tariff that permitted agriculture to enjoy a degree of Community preference similar to that accorded to other sectors. From an EC point of view, such a base line is unlikely to be acceptable if world trade continues to be dominated by the agricultural policy decisions of other countries. This is the mirror image of the reasoning that has led agricultural exporting countries to complain that the CAP destroys their markets. It means that the EC would not accept an economic base line for its agriculture based on current patterns of world trade. The solution might be to move to global disarmament in agricultural policy and trade. Such an approach would lead to more rational and probably more stable world markets. It would, however, imply a greater degree of internal price instability for the EC than do present arrangements. This would be unwelcome in the Community, and the EC might seek instead to attempt to regulate world trade through international agreements. Such commodity agreements have not worked well in the past, and there are no good reasons to believe that they would do so in the future. If they were not available, however, the implication could be that the EC would determine an economic base line for its agriculture that reflected long-run market trends but incorporated buffering arrangements against short-run fluctuations. In effect it would adjust its prices retrospectively to trends in world markets. In a crude sense that might be seen as already occurring for some products where the cost of support has exceeded politically acceptable levels.

A second approach starts from the judgement that actual world prices are so distorted by government actions that they cannot represent a long-run supply function for agricultural goods. The logic of decoupling suggests, however, that internal prices should be at a level at which there would be a secure supply available from the rest of the world. Thus, the economic base line should relate to production costs in the EC and the rest of the world rather than to current prices. The practicability of such an approach must be questioned. Attempts to measure production costs at the margin are fraught with difficulty, even within countries. International comparisons are much more difficult – exchange rate problems, cost differences related to fiscal policies, and differences in the structure of price formation – all add to the problems.

Both approaches to determining an economic base line for agricultural prices accept the notion that market prices do provide an authentic reference point. However, this too will be disputed. Externalities play a crucial role in several areas of agricultural policy. The value society derives from agricultural activity in Europe includes positive and negative benefits in the areas of landscape, recreation, pollution and rural community. To ignore such values is to make erroneous economic judgements; a policy that did so would make society and the world poorer. A properly operating market should reflect such realities; however there are problems – measuring externalities, and especially in a way that gains acceptance from other countries, is extremely difficult. If the positive benefits of agriculture are over-estimated, then an EC industry of larger than optimum size will result. If they are under-estimated the industry will be too small. Decoupling, by making explicit the level of support or taxation associated with agreed externalities, could help to achieve a better distribution of resources. However, as this paper will argue shortly, such intervention may itself have significant consequences for the base line level of price.

Justification for direct transfers

It is convenient to distinguish three types of policy instrument that might be used to achieve some of the decoupled goals of agricultural policy. First there are instruments that pay farmers to provide goods and services that society wants but that hitherto have emerged as by-products of food production. The maintenance of hedges and walls, the preservation of wildlife habitats, the retention of public footpaths are all examples of benefits that are not actually paid for by the consumer. Such benefits occur as part of an activity that also produces food. In a decoupled system the logic requires that lower food prices would be offset by payments to farmers to provide these 'products'. These payments would ensure not only that the desired benefits continued, but that food was available at the going price as a by-product. There is no logical problem. The fact that world food prices would be depressed is immaterial. However, there are severe political problems. The process enables governments to continue to subsidize farmers and could in principle leave external suppliers in no better position. Thus, although instruments that reward externalities are a proper feature of a decoupled agriculture, there needs to be some process of monitoring and agreeing on these if the system is not to be invalidated.

A second set of instruments relates to social priorities. In the EC it is accepted that direct income aids may be a necessary concomitant of any significant price reduction. Already many governments provide specially favourable social security terms for farmers. Such payments should be production-neutral. Provided the price corresponds to the value of extra output to the Community, it may be unimportant if the recipient of an income payment chooses to spend part of it in continuing to farm. However, in a world in which the extent and level of income payments would have to vary between countries, such an outcome might well lead to the distortion of markets and the diversion of trade. The contrast is likely to be particularly acute between rich countries where hobby farming by part-time farmers might be encouraged and poor countries that could not afford to shield their farmers from economic change.

A third set of problems arises from intervention designed to promote development. The logic is that of the infant industry argument. The practicality is that the 'infants' seldom grow up. Decoupled agricultural policies are likely to include structural policies that may be designed to assist long-run adjustment. Some of these may be outside the farm sector but others are likely to promote farm enlargement and rationalization. The effect is to make the industry of the country concerned more competitive. Under a decoupled policy, that implies lower prices. For farmers in countries where such aids are not available it looks more like unfair competition.

The difficulty illustrated by this brief review of some of the techniques of attempting to meet, within a decoupled policy, goals that do not relate directly to price or production is not negligible. The validity of a move toward such a policy could be destroyed if the price that ultimately prevailed for farm output was seen to be significantly depressed by payments under this head. To do so would change the focus of the current tensions between the Community and the rest of the world from price to other aids. Efficient farmers, i.e., those in other countries who were low-cost producers, would claim to be penalized in order to allow privileged high-cost producers to survive.

Decoupling and the flow of world trade

The power of the concept of decoupling is its merits in terms of domestic policy makers. In the EC, it is the Council of Ministers who have to be convinced if changes are to occur in the CAP. However, contemporary interest in decoupling owes at least as much to the need to reform the world trading system. The current pattern of world trade is grossly distorted by the operation of agricultural policies. An attempt to assess this distortion is embodied in the recent OECD study.

This showed a league table in terms of producer subsidy equivalents (PSEs). Its most important message was not that some countries were supporting their farmers more than others, but that almost every developed country was engaged in the business of farm support. The results are frequently self-defeating. World trade is distorted, justifying more protection. World prices are depressed, raising the cost of protection to all participants. Decoupling represents a means of escape from this collective absurdity. By allowing prices to move and determine production levels, surpluses will disappear, production will be located where costs are lowest, and a world price will result that reflects the costs of meeting world food needs.

The economic case for such a move is very strong. However, its political acceptability cannot be assumed. Even within the Community the notion that, on the basis of comparative advantage, a country's agriculture should contract relative to the agriculture of other member countries, has proved unworkable. Its response to monetary adjustments illustrate the difficulty.

Faced by exchange rate movements that reflected long run shifts in comparative advantage, rather than allow prices to farmers to move, the Community devised monetary compensatory amounts (MCAs). In effect these enable farmers in the strong currency country to continue to receive the same price in their own currency. Where such positive MCAs have been removed it has frequently been by raising common prices rather than cutting them in the currency of the stronger economy. Countries with declining market exchange rates for their currencies have similarly used negative MCAs to avoid, or at least postpone, raising prices in their own currency.

If adjustment problems have been so strong within the EC, it is unlikely to be less between the world's major trading partners. In both Japan and Europe, resistance to downward price adjustment is likely to be substantial. The idea of doing so in order to allow other countries to expand their market share will not make the case easier to argue. Progress will depend upon the credibility of the decoupled policy as a means of moderating the effect of price cuts for substantial but vulnerable interested groups. Two elements seem likely to dominate debate: the rate at which the new policies are applied and the degree to which they amount to an effective decoupling.

"Time to pay" is a common cry of the offenders who are found guilty. In the case of the CAP there may be some substance in such a request. Past policies have induced a pattern of investment that is inappropriate. A decoupled policy would demand not just less investment but a different pattern. Rapid dis-investment, such as that experienced recently in the U.S. mid-west, is not only politically unacceptable in Europe, it is also wasteful. Even with a decoupled policy, the skills and some of the capital of many farmers will still be needed if the EC is to produce an appropriate level of farm output. To devastate the industry by a precipitate contraction would involve avoidable waste.

The issue of the degree of decoupling assumes greater importance if the approach to a fully decoupled system is to be spread over time. One element in this is the deviation between the internal price and the economic base line price. Another is the production neutrality of other instruments or their equivalence to decoupling. In the EC this must include the implication of quotas, of structural and regional policy, and of any income aids that are provided. To enable the concept to be applied at a global level, it will be necessary to determine methods of measuring decoupling and to provide for regular comparative assessments. Recent discussions on producer subsidy equivalents and consumer subsidy equivalents point the way.

Some Practical Problems of Decoupling within the EC

The purpose of this section is to discuss some specific problems of applying decoupled policies within the Community. These arise because the Community is not a single sovereign state, but an organization in which authority sometimes lies at a centre that requires unanimity, sometimes with the institutions of the EC who may impose their decisions on its members.

Administration, complexity and cost

To many who live under its authority it may seem absurd to describe the CAP as an administratively simple policy. However, in terms of the numbers of bureaucrats involved and compared with most alternatives, it is. Regulation at the frontier and intervention purchase in the domestic market can be carried through with relatively small numbers of EC staff. Applying and monitoring detailed structural, social and regional policies that applied individually to the Community's ten million farmers would involve much more paper work, require more policing and so involve more cost.

Under present arrangements much of the detailed administration is delegated to national authorities. The cost is not avoided but transferred. A more complex policy could use the same mechanisms to avoid charges to the EC budget. However, even now concern about the efficiency of administration and accusations that avoidable fraud occurs because policing is too slack are common.[3] Ensuring that nationally financed policies, operated under EC authority, do not lead to unacceptable trade distortions is likely to give rise to more accusations of malpractice. As a result the overt role of the EC in policy administration and control would need to increase.

Financial 'borders', who pays?

The Community has attached great importance to the concept of financial solidarity in the CAP. Price support costs fall on the European Agricultural Guidance and Guarantee Fund (EAGGF). This approach seems inevitable so long as the CAP provides a single market in Europe in which goods move freely between member countries. It is less obviously applicable to structural policy. Here the Community has funded only a proportion of the total cost, the remainder being met by the national governments and farmers themselves. For a decoupled policy where income goals were met by direct payments and environmental targets by ad hoc policies, such common financing is neither inevitable nor desirable. The level at which income aids are accorded has to relate to incomes within the region of the farmer affected. These vary among EC countries. In Germany GDP per head in 1985 was 13,089 ECU, in Portugal only 5,267 ECU.[4] To provide the same level of income aid would either under-reward the German or over-compensate the Portuguese farmer.

To provide differential awards, paying more to the richer countries from common funds, would run counter to equity. The more rational solution would be to make each country responsible for financing its own farmers and use common funds to help the poorest and those with the largest adjustment problems.

Such an approach would result in a substantial shift in the balance of costs and benefits so far as member states were concerned. Lower prices would benefit agricultural importers but reduce the gains achieved by agricultural exporting member states. The difficulties of negotiating price cuts in the face of mounting surpluses and an exhausted budget have been clearly demonstrated, most recently at the Brussels summit in February 1988. A switch of support toward the poor and needy member states would greatly benefit the southern members and Ireland. The losers would be Germany, France, Holland and Denmark. Such practical realities suggest that it may be difficult even within a decoupled policy to use Community resources in a rational manner to ease adjustment.

One important reason to retain Community involvement in financing in all aspects of a decoupled policy is to ensure control. Financial participation requires information and imposes audit procedures. In its absence it is more difficult to detect abuses of the system. Thus, it may be essential to maintain Community financial participation even where the country concerned is neither poor nor needy. The financial consequences of such a commitment cannot be glossed over. If direct income aids, environmental payments and regional spending are to leave rural communities no worse off in overall income terms, the sums involved will be very large. Precisely how much would depend on the policies chosen, but at least in the short run there might be little overall saving to budget commitments.

Diversity of goals

Within Europe there exist very different perceptions of the role of agriculture in society. In many countries it is perceived as an integral part of rural community. Farmers are seen as embodying the virtues of independence, diligence and political stability. The scenery that they have created is prized and major changes regarded as undesirable. In contrast the UK and Holland have tended to see agriculture more in terms of its contribution as an industry. The case for its support has been argued in terms of economic benefits.

Neither set of attitudes is immutable. The growth of green parties has reflected an increasing urban concern about the use of natural resources, about landscape and wildlife. Such attitudes are critical of much modern farming and especially of large-scale, mechanized agriculture that relies on chemical inputs.

A decoupled policy that seeks to meet changing and different non-food production goals will have to establish priorities among these goals. Politically it will be vulnerable to the more articulate pressure group. Economically it will have to weigh each new technology against conservation interests, which vary across the Community. As a result the impact on production levels of decoupled policies may vary in different locations. It will be difficult to detect the difference between this and distortion. Experience suggests that, faced with such an opportunity, many member governments would "try to ensure their farmers were not disadvantaged",[5] in effect opting for the production-favourable type of policy.

Present policies and new opportunities for distortion

The Community operates both price support and, for milk and sugar, quota policies. Both distort production and trade and, under a decoupled regime, should be reformed. However, EC policy makers may identify different opportunities.

Quota policies permit discrimination among producers. From a world trade perspective, quotas could be used to force production down to a level that it is believed would operate at an agreed economic base line. Within the Community the vulnerable farmers might be protected by higher levels of price within quota. EC consumers and taxpayers would bear the cost, but third countries would still gain market share. Such an approach violates the economic arguments for decoupling, but it could be presented as a pragmatic way to attain broadly the same ends. The dangers of such an approach are long-run, rather than immediate. Quotas rapidly become part of the capital assets of the producer. They freeze the pattern of production and impose avoidably high costs. Globally, as well as for the EC, they imply a loss of economic welfare. Politically they sustain the isolation of the EC from world agricultural markets and so would tend to lead to continuing conflict about market share and access.

Price policies remain the principal instruments of support for most commodities within the EC. Decoupling will require an erosion of the difference between current EC prices and those of an agreed base line. From an international standpoint this process may be frustrated if the Community continues to regard certain volumes of production as appropriate for its farmers to produce. Such arguments reflect concerns about security, but they have no economic basis. The recent changes to the cereal regime, which include a budgetary stabilizer based on an EC production of 160 m tonnes, well in excess of EC consumption, illustrate the dangers. Politically, however, it may be necessary to negotiate some volume assumption as part of the definition of a global base line for a decoupled policy.

'Compensation' or 'Welfare Payments'

It is characteristic of European democracies that the state provides some form of safety net for the poor. Such systems are less fashionable than in the heyday of the welfare state, but the thinking that justified them still prevails in most quarters. Farmers faced by a loss of income as a result of a policy change would thus qualify for social security benefits. Whether as farmers they merit different treatment is an issue for debate and for each society to decide. Assuming they do, income payments would have to relate to need. Within Europe such needs are not easy to assess. Many small farms are part-time businesses, some merely convenient residences to which farming forms an appealing background. In contrast some larger farms may be in severe difficulty, facing substantial debts and a much reduced income. For them welfare payments may be more justly claimed.

An alternative adopted, for example, in the Atlantic Institute paper "A Future for European Farming",[6] is to take a compensation approach. This starts from the premise that the damage farmers suffer results from a change in an EC policy to which they have been subject. Since this change is to benefit the EC as a whole, the costs of change should fall on the Community in general, rather than on the farmers. Thus, compensation might be based on an estimate of the damage done and paid as either a capital sum or an annual payment. Such a system would lead to large payments to big producers. The Atlantic Institute proposal suggested that it would be necessary, on political grounds, to incorporate some element of degressivity.

Such differences in the conceptual basis of income aids are important. They would have very different implications for the medium-term size of EC agriculture, and hence for its role in world trade.

Epilogue – Would Decoupling Solve our Problems?

In principle decoupling seems an attractive and rational approach to the reform of agricultural policy. In practice, as this paper has attempted to demonstrate, the issues it raises are complex, the application of the policy institutionally demanding, and its effects not always predictable. In the final few paragraphs the paper seeks to assess whether this concept is likely to contribute to a solution to some pressing problems.

The most immediate issue is over-production. Current arrangements have provided too great an incentive to produce, not only in Europe but also in Japan and, at least until recently, in the United States. Decoupling has at its heart the notion that the incentive to produce must be related to markets and divorced from the other goals of farm policy. For it to create a better world trading system would require mutual action by all the major participants in world agricultural trade. It would also need a basis for assessing how far prices and other incentives have to move — what is here called an economic base line. Its application would have to be phased in over several years. Such an approach would contribute to the long-run solution of the problem of over-production. It is unlikely to resolve the immediate crisis.

For Europe the key problem has been seen as one of an excessively costly budget. Decoupling would reduce the cost of price support, but it would demand large, visible expenditures in other directions. That raises questions about the pace of change, the role ascribed to quotas and the extent to which expenditure should be EAGGF-funded or nationally based. In turn these issues become embroiled in the matrix of gains and losses among member states. In straightforward economic terms decoupling makes sense. In political terms it remains to be shown that it is possible.

Within the Community special emphasis has been given to the need to maintain farm incomes. Decoupling alone provides no solutions. Indeed it implies less income from farming. However, it does release resources to be applied to farm income welfare or compensation payments. The difficulty of implementing such payments is their visibility. Faced by the need to vote billions of ECU to aid people who, in some cases, may already own more than the average amount of capital, EC voters may prove unreliable friends of the farmers.

Some goals might well benefit greatly from a decoupled policy. Payments to protect wildlife, to provide recreation, to diversify rural economies and so on, might all be stimulated. Such gains flow from the more precisely targeted emphasis of decoupled policy. For economists there might be a boom in the evaluation of such policies.

The call for decoupling comes most insistently from those who wish to reform the world trading system. The reasonableness of their claim cannot be contested. However, for decoupling to improve trade, it is essential to devise an operational global economic base line to which prices adjust. To argue that this must be 'free trade' is to demand more of Community politicians than they can deliver. If the world wants to make progress in its trade in agriculture it will need to join the messy, uncertain business of attempting to define a price level that offers security and stability, as as well as an opportunity for low-cost producers to expand their share of the market.

Conclusions

This paper started from the premise that decoupling represents a constructive responsive to the current worldwide pressures on existing agricultural policies. It then sought to illustrate some of the conceptual and practical difficulties of translating such an idea into a new set of policies.

The supplementary paper contributed by Professor Henrichsmeyer shows that in some respects the CAP has moved toward elements of decoupling but that it remains firmly wedded to the principle of an administered, stabilized internal price. It is not just that it is difficult for all EC farmers to be exposed to open competition from the rest of the world, but that the Community does not wish this to be the case.

Some practical conclusions do emerge. First, negotiating levels of protection in a downward direction, including price reductions, is worthwhile even if the goal of zero protection is unattainable in the short run. Half a loaf is still better than no bread, and the acceptance of the principle that protection for agriculture is negotiable is itself a significant advance. Second, there are likely to continue to be policies directed primarily at social and regional goals and at economic externalities. These may have incidental protectionist effects, but are claimed to be justifiable in terms of the benefits they bring. Such policies need continuous scrutiny by impartial, international, expert groups if they are not to undo any benefits from negotiated protection reductions based on existing policies. This might be seen as an extension of GATT's traditional role or as the basis of a new institution.

Third, success in reducing existing protection and avoiding its replacement by other devices will be greatly influenced by the overall economic ambience in which world trade occurs. If low-income countries grow rapidly, if developed countries are less anxious about the impact of imports on domestic employment, and if the world's monetary crises of indebtedness and exchange rate fluctuation ease, then in developed countries political and social demands to maintain farming will be reduced. In this scenario decoupled policies become more financeable and the costs of protection less acceptable. Thus success will depend not just on sectoral negotiations about agricultural trade, but on the degree to which the global economy progresses. In that, GATT and the debate on agriculture have an important part to play.

Notes

1. See for example Bruce Trail, *Journal of Agricultural Economics* XXXIII 3 (1982).

2. See the argument of Andy Stoeckel in *Agricultural Policies in the European Community; their origins, nature and effects on production and trade* (Canberra: Australian Government Publishing Service, 1985).

3. *Panorama*, British Broadcasting Corporation, January 1988, reported examples of alleged fraud accounting for billions of ECU.

4. *Agricultural Situation in the Community 1986 Report* (Brussels: 1987).

5. John MacGregor, UK Minister of Agriculture, to NFU 1988 Annual Meeting.

6. "A Future for European Agriculture," Atlantic Institute with D. Bergmann, M. Ressi Boria, N. Kaldor, J.A. Schnittker, H.B. Krohn, C. Thompson, N. Wilbrandt and Pierre Uri (Rapporteur).

A European Community Approach to Decoupling: A Commentary

Wilhelm Henrichsmeyer

This commentary is presented in two parts: first, a brief commentary on the paper by Professor John S. Marsh, "An EC Approach to Decoupling", and second, some more general considerations about the concept of decoupling.

An EC Approach to Decoupling

John Marsh has given a balanced view of the decoupling issue and the various opinions held on it in the European Community (EC). My comments on the Marsh paper fall under two headings: the past performance of the EC with respect to decoupling and the future prospects for decoupling under the Common Agricultural Policy (CAP).

EC Performance on Decoupling

The Common Agricultural Policy has long been a textbook case of an inward-looking price support policy. Closer examination reveals that some shifts in the policy have occurred over time. Four phases can be distinguished with respect to its price and income policies.

The first phase, characterized by an income-oriented price policy, occurred between 1960 and 1978. During this phase, price policy was determined mainly on the basis of agricultural income goals. An 'objective' method was used to calculate price adjustments; agricultural prices were increased as costs increased. As a result, the growth of average agricultural per capita income corresponded closely to general income growth during this period. In West Germany, for example, the two growth rates matched exactly between 1960 and 1975.

Another consequence was that agricultural production increased rapidly in the EC relative to the growth in demand. Production grew by 2 to 2.5 per cent annually, compared to demand growth of only 1 per cent. In addition, the EC was able to close several import gaps and increase its exports on some central markets; the average degree of self-sufficiency within the EC rose from 85 per cent to 100 per cent. At the same time, of course, expenditures to purchase surplus agricultural products rose rapidly, by as much as 20 per cent each year.

Income transfer policies were applied in some areas during this first phase, whether for general purposes such as subsidizing the social security system or providing support for disadvantaged regions, or for specific reasons such as compensating German farmers during the period of adjusting prices to the Common level. These instances had only minor importance, however, within the overall context of the CAP.

In the second phase, between 1979 and 1984, awareness of the need for a policy change began to grow, but action was taken only reluctantly and slowly. By the end of the 1970s, the need for change in the CAP had been acknowledged by most of the political actors involved, in particular the EC Commission through its price proposals of 1978, 1979 and 1980. But after some years of a cautious price policy, the resulting pressure on agricultural incomes and a temporary relaxation of the budget squeeze (as a result of developments in world markets and exchange rates) led again to price 'corrections'. On the whole, then, this was a period without a clear policy orientation to give signals to farmers, with the result that the rapid growth in production continued.

Agricultural incomes also started to deteriorate during this phase, but this was more the result of slower structural change in the agriculture industry, in response to generally high unemployment, than it was the effect of restrictive price policies. In Germany, for example, the rate of reduction in the agricultural labour force fell to less than half its earlier rate, from 4 to 5 per cent in the 1960s and early '70s to less than 2 per cent annually in this period.

Between 1984 and 1987, the third phase saw a marked departure from previous policies. Escalating budget expenditures necessitated significant policy changes in 1984. Following long negotiations, the Council of Ministers agreed on the introduction of milk quotas (which most countries had opposed at the outset) and the need for more restrictive price policies for most other agricultural products.

Contrary to the expectations of most agricultural economists, these milk quotas have been enforced (and later reduced) rather strictly, with the result that small milk farming operations have been encouraged to shut down in most EC countries. The effects of the restrictive price policy announced for other products have been limited somewhat by significant declines in some input prices (for example, energy and imported feed). The effects have also varied between countries, depending on such factors as inflation rates and exchange rate fluctuations. In many countries, real price reductions have acted to shrink agricultural incomes but have had little effect on production growth.

The February 1988 EC Summit and Council decisions to introduce budget ceilings and stabilizers marked the beginning of a fourth phase. With production growth unchanged and world market prices at a low ebb, expenditures to purchase surplus products were continuing to climb, milk quotas and restrictive price policies notwithstanding.

The compromise reached in February 1988 limits the scope for action on price policy in the coming years in two ways:

- by means of an agreement that increases in expenditures for purposes of market intervention will not exceed 70 per cent of the rate of growth in the overall budget; and

- through the introduction of production thresholds, in particular for grains, oil seeds and pulses. If these thresholds are exceeded, prices will be reduced by up to 3 per cent annually (for grain) or according to the percentage of excess production (for oil seeds and pulses).

The thresholds are such that they would be exceeded even by 'normal' harvests, so that prices will be reduced automatically over the next several years.

The yearly decisions on basic administered prices and intervention rules will be of central importance in determining the path and timing of price changes. The implicit agreement by the Council at the Summit appears to have been that administered prices will not be nominally increased unless and until the increase in budget expenditures has been reduced significantly. The current price proposal by the EC Commission is in line with this assumption.

If nominal administered prices are held constant, a marked reduction in real agricultural prices must be expected over the nest few years. Assuming an average inflation rate in EC countries of 3.5 per cent a year, real grain prices, for example, would prompt corresponding adjustments in most other prices.

According to model calculations for EC agriculture, grain price reductions of this magnitude would be necessary to slow the growth of grain production and budget expenditures in the medium term (Henrichsmeyer et al. 1986). If the EC Council pursued a less restrictive price policy, the required reduction in budgetary expenditures could not be expected to materialize. In that event, the first of the agreed limits mentioned earlier (a ceiling on the rate of increase in budget expenditures) would take effect. If this fundamental decision of the Summit is taken seriously (and it seems to be difficult to get unanimous agreement on a less binding rule), then implementation of a significantly restrictive price policy seems unavoidable.

The only alternatives to a marked reduction in prices would be a significant increase in the producer 'co-responsibility levy' to finance management of the surplus (which would alter the character of this measure so that it would become an additional consumer tax) or the introduction of quota regulations to reduce grain production further.

The first alternative would be opposed by those countries that argue for a ceiling on the CAP budget; in any case, such a measure would only postpone necessary changes. The second alternative, in addition to having fundamental and far-reaching consequences for EC agriculture, would be very difficult to organize and manage. As a result, no country appears to have taken the proposal seriously, at least as yet.

Prospects for Decoupling in the EC

Decoupling is an economist's concept for solving agricultural adjustment and income problems. The principles are explained in textbooks and lectures all over Europe, and it appears possible to persuade some politicians and administrators of the rationality of a decoupling strategy. But it would be naive to believe that decoupling in its pure form could be accepted as a guiding principle for the process of formulating agricultural policy either within EC countries or at the Community level. There are simply too many interests at stake (Petit et al. 1986).

Rather, the driving force for any change in the Common Agricultural Policy will be the need to contain expenditures; the need to avoid serious trade conflicts will also play an important role. Given these two constraints, I believe that agricultural prices will be reduced significantly in the EC during the next decade and will narrow the gap to world market prices. The policy changes giving rise to these developments should not be interpreted, however, as a conscious political decision to adopt the principles of decoupling, but as a response to unavoidable constraints.

With price reductions and increasing pressure on incomes, stronger demands for direct payments can be expected to emerge, even from those farmers (or farmers' unions) that opposed direct transfers as long as they were considered a theoretical alternative to price reductions. Once price reductions take effect, however, transfers remain the only way to improve the income situation. This change in attitude can already be observed, but again, it does not reflect a belief in decoupling; instead, a shift in the relative interests at stake is responsible for the change of heart.

From this perspective, active participation in a worldwide decoupling process would be attractive to the EC. If price reductions in the EC are necessary, it may be useful to "sell" them through mutual bargaining within the framework of international trade negotiations.

General Considerations on Decoupling

If the aim were to clarify the concept of decoupling from the economist's perspective, it would be useful to begin with a broad theoretical concept that included national and international allocation, static and dynamic aspects, externalities and other considerations.

However, to develop a concept for political trade negotiations, it seems advisable to adopt a more narrow and pragmatic approach to decoupling. I would suggest an approach that concentrates on trade distortions and on the search for means gradually to reduce the extent of distortions. This would mean accepting the present imbalances and distortions as the starting point or reference situation and viewing decoupling as a process whereby national agricultural policies are adjusted and reoriented to reduce their trade-distorting effects.

If efforts to reduce trade distortions are seen in this light – as a means of advancing national goals – the suggested approach might have the advantage of changing the attitude of negotiators from some countries, who might otherwise see trade negotiations as limiting their scope for policy action.

As a result, it may be advisable to begin by considering the basic policy goals pursued in the various countries. For our purposes, several broad categories of goals and related policies can be identified:

- general factor allocation (production, consumption, international trade);
- food security (as a specific aspect of factor allocation);
- income distribution (farmers, consumers, taxpayers); and

- externalities (with respect to environment, landscape, specific farm structure, etc.)

Trade negotiations would have to concentrate mainly on measures related to general factor allocation. With respect to food security, income distribution and externalities, the task would be twofold:

- to define those types of measures that have a negligible effect on trade and that can therefore be excluded from trade negotiations (for example, direct personal income transfers); and

- to determine the minimum requirements of the trade partners with respect to the goals they want to achieve (for example, the minimum degree of self-sufficiency that is acceptable) and the extent to which they are prepared to accept the use of the various instruments available.

It might be useful to develop a scheme for classifying policy measures along the lines of the four categories outlined earlier. Doing so would require a rearrangement and revision of the list presented by William Miner at the Cologne seminar (which was based on FAO, OECD, and USDA classification procedures). Here I would offer some preliminary considerations about each of the categories.

With respect to *general factor allocation*, and bearing in mind the limited definition of decoupling suggested earlier, the following types of measures can be identified:

- measures that have a negligible effect on international trade;

- measures that support structural change and reduce trade distortions (for example, policies to improve labour mobility);

- measures that distort national allocation but reduce international trade imbalances (such as set-aside programs and quota regulations); and

- measures that distort national and international allocation (production, consumption, trade). In this case, the degree or intensity of distortion possibly should also be taken into account.

As far as *food security* is concerned, it does not appear necessary to deal explicitly with this category, because most countries will consider food security a non-negotiable goal. In practical terms, it may be difficult to separate food security measures from other factor allocation measures. During the political negotiations, however, it might be helpful to consider the extent to which national goals are being realized.

For example, agreement might be reached that food security arguments could be put forward only if the degree of self-sufficiency in a given commodity (or category of commodities) is below a certain threshold (say, 90 per cent of self-sufficiency). Below that threshold, specific negotiations would have to be undertaken if a country wanted to get the trade partners to agree to the application of measures that would otherwise be unacceptable.

On the question of *income distribution* measures, my view is that the degree of internal redistribution of income among various groups in any given country should not be a matter for international negotiation. The original concept for PSEs (as developed by Josling) therefore seems inadequate for purposes of international negotiations. Instead, a measurement concept that focuses mainly on quantifying trade distortions would have to be defined. Income support measures that can be agreed on as not significantly trade-distorting should also be identified.

The fourth category of policies is those respecting *externalities* such as environment, landscape and the protection of specific farm structures. Measures designed to take account of externalities are difficult to evaluate centrally (or even in international negotiations). An attempt should be made, however, to agree on criteria for selecting those measures that can be accepted as not noticeably trade-distorting. One criterion could be that measures favouring a certain group of farmers or certain regions, (for example, disadvantaged regions) would be admissible if they were acceptable to competing farmers in other farm groups or regions in the same country.

This suggested approach to trade negotiations could be put into effect through a series of steps. The first step is to identify those policy measures in the four categories just enumerated that can be considered non-trade-distorting or not significantly trade-distorting. Then, negotiations should concentrate on those sub-sets of measures that do have significant influence on trade. For these measures, a means of quantifying trade distortions would have to be developed. The measurement technique could involve either an expanded concept of effective protection, a more limited concept of PSEs, or a modified concept of the price adjustment gap (PAG). Which would be the best choice will depend to some extent on the outcome of the initial negotiations to identify those measures accepted as not noticeably trade-distorting.

III. Developing Country Perspectives

Contents

Agriculture in GATT Negotiations and Developing Countries   169
Nurul Islam

Effects of Trade Liberalization on LDCs   170

Food Aid and Trade Liberalization in Cereals   174

Agricultural Policy Reforms in Developing
Countries and GATT Negotiations   175

Trade Liberalization and Structural Adjustment   178

Stability in Agricultural Trade and Prices   180

Differential and More Favourable Treatment
for Developing Countries   181

Conclusions   185

Notes   186

References   189

Agriculture in GATT Negotiations and Developing Countries

Nurul Islam

The Uruguay Round of trade negotiations, under the auspices of GATT, is distinguished from the previous rounds in a number of ways. First, for the first time agriculture is high on the agenda, unlike in earlier rounds when agriculture enjoyed exceptions and waivers. Second, as a central concern in the negotiations during this round, not only import restrictions but also export subsidies, as well as various direct and indirect measures, including domestic agricultural support policies with a trade-distorting effect, are included. Third, the developing countries are expected to play a more active role. In the past, they played, on the whole, a passive role, and whatever benefits they derived from trade liberalization were a result of bargaining and negotiations among the developed countries. Fourth, in view of the current state of disarray in world agricultural trade, including threats of trade war and tension among the major trading partners, and given the high hopes placed on GATT negotiations for agricultural trade liberalization, success in negotiations on agriculture may be crucial to the success of the overall GATT negotiations.

How are the different groups of developing countries affected by the liberalization of trade in agricultural commodities? In which commodity groups have they special interests? Are there losses to set against gains from trade liberalization? Should they offer reciprocal concessions, and how effective will they be in GATT negotiations if they – or at least some among them – do not offer reciprocal concessions? Should the developing countries receive special and more favourable or differential treatment in the GATT negotiations? What are the essential components of special treatment for developing countries?[1] This paper seeks to examine these and related questions about the interests of developing countries in the Uruguay Round of Agricultural Trade Negotiations.

Developing countries have an important share in world exports and imports of agricultural commodities. They accounted for about 30 to 33 per cent of the world trade in agricultural commodities during the early 1980s. Moreover, agricultural exports constituted 37 per cent of non-oil exports of developing countries as a whole in 1980-82; agriculture's share in Africa and Latin America was 58 to 56 per cent of their total exports, and in the Near East and Far East the shares were 32 and 25 per cent respectively. Agricultural imports constituted about 19 per cent of their total imports.

One can distinguish between two groups of commodities as far as the interests of developing countries are concerned. The first group consists of those commodities in which developed and developing countries compete in world markets as well as in the national markets of each. Developed countries are major producers and exporters of many of these commodities. The group includes cereals, livestock, dairy products, sugar, oilseeds and vegetable oils. The second group of commodities are those produced predominantly by the developing countries, i.e., tropical products such as beverages, agricultural raw materials, cotton, jute, rubber, and tropical horticultural products. Fish and forest products cut across both groups.

The agricultural commodities of interest to developing countries are allocated to a number of different GATT committees. These are expected to conduct simultaneous negotiations in commodities assigned to them, and any trade-off (i.e., concessions in one committee to be offset by concessions in another) will take place at the end when the results of the negotiations in different committees will be brought together.

Effects of Trade Liberalization on LDCs

The developing countries face tariff and non-tariff barriers of various kinds on their agricultural exports to developed countries. The average tariff rate facing their exports in 1983 was about 5.5 per cent for food and 0.5 per cent for agricultural raw materials, as against 2.7 per cent for all items (3.7 per cent for chemicals and 6.7 per cent for manufactured goods). Of 20 selected agricultural imports (raw and processed) by the EEC from developing countries with average tariff rates above 5 per cent, 10 items had tariff rates higher than 10 per cent and 2 were higher than 20 per cent. Among 41 items imported by Japan, 33 had rates higher than 10 per cent and 6 higher than 20 per cent. Out of 18 items of imports by the United States, 8 had tariffs greater than 10 per cent and 2 were over 20 per cent.[2] At the same time, the percentage of all agricultural imports from developing countries that was subject to non-tariff barriers of all types in 1983 ranged from 67 per cent for Switzerland to 15 per cent for Norway, with 27 per cent for the EEC, 25 per cent for the United States and 53 per cent for Japan.[3]

Various studies of the effects of liberalizing world agricultural trade have focused attention on a few salient aspects: the effect on the level of world prices of commodities in respect of which trade liberalization occurs; the effect on the stability of prices in the world market; the effect on the export earnings of various groups of countries; and the effect on producers, consumers, tax payers and on the net welfare of the countries which undertake liberalization.

The effects of trade liberalization would depend on (a) which countries liberalize, i.e., OECD countries, or all countries including developing countries, and (b) which commodities undergo liberalization. Also, because of linkages between commodity markets, commodity price results depend upon whether liberalization is undertaken simultaneously or not. The effect of liberalization in wheat markets, for example, would be different depending on whether it is accompanied by liberalization in livestock markets. The degree of protection, the extent of liberalization, and the supply and demand elasticities of individual commodities – all influence the outcome.

Even though the various studies of the impact of trade liberalization are not comparable because of differences in commodity coverage, methodology and the degree of liberalization envisaged, the orders of magnitude are widely agreed upon. Generally speaking, world prices of most commodities would rise in varying degrees. In the case of sugar, red meats and dairy products, i.e., commodities where the degree of protection in the major producing and trading countries is significant, price increases of as much as 10 to 30 per cent have been suggested.[4]

Second, price instability is likely to be reduced, especially in cereals and livestock products, the extent of such reduction varying widely between individual commodities. To date the analysis of the impact of trade liberalization on price stability has been carried out in respect of complete trade liberalization. The estimates of the impact of partial liberalization are not available; a reduction in the level of variable import levies, for example, does not by itself reduce the degree of price variability in world markets even though it reduces the gap between domestic and world price.

Third, developing countries are expected to achieve a sizable increase in export earnings, especially if liberalization covers all commodities, including tropical and other commodities of interest to them, not just cereals and other temperate zone products in which they do not have large exports. (On the contrary, in a few of these commodities they are net importers.) The gain to developing countries will accrue mainly from sugar (the largest gain), beverages and tobacco, meat, coffee, cocoa, vegetable oils and fats.[5] Some countries may lose, especially those with heavy dependence on imports of commodities that are currently highly protected and subsidized in exporting countries, such as cereals and livestock products, and that will record a greater than average rise in world prices after liberalization.

The gains in export earnings by developing countries have all been variously estimated, ranging from $7 billion dollars for total food and agricultural commodities in 1980 prices to a much higher figure of $15.8 billion for only sugar, beef and dairy products. This wide range results mainly from widely different methodologies and prices elasticities of demand, as well as the different levels of protection on which estimates of the effects of liberalization have been based.

Because gains from trade liberalization will not be distributed equally among the different groups of developing countries, their interests will not coincide. The middle-income developing countries stand to gain more because the commodity composition of their exports is such that they gain substantially from trade liberalization. In many tropical products, such as tea and coffee, the gain in export earnings will result more from price increases than from the expansion of export volume.

A few points of clarification may be needed regarding the various analyses of the effects of trade liberalization on world prices. First, most analyze the consequences of complete rather than partial liberalization of trade, which is the more realistic possibility. Second, most of the studies are based on the nominal protection rates prevailing in late 1970s or early 1980s. In subsequent years the level of protection in the OECD countries increased, in some cases significantly, and the extent of a rise in world prices following reduction or elimination of this higher level of protection would be greater. For example, one study shows that if present policies persist in developed countries, average world prices of seven selected food products in 1995 would be 40 per cent below the levels of 1980-82. If the protection levels in 1980-82 were eliminated, however, prices would go up by 16 per cent from this depressed level. If liberalization took place in 1988 when protection levels were even higher, the world price levels reached in 1995, after long-term adjustment to effects of liberalization had taken place, would be 30 per cent higher than what otherwise would have prevailed in its absence.[6]

Third, most if not all studies of the impact of trade liberalization on world prices do not incorporate the impact of cost-reducing technological innovations which have led to the historically observed downward trend in world cereal prices. This downward trend is likely to continue, and the effects of trade liberalization will be superimposed, so that prices are likely to be higher than what would otherwise obtain without liberalization but with technological progress. At the same time, they could be lower than prices prevailing today. However, an additional aspect of technological innovations is induced or stimulated by domestic price support or incentives. A reduction in price incentives following liberalization is expected to slow down the rate of technological progress in the developed countries; in developing countries, higher price incentives, may speed up a rate of technological progress. The magnitude of such price-induced technological innovations is unknown. However, one study, on the assumption that a 10 per cent rise in prices leads to a 1 per cent rise in productivity, shows an increase in long-run supply elasticity of 0.5 but an insignificant impact on the world price level.[7]

The loss that would be incurred by cereal-importing low-income food deficit countries as a result of a rise in world cereal prices has often been emphasized in recent discussions. However, their losses may be partially or fully offset by benefits from trade liberalization in respect of other agricultural exports, including horticultural and processed agricultural commodities as well as manufactured exports. Furthermore, recovery in cereal prices from today's depressed, heavily subsidized levels would encourage domestic production in many developing countries with comparative cost advantages in the production of cereals that remain unexploited in the face of prevailing low world prices. Current low world prices are unlikely to obtain in the future; past experience indicates that levels of domestic support programs or subsidies in major developed countries or regions fluctuate over time. For developing countries to formulate food production strategies with reference to current world prices would be to sacrifice their long-term comparative advantage and to incur a loss of fixed investment resources that cannot easily be reallocated to alternative uses when prices change.

To the extent that a more efficient allocation of resources in the developed countries, resulting from trade liberalization, stimulates their long-run growth, demand and markets for developing country exports over a wide range of products should receive a stimulus. If developing countries also undertake domestic agricultural and trade policy reforms, there will be gains from increased efficiency in the allocation of resources in their economies not only within the agricultural sector but also between agriculture and rest of the economy, to set against the possible terms of trade loss incurred through a rise in import price. One of the principal advantages that the developing countries should expect to gain from trade liberalization would be opportunities to diversify and to develop new agricultural exports. In a dynamic context, trade restrictions not only limit the expansion of existing exports but also inhibit long-term investment in the development of new exports, which requires predictable market access and an open trading environment. The uncertainty of market access, or the possibility that market access would be closed abruptly, act as disincentives to the diversification of production and trade. For example, the developing countries have an increasing interest in high-value agricultural exports like horticultural products, some of which are and can be produced in a labour-intensive way in developing countries with labour surpluses. To ensure a widespread interest among developing countries in the GATT, it is necessary to liberalize trade in a very broad range of commodities that are of export interest to all or the majority of developing countries, so that gains and losses can be offset and are widely distributed.

Apart from tariff and non-tariff barriers, the developing countries have considerable interest in the sanitary and phytosanitary regulations and standards affecting their agricultural exports, particularly livestock, dairy and horticultural products. First, there is the problem of harmonizing the diverse standards or regulations imposed by developed countries. Second, the developing countries need technical assistance from countries imposing such regulations and standards to help them overcome both the substantive and the administrative problems arising from these measures.

Food Aid and Trade Liberalization in Cereals

Would the food aid-dependent developing countries be affected adversely by liberalization of trade in cereals and by elimination or substantial reduction in surplus food stocks in developed countries?

In this formulation, food aid is conceived predominantly as a surplus disposal program. In other words, food aid is a net addition to financial aid and does not compete with it. Under present conditions, this is probably to a large extent the case but not entirely so. It is difficult to quantify the extent to which it is additional. There seems to be a paradox; the price for providing food aid is to create such a large surplus that the world price is pushed down through competitive export subsidies, below the cost of production of the most efficient producers. In a more rational world, it should be possible to reduce the excess supply in the world market and to use the large production capacity in the donor countries to produce enough food to meet the needs of both commercial exports and food aid. Moreover, food aid or grants can offset any possible adverse impact, through a rise in import prices, on the poorer developing countries that are heavily dependent on food imports.

Is food aid inconsistent with attempts to strengthen GATT rules to eliminate export subsidies? Food aid amounts to concessional food sales, and this compares with subsidized exports. It may replace the commercial imports that may otherwise have taken place; it may reduce export sales by countries with comparative advantage in food production. However, the replacement of commercial sales by food aid is comparable to and is no different from replacement of other imports by non-food aid. When food aid is linked to development projects and to an employment-oriented strategy for expanding income and food consumption of the poor, an increase in demand for food matches the increased supply. To the extent that food aid is provided to the poorer developing countries, its denial would scarcely be substituted by an equivalent increase in commercial imports.

There are two reasons why enough supplies would probably be available for meeting food aid needs. First, as in the past, there will be weather-induced fluctuations in cereal production that can be matched partly by variations in domestic stocks. These stocks can be managed with a view to meeting food aid and commercial needs. Second, under the Food Aid Convention, the developed countries agreed in the aftermath of 1974 World Food Conference to provide 10 million tons of food aid annually. The commitment of food aid under this Convention fluctuated in the past, it is true, in response to variations in domestic supplies in donor countries, but it could have been and can be in the future more stable over time if donors make multi-year commitments.

Technological progress in industrial countries will continue to generate a high rate of growth in productivity in the cereal sector, which can be matched partly by (a) a fall in the real price of food, as has been happening in the past decades, and (b) food aid to promote development and alleviate poverty in developing countries.[8] Rather than being a response to an unwanted food surplus generated by a distorted price system and consequent misallocation of resources in the food sector, food aid can be provided as an instrument for development, and supply in donor countries will respond to the provision of food aid, through the utilization of their large production potential.

Agricultural Policy Reforms in Developing Countries and GATT Negotiations

Obviously, developing countries gain from trade liberalization by developed countries through enlarged market access for their agricultural exports. Should they themselves also undertake trade liberalization, i.e., change their border as well as their domestic policies affecting trade in agricultural commodities? How do their current policies, as well as concerns for rapid agricultural development, fit in with the liberalization of trade under GATT auspices?

Two aspects deserve serious consideration in this regard. First, a large number of developing countries tax their agriculture directly and indirectly. Second, a few countries, for example, among the high-income developing countries in East Asia and Latin America, protect their agriculture, especially in respect of commodities that are import substitutes. This tendency seems to be on the increase.

A distinction needs to be made between policies specific to agriculture and economy-wide policies with significant impact on agriculture in terms of the relative profitability of resource use in agriculture compared to non-agricultural sectors. Sector-specific policies that discriminate against agriculture include export taxes on agricultural products, low procurement prices offered by state marketing agencies with purchase monopolies or subsidies on agricultural output such as consumer food subsidies. In the case of import substituting products, direct sector-specific policies have become less discriminatory against agriculture in the recent years; in fact, in an increasing number of instances they enjoy a positive nominal rate of protection, i.e., domestic prices exceed world prices. Average tariff rates on food and agricultural commodities in a large number of developing countries range between 16 and 25 per cent, and non-tariff barriers affected 37 to 48 per cent of the imports in 1985.9

The economy-wide policies that discriminate against agriculture include (a) overvalued exchange rates, and (b) high protection of the industrial sector. The extent of discrimination against agriculture involved in economy-wide policies frequently exceeds, sometimes by a considerable margin, the impact of sector-specific policies on agriculture. The negative impact of economy-wide policies in many cases more than offsets the positive nominal protection provided to import substituting commodities by sector-specific policies. In the case of export commodities, in the majority of cases, both sets of policies reinforce each other and heighten the extent of discrimination against agriculture.10

Insofar as sector-specific policies are concerned, the taxation of agricultural imports and exports, or profits of state trading agencies engaged in agricultural commodities, are often the principal means for raising revenue in the developing countries. Any substantial reduction in such taxation will have to be offset by alternative sources of revenue, such as various forms of direct taxation, which in the context of developing countries are not easy to devise or implement. As economic development accelerates, reliance on taxes on foreign trade will be reduced. Until that time, reliance on this source of revenue will continue. However, efficiency considerations warrant a reduction in the current wide dispersion of the nominal rates of protection.

Discriminatory policies against agriculture in developing countries, which discourage domestic production, expand imports and hampers exports, even though they cause misallocation and inefficient use of resources, does not engage the attention of GATT, since they do not adversely affect the trade of other countries in terms of market access of export competition. Consequently, exchange overvaluation which discourages exports has not been the subject of GATT's concern or concern of trading partners, even though undervaluation which encourages exports has been.

In GATT negotiations, trading partners are greatly concerned about export subsidies; few developing countries use or can afford export subsidies. Export taxes on commodities that face elastic world demand misallocate domestic resources. However, export taxes are often imposed with a view to reducing the cost of raw materials to the domestic processing industry and strengthening its competitive strength in export markets. A reduction of import barriers in developed countries on processed agricultural commodities, which escalate in direct proportion to the degree of processing, would obviate the need for such taxation. It is important to recognize that reform of trade policy in developing countries cannot be implemented without the development of a broad-based efficient taxation system. In fact, many countries facing budgetary imbalances and the need to mobilize greater financial resources have been under pressure, often supported by international financing agencies, to raise rather than lower taxes on foreign trade, albeit reducing its dispersion.

To the extent developing countries reduce the level of industrial protection, they will reduce the extent of discrimination against agriculture. However, exchange rate policies are not part of the GATT negotiations, even though they significantly affect the relationship between domestic and world prices. The prices of tradable commodities, mostly agricultural, are depressed below what they would otherwise be in the presence of what is mostly an overvalued exchange rate. This reinforces rather than offsets or counterbalances the effect of exports subsidies provided by the developed exporting countries. This emphasizes that action on trade policies cannot be divorced from supporting action on exchange rate policies.

Should the developing countries reduce or eliminate discrimination against agriculture as a part of GATT negotiations? This will enable them to exploit their comparative advantage on resource utilization, promoting overall development through intersectoral linkages, especially in the non-tradable sectors, and expanding foreign exchange resources. They will be able to take advantage of and gain maximum benefits from trading opportunities opened up by liberalization by developed countries. It will contribute to global efficiency in the allocation of resources by encouraging low-cost sources of production. Therefore, ending discrimination against agriculture is in the interests of developing countries as well as of a more efficient world agricultural economy.

Agricultural development requires more than the elimination of discrimination against agriculture; it requires positive measures of support. In addition to providing market incentives, the state has a vital role to play in such areas as (a) research, extension and training, (b) development of infrastructure, roads, transport and communication systems, (c) marketing and distribution systems, and (d) institutions for mobilizing and allocating capital. Subsidies for inputs like fertilizer may be needed in the early stages to reduce the risks and uncertainties involved in introducing a new technology. Furthermore, so long as economy-wide policies such as overvalued exchange rates continue to discriminate against agriculture, subsidies on inputs and direct expenditures by the state on improving agricultural productivity may partly offset the adverse impact of an overvalued exchange rate.

The various measures of support for domestic agriculture, which are included in the measurement of "producer's subsidy equivalents" but are not directly trade distorting, need much greater emphasis in the context of developing countries. In fact, the Cairns Group of countries, whose 13 members include 9 from the developing world, endorsed "support measures in relation to domestic economic programs to promote economic and social development which are not explicitly linked to export measures." The process of growth and structural adjustment takes time; trade liberalization and associated policy reforms will need a longer time frame for implementation in developing countries and need to be recognized by all the parties concerned.

Trade Liberalization and Structural Adjustment

It is recognized increasingly by developing countries and the international community that the process of trade liberalization cannot be viewed in isolation from exchange rate policy, industrial protectionism and other macroeconomic policies bearing upon the allocation of resources to and within agriculture.

The implementation of policy reforms following this recognition is carried out not in relation to GATT negotiations, but in the context of negotiations on long-term development assistance and short-term balance of payments support. Many countries, in agreement with bilateral and multilateral financing institutions, have embarked upon exchange rate adjustment or trade liberalization, including a wide variety of domestic agricultural policy reforms. The structural adjustment and stabilization programs required or currently undertaken in many developing countries, reduce investment and constrain economic growth in the short run, even though greater efficiency in resource use is expected to facilitate higher growth in the long run; also, they inflict losses on some sectors of the economy which are either vulnerable or vocal or both. This may jeopardize the process of adjustment itself by endangering the social and political acceptability and hence the implementation of the adjustment programs themselves. Additional external assistance may ease the process of adjustment in developing countries, which in view of their low income or limited resources, are unable to maintain the growth momentum or compensate the losses, relying on their own recourses only.

There is, moreover, an asymmetry between developed and developing countries in this respect. Whatever concessions developed countries provide will be in the context of GATT negotiations or bilateral trade negotiations outside GATT, such as the U.S.-Canada trade agreement and the U.S. and Japan/EEC negotiations (later to be incorporated, it is hoped, in the GATT framework). To the extent, therefore, that developing countries are to bargain in the GATT for access to markets in developed countries, their prior and unilateral liberalization reduces their bargaining strength.

In an ideal world, unilateral liberalization, be it in a developed or a developing country, promotes its welfare and efficient allocation of resources, independently of what its trading partners do. Admittedly, welfare gains from world trade are greater if all liberalize, and the extent of readjustment in the allocation of resources within any production sector is also less following multilateral liberalization. However, in the real world, or at least in the GATT world, liberalization is considered a concession to the trading partners in return for reciprocal concessions. Furthermore, governments embarking on trade liberalization face stiff opposition from domestic pressure/interest groups that are hurt by the reduction of trade barriers in the short run and are obliged to readjust; exchanging concessions in export markets enables governments to win the support of the exporters who are the gainers, thus offsetting pressure from the losers. Developing countries, especially the middle-income countries among them, to the extent that they will be called upon to make reciprocal concessions, should be able to claim credit for the trade liberalization that they have already introduced under various structural adjustment programs in the last few years. The time period for allowing credit for such liberalization measures can be linked to the timing of their undertaking adjustment programs in agreement with the World Bank or the IMF. These two sets of negotiations on the part of developing countries are also related in respect of policy instruments, for example, the use of quantitative controls for balance of payments purposes, where developing countries traditionally have been given greater flexibility under the GATT rules.

Stability in Agricultural Trade and Prices

The Uruguay Round remains silent on the issue of stability in world prices and on the related issue of International Commodity Agreements. Trade liberalization contributes to a reduction of instability, but most analyses of a decline in price instability are based on the assumption of complete liberalization – an unlikely possibility. Furthermore, even under complete trade liberalization, a reduction in price stability, strengthened by future markets wherever they are effective, may be less than what is considered desirable by developing countries. This is of some importance to a large number of developing countries heavily dependent on commodity exports.

Ideally, international commodity agreements, based upon buffer stocks and price ranges that closely follow long-term market trends, should neither create surplus nor misallocate resources, but those based on quotas are likely to do so, unless quotas are revised frequently to follow changing market shares. Not only are such ideal conditions never met, but as past experience indicates, consensus on price ranges, quotas or stock financing arrangements is extremely difficult to reach; if consensus is reached, it is rarely sustained for any length of time. Furthermore, at the level of individual countries, exchange earnings fluctuate because of weather-induced variations in supply, lags in supply response, and so on.

The developing countries should therefore evince a greater interest in the availability of compensatory financing facilities for export shortfalls, as well as for meeting a rise in food import prices, for example, rather than in commodity agreements that seem continually to elude their grasp. These financing facilities as for example the IMF Compensatory Financing Facility for export shortfalls or Cereal Financing Facility, with further improvements and with enlarged access, will help them meet the consequences of supply and price fluctuations. To the extent, however, that they seek to stabilize domestic market prices for consumers or producers, they have no option but to resort to domestic stock management supported by border measures such as taxes on imports or exports. It may, however, be possible to keep short-term variations in border measures within limits, while ensuring that long-term trends in domestic prices are in line with and do not diverge from world price trends.

Differential and More Favourable Treatment for Developing Countries

Should developing countries receive "differential and more favourable treatment"? There are several aspects of this problem. One is the question of reciprocity. The Uruguay declaration confirmed that the "developed countries do not expect reciprocity for commitments made by them in trade negotiations to reduce or remove tariffs and other barriers to trade of developing countries. Developed contracting parties shall, therefore, not seek neither shall less developed contracting parties be required to make concessions inconsistent with the latter's development, financial and trade needs." It was agreed that the latter's "capacity to make contributions or negotiated concessions or take other mutually agreed action [would] improve with the progressive development of their economies and improvement in their trade situation;" and that special attention be given to "problems of least developed countries and to the need to encourage positive measures to facilitate the expansion of their trading opportunities."

Two other related aspects of the role of developing countries in the GATT system are (a) the Generalized System of Preferences for developing countries in trade concessions, and (b) the creation among developing countries of preferential trading arrangements on either a regional or worldwide basis.

Within the GATT framework of negotiations, trade liberalization and concessions are reciprocal. In the past, developing countries did not offer any concessions; concessions exchanged among developed countries were extended under the Most Favoured Nation clause to other contracting parties, including developing member countries. However, the developing countries are often obliged to make reciprocal concessions in bilateral trade negotiations or agreements, as for example, when they agree to voluntary export constraint; sometimes concessions cut across sectors as, for example, when textile quotes are linked to food imports from quota giving country even if the latter is not the cheapest source. Since concessions were exchanged among developed countries, the commodities involved were necessarily those of interest to them and not to developing countries. Furthermore, developing countries faced discriminatory export restraint arrangements in commodities where they demonstrated substantial comparative advantage.

In the forthcoming negotiations, the developing countries can continue past practice and not grant reciprocal concessions. Since changes in the rules and procedures of GATT require agreement by all the GATT member countries, their bargaining strength consists of merely slowing down or blocking such changes. But if rules cannot be changed because of lack of agreement by the developing countries, the developed countries may resort to codes that require agreement only of the countries subscribing to the codes. Moreover, such steps by developing countries may encourage bilateral or plurilateral deals among developed countries – the beginnings of which are already visible. The developed countries, faced with import competition from middle-income developing countries in specific sectors, would be able to fend off more successively domestic opposition by affected interest groups to multilateral trade liberalization if they secure some reciprocal trade concessions. In the ultimate analysis, if GATT negotiations fail, the Most Favoured Nation Treatment in trade concessions will be jeopardized to the great disadvantage of the developing countries.

The developing countries might find it more advantageous to participate on the basis of reciprocity – at least limited reciprocity – and exercise their bargaining power, which could be greatly enhanced if they could act together in the GATT negotiations. Potentially they provide the expanding market of the future, if their state of economic growth is accelerated. Furthermore, active participation will enable them to obtain liberalization of trade in commodities of special interest to them. Most of them will be or are in the process of liberalizing, because of efficiency considerations and/or in the course of negotiations with lending agencies, so it would be to their advantage to link it up with or do so under GATT auspices. They may offer reciprocity in terms of eliminating or substantially reducing discrimination against agriculture, which will promote their own growth and is in their long-term interest. The developing countries have a vital interest in trade liberalization in labour-intensive manufactured goods, in which they are expanding production and have comparative advantage; this is also true of labour-intensive agricultural commodities like horticultural products. Also, the elimination of certain internal taxes in developed countries that constrain consumption of commodities of export interest to developing countries will be helpful to the expansion of their commodity trade. They are likely to gain from cross-commodity/cross-sectoral concessions and need skillful balancing of one set of concessions against another.

While participating effectively in GATT negotiations, the developing countries will need to obtain recognition of their special circumstances because of their relative underdevelopment; this includes, among others, agreement on a broader range of domestic support measures for promoting their agricultural and rural development, reliance on taxes on foreign trade for mobilizing financial resources until economic development widens their tax base, border measures to support domestic price stabilization efforts, and credit for unilateral policy reforms, both border and domestic policy measures affecting trade, that have already been or are being undertaken.

It needs to be recognized that growth in income and demand in developing countries is crucial for the expanding world trade in agriculture. It is necessary, therefore, to put in proper perspective the role of trade liberalization by developing countries in the expansion of world or developed country exports. The largest portion of the trade of developed countries is with each other. For the developing countries, on the other hand, the major sources of imports and major export markets are the developed countries. Thus the liberalization of trade by developed countries is vital for the trade expansion of the developing countries but the reverse is not true. For the majority of developing countries (the exceptions are a few high-income countries and selected sectors) it is not the level of their import restrictions as much as the size of their domestic market, as determined by low per capita income and limited import capacity, that limits the expansion of agricultural imports from developed countries.

In the light of the foregoing analysis, what will be the role of the Generalized Scheme of Preferences for developing countries? This is not a part of the GATT system of reciprocal trade concessions and hence is considered a voluntary measure, which can be changed at the discretion of the country giving preference in terms of coverage of both the countries and the commodities eligible for preferential concessions.

It is noteworthy that GSP includes only tariffs and excludes non-tariff barriers, whereas non-tariff barriers are more rampant for agricultural than for manufactured goods. Moreover, commodities with higher tariff rates in the developed countries tend to have higher non-tariff barriers as well, and GSP coverage is narrower on imports with higher tariff rates. Secondly, GSP covers a smaller proportion of agricultural commodities than of manufactured goods. For example, the share of GSP-covered commodities in all MFN dutiable agricultural imports in 1980 was 30 per cent for the EEC, 21 per cent for Japan, 43 per cent for the United States, 30 per cent for Canada; the corresponding percentages for manufactured imports were 87 per cent, 94 per cent, 55 per cent, and 55 per cent respectively.[11] The net increase in exports, both agricultural and manufactured, of the GSP recipient countries resulting from the implementation of GSP is relatively small; in 1983 it was estimated at about $6.5 billion above what would otherwise have taken place in the absence of GSP; this compared with $280 billion in total imports by the preference giving countries from the recipient countries.[12]

With the flexibility and freedom of action allowed by the GSP scheme, the developed countries found it a better — less costly — alternative to (a) a commitment of non-discriminatory treatment of developing countries and strict adherence to MFN, and (b) a substantial reduction in the tariffs on commodities that are important exports of developing countries. Graduation is already being practised by changing the coverage and extent of concessions under the GSP scheme according to the stage of development or level of income of the recipient country. There is nothing in the current GATT rules that prohibits or prevents such a policy.

A recent study found that if developed countries were to extend GSP to all products and implement them at zero rates, the countries now receiving preference would gain an increase in exports not significantly higher than what they would gain if developed countries were to eliminate all duties on an MFN basis.[13] Particular groups of countries may lose as a result of the termination of existing preferential arrangements such as the ACP countries under the Lome Convention of the EEC or preferential quotas enjoyed by the Caribbean countries or the Philippines in the U.S. market. These losses are expected to be more than offset by world-wide trade liberalization. However, so long as tariff barriers remain, their elimination on a preferential basis in respect of all exports from developing countries could result in a substantial increase in the exports of developing countries — a most unlikely possibility. If GSP were to yield its expected benefit, it needs to be a binding and predictable obligation to be implemented in full through a substantial reduction or elimination in tariff barriers. It seems that, at most, such a major preferential scheme could be only a part of much broader international action to transfer resources to the developing countries, and not just a part of GATT negotiations. So long as this likelihood is very small, especially for the middle-income and high-income developing countries, it may be more advantageous to opt for a substantial reduction on an MFN basis of tariffs on commodities of special interest to developing countries.

They may need to make coalitions with like-minded countries or countries with common interests. The Cairns Group of developing countries has combined with a few developed countries for liberalizing agricultural trade; the former should be able to receive the support of the latter to liberalize trade in their manufactured exports as well. Developing countries can strengthen efforts of the United States to liberalize agricultural imports of the EEC and Japan, while securing U.S. support to liberalize manufactured imports of all industrial countries, including the United States.

The least developed countries constitute a distinct category and have been recognized as such not only in the Uruguay declaration but also in other forms of international negotiations in the UN system. They should continue to receive preferential access at zero rate from developed countries; in most cases, they do so now. It is necessary not only to adhere to the strict definition of least developed countries as accepted by the international community but also to rule out any arbitrary change in the definition by the preference giving country. Secondly, the lease developed countries should receive preference on all their exports without exception. The sacrifice incurred by the preference giving countries is small, but the gain for the least developed countries will be considerable, given the importance of agricultural products in their trade.

Conclusions

The developing countries have a vital interest in GATT negotiations to liberalize of agricultural trade (i.e., eliminate both tariff and non-tariff barriers) in a broad range of agricultural commodities of interest to them. The countries heavily dependent on food imports may incur higher import costs as a result of a rise in world prices of cereals and livestock products, but this is likely to be compensated by a substantial reduction in restrictions on a wide range of their agricultural and manufactured exports, as well as by food aid so far as the poorer developing countries are concerned.

It may be advisable for the developing countries, especially the high-income countries among them, to grant limited reciprocal concessions in the GATT negotiations so as to exercise their bargaining strength and ensure trade liberalization in commodities of special interest to them. This does not preclude bargaining for a speedier and greater reduction in barriers on their exports as worldwide or restrictions on an MFN basis are being lowered. The GSP for developing countries in its present voluntary form does not bring much gain and is highly uncertain.

Many developing countries are already engaged in liberalizing trade and domestic agricultural policies, both because of efficiency considerations and as part of negotiations with external financing agencies. They should receive credit for such liberalization efforts in GATT negotiations. However, they should seek a longer time frame for implementation of reforms agreed to under GATT. They should be entitled, in view of their current state of underdevelopment, to a wider range of domestic support measures for promoting their agricultural rural development, including, for example, a recognition of their need for reliance on taxes on foreign trade as a source of revenue and for measures to stabilize prices and income in their highly volatile agricultural sector. At the same time, the special case of the least developed countries needs to be recognized; the implementation of an effective preferential scheme for both tariffs and quotas on all their exports deserves high priority.

Notes

1. It is noteworthy that GATT, unlike in the United Nations system, does not have a clear definition of the category of countries called developing countries. The UN not only defines the developing countries but also a category of countries called the least developed countries. This latter definition seems to be accepted by the GATT.

2. C. Nogues, J. Olechowski, and L. Winters. "The Extent of Non-Tariff Barriers to Imports of Industrialized Countries," World Bank Working Paper No. 789 (1986).

3. *Protection in Developed and Developing Countries: An Overview.* World Bank and Thai Development Research Institute Conference, Bangkok (1986). UNCTAD, *Liberalization of Barriers to Trade in Primary and Processed Commodities,* (January 1983).

4. A sample of estimates of the extent of increase in world prices for selected commodities following trade liberalization is as follows: meat (5-18 per cent), dairy products (8-27 per cent), wheat (5-18 per cent), sugar (8-29 per cent), roasted coffee (11 per cent), cocoa powder (14 per cent), tea (3 per cent) and palm oil (3 per cent). All estimates refer to protection levels of the late 1970s or early 1980s.

5. J. Zietz and A. Valdes. "The Costs of Protectionism to Developing Countries: An Analysis for Selected Developing Countries," World Bank Staff Working Paper 769 (Washington, D.C., 1986); A. Valdes, " Agriculture in the Uruguay Round: Interests of Developing Countries," *The World Bank Economic Review* 1:4 (1987); R. Tyers and K. Anderson, "Distortions in World Food Trade: A Quantitative Assessment," Background Paper for the World Development Report 1986.

6. It should be noted that price levels in these analyses refer to world prices; not domestic prices. Protectionism shifts the location of production to the high-cost producers, whose domestic

prices are raised in order to cover their high production costs, by driving a wedge between domestic and world prices. High domestic prices in the protectionist countries restrain consumption, expand production, reduce import demand, and consequently have a depressing effect in the world market; furthermore, high domestic prices soon produce surpluses for export, as in the EEC, which can be sold in the world market only at subsidized prices. The cumulative effect of an excess supply in the world market is a fall in world prices. The elimination of protectionism therefore results in a fall in domestic prices as high support prices are reduced, but it leads to a rise in world prices through an expansion of demand and contraction of supply in the world market. The largest percentage fall in domestic prices would occur in the EEC and Japan, and the smallest in the United States. The self-sufficiency ratio of the EEC and Japan would be substantially reduced, and exports by low-cost producers like the United States, Canada and Australia would expand. R. Tyers and K. Anderson, "Liberalizing OECD Agricultural Policies in the Uruguay Round: Effects on Trade and Welfare", forthcoming in *Journal of Agricultural Economics* 30:2 (May 1988).

7. R. Tyers, "Developing-Country Interests in Agricultural Trade Reform," Conference on Directions and Strategies of Agricultural Development in the Asia-Pacific Region, Taipei, (January 1988).

8. This is not inconsistent with a rise in world prices following trade liberalization. World prices following trade liberalization would be higher than what they would be in its absence, but at the same time could be lower than what they were prior to the cumulative rise in domestic support programs and competitive export subsidies that commenced in early 1980s. In other words, the long-run downward trend would be less than what would occur with the continuation of present policies.

9. These figures relating to protection rates and non-tariff barriers are not strictly comparable to those given earlier for developed countries; first, the commodity coverage is not the same and second, for non-trade barriers the methodology is not exactly the same, even though in both cases the percentage of items subject to NTBs is weighted by the volume of imports. But the orders of magnitudes are comparable. Moreover, average tariff rates on agricultural products in developing countries are lower than on manufactured goods as it is in developed countries, whereas

NTBs are roughly comparable between agricultural and non-agricultural products in developing countries, but in developed countries NTBs on agriculture are higher than that on non-agricultural imports. UNCTAD. "The Profile of Protectionism in Developing Countries." Discussion Paper 21.

10. Ann Krueger, M. Schiff, and A. Valdes, "Measuring the Impact of Sector-Specific and Economy-Wide Policy on Agricultural Incentives in LDCs", *The World Bank Economic Review* (forthcoming 1988).

11. In the case of the United States the figures refer to those imports that actually received preference rather than only being eligible for preference. Imports eligible for GSP do not always actually receive such preferences; for example, the ratio of imports actually receiving preference to the total imports covered by GSP was 57 per cent for the EEC (1980), 92 per cent for Japan (1980), 66 per cent for Canada (1976). This is because in the implementation of GSP scheme, restrictions or conditions are imposed regarding ceilings on imports, tariff quotas, maximum amount allowed per country, competitor status, etc., which limit the amounts actually receiving preferences. UNCTAD, *Liberalization of Barriers to Trade, op. cit.*

12. G. Karsenty and S. Laird, "The Generalized System of Preferences – A Qualitative Assessment of the Direct Trade Effects and of Policy Options," UNCTAD, Discussion Paper No. 18.

13. *Ibid.*

References

Hathaway, Dale E. "Agriculture and the GATT: Rewriting the Rules." Washington, D.C. Institute for International Economics, September 1987.

Krueger, Anne O.; Maurice Schiff; and Alberto Valdes. "Measuring the Impact of Sector-Specific and Economy-Wide Policies on Agricultural Incentives in LDCs." Washington, D.C., January 1988 (forthcoming in *The World Bank Economic Review*, May 1988).

Valdes, Alberto and Joachim Zietz. "Agricultural Protection in OECD Countries: Its Cost to Less-Developed Countries." Research Report 21. Washington, D.C.: International Food Policy Research Institute, December 1980.

Valdes, Alberto. "Agriculture in the Uruguay Round: Interests of Developing Countries." *The World Bank Economic Review*, 1:4, (September 1987) pp. 571-593.

Wolf, Martin. "Differential and More Favorable Treatment of Developing Countries." *The World Bank Economic Review*, 1:4, (September 1987), pp. 647-668.

Zietz, Joachim and Alberto Valdes. "The Costs of Protectionism to Developing Countries: An Analysis for Selected Agricultural Products." The World Bank Staff Working Papers, No. 769. Washington, D.C., January 1986.

IV. Exchange Rate Issues

Contents

Exchange Rates and Their Role in Agricultural Trade Issues   **193**
G. Edward Schuh

Some Background   **194**

The Simple Economics of Distortions to Trade Caused by Distortions in Exchange Rates   **197**

Some Complicating Issues   **198**
     Monetary and Fiscal Policies as Sources of Distortions in Foreign Exchange Markets   **199**
     Monetary Unions as Distortions to Foreign Exchange Markets   **200**
     Green Currencies   **201**
     Bloc Floating Exchange Rates   **201**
     Masking of Underlying Comparative Advantage   **202**
     Instability in Exchange Rates   **203**

Elements of a Code for Foreign Exchange Markets   **204**
     The need for generalized floating   **205**
     The need for neutral monetary and fiscal policies   **205**
     The need for open international capital and investment markets   **205**
     The need for free trade   **206**
     The need for codes governing distortions in foreign exchange markets   **206**
     The need for surveillance and monitoring   **206**

Living in a Less-Than-Perfect World   **207**

Concluding Comments   **209**

Exchange Rates and Their Role in Agricultural Trade Issues: A Commentary   211
Murray G. Smith

Policy Surveillance and Coordination for Industrial Countries   **212**

Exchange Rate Volatility and Safeguards   **212**

Exchange Rate Issues in Developing Countries   **213**

Concluding Observation   **214**

Exchange Rates and Their Role in Agricultural Trade Issues

G. Edward Schuh

Although it is well known that distortions in foreign exchange markets are equivalent to distortions in trade, this reality is seldom reflected in trade negotiations or in discussion of trade conflicts. Instead, exchange rates tend to be viewed as part of the international monetary system and separate from the trade system. Although generally recognized as an important factor influencing the volume of international trade, the role of exchange rates in distorting trade is generally neglected.

Several changes in what can be best described as the structure of the international economy over the last 25 years have increased the importance of exchange rates as factors affecting trade flows. In addition, the international debt crisis and other problems in the international economy increase the likelihood that the exchange rate will be used as an instrument of economic policy and thus as a conscious means of distorting international trade flows.

This paper is organized in five parts. Part one provides general background on the current exchange rate system. This material is essential to understanding subsequent material. The second provides a synthesis of the simple economics of distortions to trade caused by distortions in exchange rates. This is followed in part three by a discussion of the issues that complicate exchange rate management and that give such a great role of distortions in exchange rates as a factor influencing international trade. Part four describes the main elements of a code for the management of exchange rates in a non-distorting fashion, while the fifth "Living in a Less-Than-Perfect World", suggests some measures that might help keep distortions in exchange rates from being as large as they have been or from having such large effects.

Some Background

From the end of World War II until 1973 the world was on a fixed exchange rate system, a system agreed to at the Bretton Woods Conference in the New Hampshire town of that name. The system was agreed to because many observers believed that the depth and breadth of the Great Depression was caused by the use of competitive devaluations during that decade. Individual countries would devalue their currencies in an attempt to gain a competitive edge in foreign markets and thus to dump their domestic problems abroad. The notion of trade diversion is already established by that proposition.

The idea of the fixed exchange rate system was that governments would re-establish equilibrium in their external accounts – when disequilibrium occurred – by changing their domestic macroeconomic policies. Countries that were running deficits in their external accounts were expected to pursue restrictive domestic policies until balance in the external accounts was re-established. Countries that were incurring surpluses in their external accounts were expected to pursue stimulative policies until balance was achieved. Exchange rates per se were to be changed only when all else failed.

This system worked reasonably well through the 1950s and the 1960s. International trade grew consistently throughout this period, and it grew at a faster rate than did global GNP. One should not conclude that this was the best of all possible worlds, however, since we have no counter-factual evidence on how an alternative world might have performed. We do know that the fixed exchange system involved significant distortions and thus may have been more restrictive of trade expansion than is generally believed. The U.S. dollar, for example, was persistently overvalued in this period, as were the currencies of many, if not most of the developing countries, especially in relation to the U.S. dollar.

Stresses and strains on the exchange rate system grew significantly over the 1960s and provoked a particularly rancorous debate among Japan, West Germany, and the United States over their respective exchange rate policies. The United States incurred increasingly large trade deficits as it simultaneously pursued the Vietnam War and financed the programs of the Great Society – both without raising domestic taxes.

The deficit in the United States external accounts was offset in large part by surpluses in the external accounts of Japan and West

Germany. The United States argued that since the dollar was the principal reserve currency of the international economy, Japan and West Germany should revalue their currencies or stimulate their economies. Japan and West Germany, on the other hand, argued that since the United States was the principal source of the international imbalance, it was the country that should change its policies.

Pressures in foreign exchange markets built up, and the United States finally devalued the dollar in 1971. By 1973 pressures had built up again. The United States formally devalued again, but also announced that henceforth the value of the dollar would be determined in foreign exchange markets and not by government efforts to establish some predetermined value. This gave rise to what can best be described as a bloc floating exchange rate regime for the international economy. The system is 'floating' in the sense that the major currencies (the U.S. dollar, the West German Deutschmark, the French franc, the British pound sterling, etc.) float relative to each other, but 'bloc' in that a large number of smaller countries peg the value of their currencies to one of the major reserve currencies.

On the surface, the system has a great deal of rigidity. However, there is more flexibility than meets the eye, because many of the pegged currencies flex implicitly relative to each other as the values of the major reserve currencies float relative to each other. Implications of this system are discussed below.

A second significant development in the international economy was the emergence of a well-integrated international capital market. The original impetus for this market was the emergence of the Eurodollar market in the 1960s, followed by the emergence of the Eurocurrency market. By the end of the 1960s and the beginning of the 1970s, the size and scale of this international capital market were already of unprecedented proportions. In fact, the main reason the old fixed exchange rate system eventually broke down was that the international capital market was so large that it was no longer feasible to peg the major reserve currencies.

The increase in petroleum prices in 1973 and again in 1979 gave further stimulus to this market. Trade in petroleum is transacted for the most part in U.S. dollars. Increases in the price of petroleum generated a flood of petrodollars, which commercial banks were enjoined to recycle in order to keep the international economy from collapsing.

By the mid-1980s, the international capital market had grown so large that it literally dwarfed international trade. In 1984, for example, total international trade flows were on the order of U.S. $42 trillion, while international capital flows were only about U.S. $2 trillion. The significance of these numbers is that it is international financial flows, not international trade, that tends to drive foreign exchange markets.

The implication of this development is explored below. For now we want to discuss another set of issues – the implication of the simultaneous shift to a flexible exchange rate system and a well-integrated international capital market. In an international system of this kind, changes in monetary and fiscal policy affect domestic economies in ways completely different than in an international economy characterized by fixed exchange rates and an international capital market of little significance.

In the old system (the 1950s and 1960s), changes in monetary and fiscal policy affected the economy broadly, with any differential impact determined largely by the capital intensity of the sector. In the system that emerged in the 1970s and 1980s, however, adjustments to changes in monetary and fiscal policies are forced on to the trade sectors – export and import-competing sectors. Changes in the tightness or easiness of monetary policies, for example, are reflected in changes in the value of national currencies, not in interest rates. Thus the conditions of trade are changed as monetary and fiscal policies change.

Moreover, it isn't just the change in home-country monetary and fiscal policies that matter, but those in other countries as well. This was illustrated in the extraordinary rise of the dollar in the first half of the 1980s. The contradictory monetary and fiscal policies of the United States – a highly stimulative fiscal policy and a tight monetary policy – caused interest rates to be high in the United States. This caused a shift out of non-U.S. dollar assets into U.S. dollar assets, causing the value of the dollar to rise in foreign exchange markets. However, this problem was exacerbated by the macroeconomic policies of Europe and Japan, where fiscal policies were conservative and monetary policies relatively easy.

This large rise in the value of the U.S. dollar imposed large shocks on the tradeable sectors in the United States, both the export sectors (such as agriculture) and the import-competing sectors (such as smokestack industries). There were offsetting adjustments in these same sectors in other countries. The extent to which the dollar was overvalued in this period, despite being 'free' to fluctuate in response to market forces, is discussed below.

Finally, it should be noted that international monetary conditions became much more unstable starting in about 1968. The reason for this increased instability is not well understood, but U.S. monetary policy in particular became quite unstable. This instability is reflected both in the international monetary aggregates and in real interest rates. Instability in monetary conditions has led to instability in exchange rates and in turn to trade. It has also given rise to strong protectionist pressures as fluctuations in the exchange rate masked underlying comparative advantage.

The Simple Economics of Distortions to Trade Caused by Distortions in Exchange Rates

Assume a world in which there are no distortions to trade and in which monetary and fiscal policies are neutral in the sense that the budget is balanced and monetary policy is producing a stable price level. Under these conditions, the equilibrium exchange rate is the rate that will establish balance in the external accounts, with no deficit or surplus in the overall balance of payments.

Under these conditions, a distortion in the value of the currency will have trade-distorting effects. (It will have effects in the international capital market as well, but these effects are beyond our present interests.) An overvalued currency is equivalent to a tax on exports and a subsidy on imports. (An overvalued currency means that foreign currencies are valued at a lower price in terms of the domestic currency than they would otherwise be, say, 30 *cruzeiros* to buy a dollar when the equilibrium rate would be 40 *cruzeiros*.)

Under these conditions, if the country is unimportant in international markets, so that its exports and imports do not affect international prices, the overvalued currency will cause export commodities to be valued lower in the domestic market than they would be worth if the value of the domestic currency were at its equilibrium level. Similarly, imports will also be valued lower in terms of the domestic currency than they would be if acquired at the equilibrium exchange rate. It is in these senses that an overvalued currency is equivalent to an export tax and an import subsidy.

In the same way, an undervalued currency is equivalent to a general export subsidy and to a general tariff. (The *cruzeiro* would be undervalued, for example, if its price were fixed so that it took 50 *cruzeiros* to buy a dollar when the equilibrium rate was 40 *cruzeiros* per dollar.) In this case exports would be valued in the domestic currency at prices greater than they would be at the equilibrium exchange rate. The same would be true for imports. In the case of exports, for given costs of production, the product or service would be sold at a lower price in foreign markets than would be the case at the equilibrium exchange rate.

There are important connections between distortions in the exchange rate and trade distortions. For example, an overvalued currency can lead to protectionist pressures and the imposition of limitations on market access by tariffs or quantitative restrictions on imports. In fact, much of the high protection against imports in developing countries is a consequence of their persistent tendency to overvalue their currencies significantly.

An undervalued currency elicits similar barriers to imports from countries that undervalue their currencies, as Japan has learned. Thus distortions in both directions provide incentives to impose barriers to trade. That is one of the reasons why establishing discipline in the distortion of exchange rates should be an important part of general trade liberalization.

It is equally as important to note that trade distortions can lead to distortions in the exchange rate. For example, other things being equal, protectionist measures will cause a domestic currency to be overvalued. Countries that systematically raise their tariffs and other forms of protection as part of import-substituting policies will simultaneously increase the implicit tax on their export sector. Countries that subsidize their exports by explicit means similarly subsidize their imports implicitly.

It is for these reasons that trade liberalization measures require liberalization of foreign exchange markets if the full benefits of the liberalization are to be realized. Similarly, liberalization of foreign exchange markets could induce a significant amount of trade liberalization.

The so-called "Dutch disease" is a final aspect of the simple economics of exchange rates. This occurs when a country has an unusual comparative advantage in a particular sector such as petroleum. This advantage may give it a very strong currency, which in turn will have deleterious consequences on other export and import-competing sectors. This may give the country a higher degree of specialization than it otherwise would have. Moreover, if such a sector emerges as a result of contemporary developments, its emergence may impose significant adjustments on other sectors in the economy.

Some Complicating Issues

There are a number of complicating issues associated with exchange rates that give added importance to bringing them under some system of codes and discipline if much progress is to be made in liberalizing international trade. We saw in the previous section how distortions in trade and in foreign exchange markets can be interrelated. We also saw how distortions in exchange rates can give rise to protectionist pressures, thus adding to distortions of trade or making it difficult to reduce barriers to trade.

This section focuses on complications that at one level point to the difficulties of determining what an equilibrium exchange rate is, while at a different level point to further reasons why reaching agreement on the management of foreign exchange markets is so important to making progress in trade liberalization. Six issues are discussed: monetary and fiscal policies as sources of distortions in foreign exchange markets; monetary unions as sources of distortions; green currencies; bloc floating exchange rates as a source of distortions; distortions in exchange rates as a mask to underlying comparative advantage; and the problem of instability in exchange rates.

Monetary and Fiscal Policies as Sources of Distortions in Foreign Exchange Markets

The particular configuration of monetary and fiscal policies a country pursues can create distortions in foreign exchange markets. Perhaps the best example in recent history are the contradictory monetary and fiscal policies pursued by the United States in the 1980s. Those policies have consisted of highly stimulative fiscal policies, reflected in a large federal deficit, and a highly restrictive monetary policy as the U.S. Federal Reserve essentially refused to monetize the debt created by the federal deficit. This particular policy configuration caused interest rates to be much higher than they would have been with neutral monetary and fiscal policies. High interest rates induced a shift out of non-dollar assets and into dollar assets, thus bidding up the value of the dollar and causing it to be higher than it otherwise would have been.

The configuration of monetary and fiscal policies that would be neutral in its effect on foreign exchange markets would consist of a balanced federal or national budget and a monetary policy that resulted in a stable aggregate price level. Any drifts from either of these goals would lead to distortions in exchange rates, since they would lead to capital flows that would distort the exchange rate.

It is important to note that it is not just own-country monetary and fiscal policies that lead to distortions in the value of a nation's currency. For example, as noted above, the dollar became highly overvalued in the first half of the 1980s, in part because Japan and the countries of Western Europe were pursuing a configuration of monetary and fiscal policies that was the reverse of U.S. policies – a conservative fiscal policy and a relatively easy monetary policy. This widened the interest rate differential between the United States and the other countries and caused a greater shift out of non-dollar assets into dollar assets than U.S. policies alone would have induced.

There is also a corollary point. In the same way that the dollar was overvalued, the currencies of Japan and Western Europe were undervalued. This influenced trade performance in important ways on both sides of the relationship.

Finally, it should be noted that not all capital flows lead to distortions in exchange rates. Interest rate differentials that reflect productivity differentials and differences in propensities to save among countries are perfectly consistent with non-distorting exchange rates. However, differentials that reflect non-neutrality in monetary and fiscal policy within a country or between countries result in distortions in foreign exchange markets that produce equivalent distortions of trade.

Monetary Unions as Distortions to Foreign Exchange Markets

A number of monetary unions have been created in various parts of the world. One of the more prominent is the European Monetary System, which was created as a reaction to instability in foreign exchange markets. This system is based on the European Currency Unit (ECU), which is used as an accounting unit for international trade purposes. The ECU does not actually circulate, although it is used as a monetary reserve.

As part of the European Monetary System, the values of national currencies are limited to fluctuating within a narrow band, called the 'snake'. The limits of this band are changed from time to time for individual currencies as they get out of balance with underlying economic conditions.

The problem with this system is that there is no unified monetary policy and fiscal system to back it up. Member countries continue to pursue independent monetary and fiscal policies, although part of the original goal was that this modified fixed exchange rate system would impose a discipline on macroeconomic policies similar to that imposed by the old Bretton Woods fixed exchange rate system.

A consequence of a unified system without unified macroeconomic policies to back it up is that most currencies will be out of equilibrium at any given point in time. Countries, such as West Germany, that pursue conservative fiscal and monetary policies will find their currency undervalued for extended periods of time. Countries that pursue less conservative monetary and fiscal policies will tend to find their currencies chronically overvalued. Only those currencies that are the consequence of the 'average' monetary and fiscal policies will be close to being in equilibrium. The consequence is that the monetary union results in distortions in foreign exchange markets, which in turn lead to distortions in trade.

A somewhat different monetary union has been established in Africa with the French franc as the basic currency. This system does not have a separate unit of account, nor does it make use of a band (or snake). The goal was to foster exchange rate stability and to foster trade within a French bloc of African countries.

This system has fostered distortions in exchange rates that are even wider than those in the European system, largely because the African member countries have done less well than the European nations in the EMS in managing their monetary and fiscal policies. As a result, some of the currencies are badly out of line in the sense of being overvalued, and distortions to trade are even larger.

Green Currencies

Members of the European Economic Community, as well as a number of other countries, use what are called green currencies. These are special rates applied to the trade of agricultural commodities and constitute multiple exchange rate systems.

The most extensive system of green currencies is in the EEC. The original goal of the EEC's Common Agricultural Policy (CAP) was to unify agricultural prices within the community behind a common external barrier. That goal was accomplished for approximately one year, but domestic pressures arising from the changes in prices were ultimately too great. France was the first to break out of the system by creating a green currency that was overvalued compared to its regular currency and thus taxed its agriculture. A short time later West Germany created a green currency for its agriculture that was undervalued in relation to its general exchange rate, thus constituting an export subsidy and an implicit tariff – a return to its long-held practice of strongly protecting its agriculture.

Eventually every member state except one established a green currency for its agriculture. The disparity between over- and undervaluedness was as much as 40 per cent at times. The result was a considerable degree of trade distortion within the Community, and a failure to obtain the goal of uniform commodity prices and resources efficiently within the Community, even though variable levies kept a common price to the external market.

Green currencies were thus a distortion to trade within the EEC at the same time as variable levies (and a variable export tax in the mid-1970s) distorted EEC agriculture in the aggregate vis-à-vis the rest of the world.

Bloc Floating Exchange Rates

An important feature of the present exchange rate system is its bloc floating character. For example, a fairly large number of countries keep the value of their currency pegged to the value of the U.S. dollar, either in nominal terms or in real terms according to purchasing power parity principles. In the latter cases, some form of a crawling peg policy is usually followed. A significant number of countries tie the value of their currency to the French franc (especially in Africa), some tie to the British pound sterling, some to the Special Drawing Right (SDR), and still others to a variety of 'baskets' of currencies.

This pegging of currencies leads to trade distortions. It also can impose significant external shocks on an economy if policy makers are not alert. Perhaps the outstanding example of the latter occurred in the case of Brazil, which in the 1970s was using a crawling peg to keep the value of the *cruzeiro* pegged to the value of the U.S. dollar according to purchasing power parity principles. This policy enabled Brazil to escape the consequences of the large rise in petroleum prices in 1973, because the value of the dollar fell during the 1970s. Thus the value of the *cruzeiro* fell relative to other currencies that were floating and relative to the currencies tied to those floating currencies, and Brazil benefited relative to 'third' countries.

When the 1979 petroleum price increase occurred, Brazil – after a maxi-devaluation whose effect was soon dissipated because of a failure to follow proper monetary policies – again followed the same policy as before. This time, however, the value of the U.S. dollar did not decline. Instead, it went on an unprecedented rise as a result of a change in U.S. monetary policy. This time the fact that the real value of the *cruzeiro* was pegged to the U.S. dollar worked against Brazil, eventually leading to its debt crisis of 1982.

More recently, this pegging of other currencies has been recognized for what it is – a trade distortion. As the value of the U.S. dollar has fallen since May 1985, a number of countries have benefited significantly, including South Korea, Taiwan and other Southeast Asian countries. These countries have consequently accumulated large foreign exchange reserves. In effect, they have been riding free, because they have not been bearing the adjustments that the productivity of their respective economies and the corollary capital flows would have required. After they failed to respond to U.S. requests that they revalue their currencies, the United States eventually took away their generalized preferences privileges. These countries were (are) in effect benefiting from undervalued currencies, which as noted earlier are equivalent to implicit export subsidies.

Masking of Underlying Comparative Advantage

The failure of countries to pursue neutral fiscal and exchange rate policies, together with the system of bloc floating currencies, has caused effective exchange rates to mask underlying comparative advantage and to mask it for significant periods of time. This was implicit in what has already been said, but it is worth addressing explicitly, for it illustrates the significance of distortions in exchange rates to distortions in trade.

Again, U.S. experience is perhaps the most useful example. That country experienced an unusual agricultural export boom in the 1970s, driven in large part by the fall in the value of the dollar over that period. (The dollar fell because of inappropriate monetary and fiscal policies and a bad energy policy.) As predicted by economic theory, not only did U.S. exports grow in an absolute sense, the U.S. share of global markets grew significantly as well.

Interestingly enough, everybody was willing to take credit for the growth in exports – U.S. farmers, exporters, policy makers, St. Peter for the weather, and anybody else who was involved. When the dollar went the other way, however, and took off on an unprecedented rise toward the end of 1979, the fall in exports was a fatherless child, and the rise in the value was (properly) given its due (complicated, of course, by U.S. commodity policies).

Ironically, the United States (and others) developed the idea in the 1970s that nobody could compete with it in agricultural trade. By 1985, just the opposite conclusion was being reached – that the United States could compete with no one. The truth, of course, lies somewhere between. Distortions in the value of the dollar were affecting U.S. trade performance in both the 1970s and the 1980s. Moreover, not only were they affecting U.S. trade performance, they were affecting the trade performance of other countries as well. This masking of underlying comparative advantage resulting from distortions in exchange rates has sent misleading signals to policy makers and the private sector, generated protectionist pressures, sacrificed global resource efficiency, and made trade liberalization difficult.

Instability in Exchange Rates

As much of the earlier discussion implies, currency exchange rates have been characterized by a great deal of instability since the end of the Bretton Woods fixed exchange rate system in 1973. Some of this instability has been of a short-term nature – something that can be handled by future markets for foreign exchange. The more difficult instability has been the long swings in exchange rates resulting from shifts in monetary and fiscal policies and from large shifts in capital from assets denominated in one currency to those denominated in another.

This instability, with its attendant increase in transaction costs and protectionist pressures, has led to growing pressure to go back to the old fixed exchange rate system or to introduce greater co-ordination of macroeconomic policies among those countries with major reserve currencies. The first of these is not feasible and, even if it were, could lead to significant distortions in international trade and a global loss in resource efficiency. It is not feasible because the international flow of capital would quickly swamp the ability of central banks to stem pressures for realignment. After all, the shift to a floating exchange rate system in 1973 was de facto recognition that exchange rates could no longer be fixed.

Co-ordination of macroeconomic policies is, in the final analysis, no more feasible. When push comes to shove, national policy makers eventually respond to their own best (political) interests. Moreover, the possibility of error in fixing target ranges of exchange rates is great and can lead to distortions in its own right. What policy makers, or group of policy makers, has the wisdom to pick the right rate, even with an ample selection of indicators?

Fundamentally, exchange rate stability will be obtained only when there is agreement on rules and codes that establish proper monetary and fiscal policies on the part of national governments and a proper international monetary environment. What is required goes beyond the confines of this paper.[1]

However, it is important to note that an important part of the necessary reforms is the need for a shift in the opposite direction from fixity. A significant share of the instability in foreign exchange markets results precisely from the existing fixity. Just as in commodity markets, when the forces of demand and supply are not permitted to influence price and quantities traded, the effects of any given shock are channelled to those parts of the market that are open. This in turn makes those parts of the market appear unstable. In the case of the foreign exchange markets, it is the presence of monetary (exchange rate) unions and the bloc floating nature of the system that create the instability. The solution is to go to more generalized floating, not to add more fixity or rigidity to the markets.

Elements of a Code for Foreign Exchange Markets

Space does not permit a complete discussion of the codes needed to establish non-distortionary foreign exchange markets. However, the elements of a code follow logically from the preceding discussion. It is useful to spell out six elements here so as to facilitate further discussion.

The need for generalized floating

Shifting from a highly distorted, fixed exchange rate policy to one of flexible exchange rates is not a painless or costless process. The real value of foreign debt may increase significantly; the decline in real exchange rates (which is what will be needed for many countries) will involve losses in real incomes for many countries; domestic income will be significantly redistributed; domestic resources will have to be reallocated; and new institutional arrangements, such as futures markets for foreign exchange, will be needed. However, the negative externalities associated with the present rigidities are such that the international community could afford to commit significant resources to help individual countries shift their policies in the right direction. The potential benefits from improved resource allocation would indeed be great.

The need for neutral monetary and fiscal policies

It is widely believed that a world of freely floating exchange rates will result in distortion-free exchange markets. That is not the case. National budgets that involve either deficits or surpluses can lead to distortions in exchange rates because, among other things, they lead to capital flows or shifts into and out of assets denominated in various currencies. Similarly, monetary policies that lead to either deflation or inflation can also lead to capital flows, thus causing exchange rates to be different from their monetary- and fiscal-policy-neutral rates.

To provide a world free from distortions in exchange rates, it is thus necessary to have codes that require countries to pursue fiscal policies that balance national budgets and monetary policies that result in stable price levels. In this regard it is important to note that distortions in exchange rates arising from non-neutral fiscal and exchange rates do not create trade and capital market distortions just for the countries that pursue them, but for other countries as well. Moreover, the more important the country is in international commerce and capital markets, the more extensive these consequences will be.

The need for open international capital and investment markets

Barriers to international capital flows can be as important in distorting foreign exchange markets as barriers to trade are. Such barriers are legion in the international economy. Although it is difficult to restrain financial capital flows per se, because under- and over-invoicing on the trade side can be used to shift capital, it is easier to restrict capital flows by means of foreign investment policies.

Distortion-free foreign exchange markets require distortion-free international capital markets. Hence, codes to that effect are needed.

The need for free trade

The theme of this paper has been to understand how distortions in exchange rates act as distortions to trade. However, the discussion in an earlier section noted that barriers to trade also lead to distortions in foreign exchange markets. This brings about the reciprocal nature of the distortions in trade markets and the distortions in foreign exchange markets. In reality, not much progress will be made in liberalizing one set of markets without liberalizing the other set. Hence, the liberalization of markets will need to proceed simultaneously.

The need for codes governing distortions in foreign exchange markets

If each of the previous four elements of a code governing international economies relative could be obtained, there would probably be no need for a code governing explicit intervention in foreign exchange markets. However, given that we are likely to be living in a less-than-perfect economic world in the foreseeable future, it is worth having a code that prevents direct intervention in foreign exchange markets for other than sterilization purposes.

The need for surveillance and monitoring

Given the extensive interactions among capital markets, foreign exchange markets and trade, a comprehensive system of monitoring and surveillance is needed if the codes proposed above are to be enforced. Much of the apparatus for such monitoring and surveillance is already in place in the form of the International Monetary Fund and the General Agreement on Tariffs and Trade. However, to foster distortion-free foreign exchange markets, coverage will need to be both more comprehensive and more extensive. Moreover, somewhat different questions will need to be asked than has been the case in the past. Integration of these monitoring and surveillance functions will also be needed.

These more comprehensive and detailed monitoring and surveillance functions in effect amount to a significant research effort on international economic relations. Given the limited knowledge available on the impact of the various kinds of distortions, it is essential that monitoring and surveillance efforts be backed up with a more basic research program designed to add to our knowledge about the effects of various distortions and their inter-relationships.

Living in a Less-Than-Perfect World

The main elements of a code that would keep exchange rates from being a distortion to trade constitute a goal or ideal. In the near future we will need to live with something less than ideal. Some suggestions that would help limit distortions in foreign exchange markets or keep them from having as large a distortionary effect on trade are presented here.

Expand the surveillance of exchange rates and monetary and fiscal policies.

A comprehensive surveillance system that identifies when monetary and fiscal policies are non-neutral and when exchange rates are out of line could help develop moral suasion against such policies. The International Monetary Fund already does a great deal of this. However, the distortions are not linked all that directly to distortions in trade. Making a more comprehensive effort at such surveillance will require a significant commitment of additional resources. A significant educational effort will also be needed so that there is a broader understanding of the issues. Even then, such an effort will not be a panacea. It is worth doing, however, both for the increased understanding it will provide and for the increased information it will generate.

In the case of monetary unions, establish a more direct linkage between balance of payments imbalances and corrective domestic policies.

The rules of the game for the European Monetary System imply that imbalances in external accounts will be corrected by changes in domestic monetary and fiscal policies. This is a carry-over from the old Bretton Woods system, and it is best-efforts measures that are called for. These rules could be tightened so there is a more direct, rigid linkage between the imbalances and the corresponding corrective measures.

The rules of the monetary unions might also be altered so as to reduce potential distortions.

One such measure would be to widen the band within which fluctuations in exchange rates are expected to be confined. This would provide more room for adjustment and thus bring about corrective action at an earlier date. A second measure would be to require quicker adjustments in the bands themselves. This, too, would provide for more adjustment and thus reduce the size of distortions.

For countries that use pegged exchange rates, establish a linkage between balance of payments imbalances and the level of the peg.

This would retain some elements of the stability in exchange rates that so many countries seem to desire, while at the same time avoiding the large distortions that occur from a rigid adherence to pegged rates. Adjustments would come about more quickly, and distortions to trade would be reduced.

Require that support levels be indexed to rates of exchange.

Target prices and deficiency payments can be left to be whatever governments want them to be or can afford. However, support prices such as those determined by loan levels, in the case of U.S. commodity programs, and the prices protected by the variable levy, in the case of EC policies, could be adjusted inversely with the value of a nation's currency. This would keep distortions in exchange rates from creating such large distortions to trade.

Require that the effects of changes in exchange rates be passed through to the domestic economy.

This is related to the previous point, although addressed to a somewhat different issue. In particular, it focuses on the consumer side of the market and seeks to ensure that consumers bear the costs and share in the benefits of exchange rate realignments. Japan is perhaps the best example. Had Japanese consumers, for example, been able to benefit from the rapid rise in the yen in recent years, a great deal of stress could have been removed from international commodity markets.

Include distortions in exchange rates as an integral part of the GATT negotiations.

This should be self-evident at this point and thus requires no further explanation. However, the incentives for developing countries to pursue undervalued currencies, with the implicit export subsidies they imply, give a sense of urgency to introducing these issues into the negotiations.

In the case of developing countries, more effective adjustment policies will help induce more rational exchange rate policies.

Developing countries needed devaluations of their currencies out of fear that such realignments will cause domestic food prices to rise and thus bring politically volatile urban consumers into the streets in protest. Targeted feeding programs that benefit the low-income disadvantaged are at least a partial solution to this problem. Other elements of a program to alleviate this problem include changes in wage policies and privatization of publicly held companies.

No one of the policies suggested here constitutes a panacea, and some have their own costs and potential for distortion. Collectively, however, the full range of measures could help keep exchange rates from getting very far out of line, while at the same time reducing the distortionary effects on trade of any exchange rate distortions that do emerge.

Concluding Comments

It is difficult to conclude this paper without emphasizing how important the monetary and exchange rate aspects of international trade really are. It may in fact be chasing a will-o'-the-wisp to believe that any significant amount of trade liberalization can be obtained without establishing more stable monetary conditions in the global economy and without the reforms that will give more stability to foreign exchange markets. Steps toward trade liberalization taken without the more general reforms are likely to be short-lived, as monetary and exchange rate disturbances give rise to protectionist pressures that cannot be resisted.

Note

1. For a discussion of how a proper international monetary environment might be obtained, see G. Edward Schuh, *The United States and the Developing Countries: An International Perspective* (Washington, D.C.: National Planning Association, 1986).

Exchange Rates and Their Role in Agricultural Trade Issues: A Commentary

Murray G. Smith

Dean Schuh's paper on "Exchange Rates and their Role in Agricultural Trade Issues" indicates the complexity of the Gordian knot of government policies influencing agricultural trade. Limiting the use of agricultural subsidies is widely recognized as a difficult but essential step toward more rational agricultural trade. Schuh raises the stakes further by arguing that co-ordination of macroeconomic policies – specifically, moderating fiscal deficits and co-ordinating monetary policy – is a prerequisite to exchange rate stability and, by inference, is also a prerequisite to liberalization of agricultural trade.

Schuh has a persuasive case that the negotiation of agricultural trade issues in the Uruguay Round must deal with exchange rate issues, but trade negotiators are likely to be in a quandary about how to deal with this reality. In this note I suggest some ways in which the GATT negotiations on agriculture could respond to exchange rate issues. Specifically, in the Uruguay Round negotiations the industrial countries should

- recognize that new mechanisms within GATT to monitor national trade and domestic agricultural policies and to promote policy co-ordination need to be co-ordinated with IMF surveillance of national monetary and fiscal policies; and

- revise the GATT rules that currently permit quantitative restrictions, as well as reform GATT to bring practices such as variable levies under the rules, and then replace these measures with safeguard mechanisms subject to specific constraints.

For their part, higher-income developing countries should

- recognize that giving up their rights under Article XVIII of the GATT would promote greater stability in their external trade and payments regime.

Policy Surveillance and Co-ordination for Industrial Countries

In the industrial countries, exchange rates, in most cases, are not subject to direct manipulation, but divergent national monetary and fiscal policies have led to great and sustained misalignments in real exchange rates. Proposals to have the GATT Secretariat and a Committee of Trade Ministers monitor the effects of national agricultural policies, such as the domestic target price for buffer stocks or price supports, must take account of Schuh's proposal for a code of conduct on macroeconomic policies influencing exchange rates.

Yet, the IMF, in conjunction with bilateral consultations among the group of seven industrial democracies, is likely to continue to be the principal vehicle for implementing efforts to co-ordinate national macroeconomic policies. Nonetheless, it will be essential that the new GATT process monitor both macroeconomic and sector-specific national policies. To evaluate the effects upon international trade of general policy commitments to limit agricultural support as measured by producer subsidy equivalents (or alternative measures), or specific policy commitments such as support prices for buffer stocks, it is necessary to have an implicit or explicit view about the 'appropriate' movement of exchange rates. Thus, it would be desirable to build close links between IMF surveillance of national monetary and fiscal policies and a proposed GATT process to monitor national trade and domestic agricultural policies.

As the Hathaway-Miner paper makes clear, new institutional mechanisms for the surveillance and co-ordination of national policies need to be buttressed by strengthening existing GATT rules and dispute settlement procedures as they apply to border measures. If too great a burden is placed on policy coordination mechanisms, there is risk that they may fail or create additional conflicts.

Exchange Rate Volatility and Safeguards

Schuh has a strong case in political economy to support his contention that instability in exchange rates makes it much more difficult to liberalize agricultural trade. Clearly, highly protected domestic industries that are sheltered by quantitative restrictions, state trading practices, or variable levies are even less enthusiastic about the prospect of being exposed to the vagaries of the world market in a world of fluctuating exchange rates. Part of the response to this problem could involve decoupled income stabilization measures that help insure farmers against risks of all sorts, not just exchange rate risk.

A complementary response would be to replace border measures such as quantitative restrictions and variable levies with permanent tariff bindings and a safeguards mechanism. The essential elements of the safeguards mechanism would be, first, that temporary surtaxes that partially offset exchange rate movements would be applied – for example, a surtax in the amount of 50 per cent of the change in world price (as measured in the national currency) could be permitted; and, second, that the measures would be time limited – for example, phased out over three years. Thus in the example cited, if the world price (measured in the national currency) fell by 20 per cent, then a surtax of 10 per cent would be applied in the first year and that surtax would be reduced by one-third per year until it was eliminated. Of course, if world prices in the national currency subsequently rose, then the surtax would cease to apply. The advantage of this type of mechanism is that it would provide farmers some buffer against volatility in exchange rates and world commodity prices, but they would receive clearer market signals in planning their production and investment decisions. At present producers selling into local markets sheltered by quotas or variable levies are largely insulated from movements in world market prices.

Exchange Rate Issues in Developing Countries

Developing countries often have restrictive payments regimes that create the potential for manipulation of exchange rates. Many developing countries maintain foreign exchange and import controls on non-agricultural products in order to sustain overvalued exchange rates. These measures impede the development of their agricultural sectors in a less visible manner, but with the same effects as explicit export taxes. As Schuh points out, however, countries with restrictive payments regimes can also follow a policy of deliberately under-valuing their exchange rates in efforts to restrict imports and promote exports.

The provisions of Article XVIII of the GATT give developing countries wide latitude in their trade regimes; this can be justified on balance of payments or developmental grounds. Now many developing countries have 'unilaterally' liberalized their trade regimes or adjusted their exchange rates in response to the problems of the debt crisis and pressure from the IMF and the World Bank.

Developing countries seek advance credit in the Uruguay Round for some of the unilateral steps they have taken to liberalize their trade regimes. At least for the more advanced developing countries, 'GATT bindings' of specific unilateral steps to liberalize trade need to be accompanied by a commitment to give up their 'rights' under Article XVIII, if their 'concessions' are to be regarded as having value by the industrial countries or other developing countries.

Forgoing their rights under Article XVIII offers two benefits to the larger higher-income developing countries. First, simply entering into GATT-bindings with respect to their current policies may give them greater influence over the trade policies of the industrial countries through GATT negotiations. Second, accepting some commitments on their external trade regimes, such as limiting the use of quantitative restrictions, will encourage them to implement more appropriate and sustainable exchange rates for their currencies; this is likely to be of considerable benefit to their traded goods sectors, and in particular their agricultural sectors, as well as contributing to a more stable trade and payments regime and economic growth and development.

Concluding Observation

Recognizing the complexity of agricultural trade and related exchange rate issues should not be an excuse for inaction. Better coordination of macroeconomic policies by the developed countries could lead to greater exchange rate stability and thus facilitate liberalization of agricultural trade. At the same time, liberalization of agricultural trade will help alleviate the pressing debt burden for many countries in Africa and Latin America who depend upon agricultural exports. The GATT negotiations must seek incremental reforms that will gradually unravel these difficult problems and steadily unwind the economic and political obstacles to their solution.

Institute for International Economics

The Institute for International Economics is a private nonprofit research institution for the study and discussion of international economic policy. Its purpose is to analyze important issues in that area and to develop and communicate practical new approaches for dealing with them. The Institute is completely nonpartisan.

The Institute was created by a generous commitment of funds from the German Marshall Fund of the United States in 1981, and continues to receive substantial support from that source. In addition, major institutional grants are now being received from the Ford Foundation, the William and Flora Hewlett Foundation, and the Alfred P. Sloan Foundation. A number of other foundations and private corporations are contributing to the increasing diversification of the Institute's financial resources.

The Board of Directors bears overall responsibility for the Institute and gives general guidance and approval to its research program — including identification of topics that are likely to become important to international economic policymakers over the medium run (generally, one to three years) and which thus should be addressed by the Institute. The Director, working closely with the staff and outside Advisory Committee, is responsible for the development of particular projects and makes the final decision to publish an individual study.

The Institute hopes that its studies and other activities will contribute to building a stronger foundation for international economic policy around the world. Comments as to how it can best do as are invited from readers of these publications.

Institute for International Economics
11 Dupont Circle, N.W., Washington, D.C. 20036

The Institute for Research on Public Policy

Founded in 1972, the Institute for Research on Public Policy is a national organization with offices in Victoria, London, Ottawa, Montreal, Quebec, and Halifax.

The *raison d'être* of the Institute is threefold:

- To act as a catalyst within the national community by helping to facilitate informed public debate on issues of major public interest
- To stimulate participation by all segments of the national community in the process that leads to public policy making
- To find practical solutions to important public policy problems, thus aiding in the development of sound public policies.

Its independence and autonomy are ensured by the revenues of an endowment fund supported by the federal and provincial governments and by the private sector. In addition, the Institute receives grants and contracts from governments, corporations, and foundations to carry out specific research projects.

The Institute is governed by a Board of Directors, which is the decision-making body, and a Council of Trustees, which advises the Board on matters related to the research direction of the Institute. Administration of the Institute's policies, programs, and staff is the responsibility of the president. The Institute operates in a decentralized way, employing researchers located across Canada. This policy ensures that research undertaken will include contributions from all regions of the country.